Gabriel García Márquez's
One Hundred Years of Solitude

A CASEBOOK

CASEBOOKS IN CRITICISM

General Editor, William L. Andrews

GABRIEL GARCÍA MÁRQUEZ'S

One Hundred Years of Solitude

◆ ◆ ◆

A CASEBOOK

Edited by
Gene H. Bell-Villada

UNIVERSITY PRESS

2002

OXFORD
UNIVERSITY PRESS

Oxford   New York

Athens   Auckland   Bangkok   Bogotá   Buenos Aires   Cape Town
Chennai   Dar es Salaam   Delhi   Florence   Hong Kong   Istanbul   Karachi
Kolkata   Kuala Lumpur   Madrid   Melbourne   Mexico City   Mumbai   Nairobi
Paris   São Paulo   Shanghai   Singapore   Taipei   Tokyo   Toronto   Warsaw

and associated companies in
Berlin   Ibadan

Copyright © 2002 by Oxford University Press, Inc.

Published by Oxford University Press, Inc.
198 Madison Avenue, New York, New York 10016

Oxford is a registered trademark of Oxford University Press

Library of Congress Cataloging-in-Publication Data
Gabriel García Márquez's One hundred years of solitude : a casebook / edited by Gene Bell-Villada.
p.   cm. — (Casebooks in criticism) Includes bibliographical references. Contents: A conversation with
Gabriel García Márquez / Gene Bell-Villada—García Márquez, on second reading / Carlos Fuentes—
Gabriel García Márquez, One hundred years of solitude / James Higgins—The humor of One hundred
years of solitude / Clive Griffin—The sacred harlots of One hundred years of solitude / Lorraine Elena
Roses—Aureliano's smile / Michael Wood—The limits of the liberal imagination: One hundred years of
solitude and Nostromo / Jean Franco—One hundred years of solitude as chronicle of the Indies /Iris
Zavala—Banana strike and military massacre: One hundred years of solitude and what happened in
1928 / Gene H. Bell-Villada—The dark side of magical realism : science, oppression and apocalypse in
One hundred years of solitude. / Brian Conniff—Streams out of control : the Latin American
plot / Carlos Rincon.
ISBN 0-19-514454-6;   0-19-514455-4 (pbk.)
1. García Márquez, Gabriel, 1928– Cien años de soledad.   I. Bell-Villada, Gene H.,
1941–   II. Series.
PQ8180.17.A73 C5323 2002
863'.64—dc21   2001035849

1 3 5 7 9 8 6 4 2

Printed in the United States of America
on acid-free paper

ad castoram

Credits

Gene H. Bell-Villada, "Tracking García Márquez: A Journey to Macondo," *Boston Review* 2 (April 1983): 26–27.

Gene H. Bell-Villada, "Banana Strike and Military Massacre: *One Hundred Years of Solitude* and What Happened in 1928," in *From Dante to García Márquez: Studies in Romance Literature and Linguistics*, ed. Gene H. Bell-Villada, Antonio Gimenez, and George Pistorius (Williams College, 1987), pp. 391–402. Presented to Anson Conant Piper. Copyright © 1987 by the President and Trustees of Williams College. Reprinted by permission.

Brian Conniff, "The Dark Side of Magical Realism: Science, Oppression, and Apocalypse in *One Hundred Years of Solitude*," *Modern Fiction Studies* 36 (1990): 167–179. By permission of the Purdue Research Foundation.

Jean Franco, "The Limits of the Liberal Imagination: *One Hundred Years of Solitude* and *Nostromo*," *Punto de Contacto* (December 1975). Reprinted by permission of the author.

Carlos Fuentes, "García Márquez: On Second Reading," excerpt trans. Gene H. Bell-Villada, *La nueva novela Hispanoamericana* (Joaquín Mortiz, 1970), pp. 58–67. Translation printed by permission of Agencia Literaria Carmen Balcells, S. A.

Clive Griffin, "The Humor of *One Hundred Years of Solitude*," in *Gabriel García Márquez: New Readings*, ed. Bernard McGuirk and Richard Cardwell (Cambridge University Press, 1987), pp. 81–94.

Contents

Gabriel García Márquez's
One Hundred Years of Solitude

A CASEBOOK

Introduction

GENE H. BELL-VILLADA

❖ ❖ ❖

*O*NE HUNDRED YEARS OF SOLITUDE initially was published in Spanish (Buenos Aires, 1967). Its author, a fortyish Colombian by the name of Gabriel García Márquez, was at the time an experienced journalist and a little-known if respected fiction writer, living with his wife and two young sons in Mexico City.

Since then, everything about that novel and its maker has grown into the stuff of legend. Critical acclaim shortly after publication of the book was widespread and sometimes ecstatic or awed. The initial printing from the prestigious Editorial Sudamericana ran out within a month, the volume quickly becoming an item that everybody in Spanish America who read simply *had* to read. Spanish-language sales of *One Hundred Years of Solitude* now stand somewhere around the 20 million mark, and of course those copies are often shared among family and friends.

Translations followed, and the pattern was frequently replicated abroad. The book won major French and Italian prizes. It was the first Latin American literary work ever to appear on U.S. best-seller lists. Critical reception was often lavish. ("Dazzling," read the simple, concluding sentence in John Leonard's review for the March 3, 1970, edition of the *New York Times*.) The noun "Macondo" and the author's name soon started cropping up as casual references in international movies, commerce, and popular culture. There is a Hotel Macondo in the Colombian beach resort town of Santa Marta and a Macondo Books store in Manhattan. A copy of *One Hundred Years of Solitude* sits as a background prop throughout much of the light French film comedy, *Like a Turtle on Its Back* (1978).

These miraculous instances of success and visibility would count as little more than ephemera were it not for the special literary qualities of *One Hundred Years of Solitude*. To an unusual degree, the volume combines a complex and sophisticated artistry with an easy, reader-friendly accessibility. Blending Euro-American Modernist methods—gleaned from Kafka, Faulkner, and Woolf (among others)—with Colombian folk elements, select colloquialisms, and good old-fashioned storytelling, the book reinvents prose narrative, its rich panoply of techniques and contents making available a whole new set of assumptions as to what can be done with the novel in our time.

The immediate, personal origins of *One Hundred Years of Solitude* constitute a dramatic legend in their own right. Between 1961 and 1964, García Márquez had been suffering from writer's block, had even been saying to his friends, "I'll never write again." How he pulled out of his slump has been told countless times—yet it bears retelling. According to the author (and no one has substantially challenged his version), he was driving his wife and two sons to Acapulco. It was early in 1965. Suddenly, he could hear the first chapter of the novel resounding in his head.

He turned the car around, headed back for Mexico City, and asked his spouse, Mercedes, to handle the household finances over the next six months while he finished writing the novel that he had always been carrying inside of him. Holed up in his room, García Márquez wrote eight hours a day while his wife sold all of their possessions and incurred total debts upward of ten thousand dollars. The thick manuscript was completed eighteen months later. By sheer happenstance, Editorial Sudamericana had recently queried the author about reissuing his previous titles. After some mishaps, García Márquez sent them his new novel, instead. The book, its surprise success, and its subsequent legend were launched.

The life of García Márquez prior to 1967 is concisely summarized in James Higgins's fine contribution to this volume. (I also refer readers to chapter 3, "The Writer's Life," in my *García Márquez: The Man and His Work*.) Here I only touch on the high points that followed publication of *One Hundred Years of Solitude*.

Seeking escape from the relentless media barrage, the author in 1968 moved quietly with his family to Barcelona, where he spent the next seven years crafting his most difficult—yet also his funniest—novel, *The Autumn of the Patriarch*, about a Caribbean dictator. He also worked on the shorter, practice pieces, which were gathered in the *Eréndira* volume (1972). He then moved back to Mexico City; over the next two decades, he would produce three novels focusing on aspects of romantic love: *Chronicle of a Death Foretold* (1981), *Love in the Time of Cholera* (1985), and *Of Love and Other Demons* (1994), in addition to a brilliant one-act play, *Diatriba de amor contra un hombre sentado* (A diatribe of love against a seated man) (1994; still untranslated). García Márquez's 1982 Nobel Prize for Literature neither softened him nor dulled his judgment.

Yet another novel, *The General in His Labyrinth* (1989), furnishes an intimate portrait of Simón Bolívar, humanizing the great South American liberator. A volume of twelve stories, entitled *Strange Pilgrims* (1992), recounts the assorted experiences of Latin Americans who, for any reason, find themselves temporarily stationed in old Europe. Meanwhile, the author kept up his journalistic labors in the press and in books. His *News of a Kidnapping* (1996) tells of the terrible, cruel abductions spawned by the Colombian drug trade and of the dilemmas such crimes create for the governing elites.

Two other ongoing aspects of García Márquez deserve mention: his left-wing commitments and his film activities. Of his socialist beliefs the author has never made a secret. In the 1980s, he wrote on behalf of Central American leftist struggles; to this day he continues to defend the Cuban Revolution's positive aspects. After three decades spent on the U.S. Immigration blacklist owing to his Marxist ties, the novelist finally saw the curious travel ban lifted by the administration of President Bill Clinton (whose favorite novel, it seems, is *One Hundred Years of Solitude*).

García Márquez's involvement with film has a long history. He briefly attended Rome's renowned Experimental Film Center in the 1950s and wrote numerous scripts for Mexican potboilers early in the next decade. In the 1980s, he began serving as an adviser to Cuba's national film school. Around that time, six of his scripts were made into movies by the Spanish National Television network under the general title *Amores difíciles*. Some of those half-dozen pictures are arguably among the subtlest, most lyrical such works in Hispanic film.

In the early 1990s, heeding the call of the tropical, northern Colombia of his youth, the author had a modernistic, ochre-colored house built in coastal Cartagena. Currently, he spends a good part of the year in that venue, where local folk regard the man as one of their own, chatting with him as he goes for his late-afternoon walks, and the press still refers to him by his nickname, "Gabo." With grand-old-man status there come inevitable perils: in 1998 he contracted lymphatic cancer, and the long-term effectiveness and consequences of the high-tech treatments (some of them undergone at the Mayo Clinic) are not certain as of this writing. In the wake of his illness, an odd episode took place when a "Farewell" under the novelist's byline started circulating widely on the Internet, and not just in Spanish. The wistful, uncharacteristic document, after being perused probably by millions, turned out to be a hoax and within months was publicly repudiated by García Márquez, who described it as *cursi* (roughly, "affected," "corny," "in pretentious bad taste"). Meanwhile, he worked on his own, much-awaited memoirs, portions of which he published in 2001.

One Hundred Years of Solitude appeared at a time when writers and critics in Europe and the United States had been deploring what they then saw as "the death of the novel." The cramped, tired quality of much new, mainstream fiction in first-world nations seemed to support such a judgment. Their lamentations were proved premature, however, by the impressive, grand-scale output of the Latin American "boom" novelists of the time and especially by the arrival of García Márquez's astounding masterpiece. Covering what seemed every possible human experience and offering with its huge cast of characters a vast array of human types, the book dramatically showed prose narrative still capable of capturing life in its full range of manifestations. Last but not least, it reminded us that literary novels could be not just beautiful, moving, and profound but also exciting, entertaining, and *fun*. The Colombian's learned, secular magic evoked both military battles and love affairs, depicted both exploration adventures and bedroom romps, all without so much as a hint of the maudlin, the puerile, or the vulgar.

The broader historical plot sequence of *One Hundred Years of Solitude* is based on actual key events in Colombia's past. Indeed, the novel often crops up on reading lists for U.S. courses on Latin American politics and history. The inner, hidden structures of the book, however, are far from strictly chronological. In this regard the author fully assimilated the lessons learned from Faulkner (who is perhaps the most influential foreign novelist in Latin America). The great Mississippi fabulator, as we know, hit upon a radically new way of representing fictive time, in which the story line moves freely back and forth from present to past to future, or any combination thereof. Though the technique can still seem daunting to first-time readers of *The Sound and the Fury*, over the past seventy years such an approach has become simply another of the many indispensable resources available to practicing novelists throughout the world.

García Márquez's youthful first novel, *Leaf Storm* (1953), was written in frank imitation of his American mentor's *As I Lay Dying*. In *One Hundred Years of Solitude*, by contrast, the use of "Faulknerian" time is so seamless, so thoroughly imbedded, as to be inconspicuous and feel all but natural. As an instance, chapter 1 of the book shows us Macondo in its initial, Edenic state. Chapter 2, in turn, moves back to events that took place more than two centuries earlier (the attack by Francis Drake on Riohacha) and then leaps ahead to certain matters (the dispute with and the murder of Prudencio Aguilar) that would ultimately prompt the Buendías' exodus from Riohacha and their founding of Macondo.

The oft-cited opening sentence in the book,

> Many years later, as he faced the firing squad, Colonel Aureliano Buendía was to remember that distant afternoon when his father took him to discover ice.

contains three different time frames. The reference to ice is immediately abandoned and is not picked up on until the end of that same chapter. The "distant afternoon" alludes to Macondo's days of innocence, evoked with wonder in the sentence that follows ("At that time Macondo was a village . . ."). And the ominous firing-squad episode does not take place until chapter 7—an attempted execution that fizzles out and spares the Colonel's life, to boot. Such a pattern of zigzagging time recurs repeatedly in the course of the narration.

In addition to these structuring features, the constant repetition of sorts of events and also of names in *One Hundred Years of Solitude* conveys a sense of time that is circular, cyclical, and looped, rather than forward-moving, sequential, or linear. This is not a single-thread, "and then, and then" book but rather a multilayered tapestry that tells about "Back then, and before that, yet some years into the future, whereas right now," and so on until world's end.

The other epoch-making trait in *One Hundred Years of Solitude* is its artful interweaving of unlikely, even impossible events with recognizably real experiences and situations. In critical parlance, the device has become widely known as "magical realism." Because the term is subject to frequent misunderstanding and abuse, some clarification may be in order. "Magical realism" should be distinguished from "fantastic literature," a genre that reached a kind of classic status in the short fiction of Borges and Cortázar, both Argentines. In the specific case of "the fantastic," unreal happenings intrude upon daily life and unsettle the reader, who hesitates as to how to interpret such strange, uncanny doings and indeed may wonder whether they've happened at all.[1]

In addition, García Márquez's magic making is to be differentiated from the formulaic, escapist "sci-fi/fantasy" that we typically associate with cheap, bright-colored paperbacks stocked on revolving racks in megastores. García Márquez personally dislikes fantasy; he balks at the facile label "fantastical writer" and defines himself above all as a realist in his art. The term "magical realism" quite obviously juxtaposes two distinct, indeed mutually contradictory strands. What is crucial to García Márquez's art is their deft and vivid fusion in his hands.

Throughout *One Hundred Years of Solitude*, magic and reality reinforce, support, and depend on each other. Father Nicanor Reyna levitates only after having sipped hot chocolate and for fundraising purposes. Remedios, the Beauty, rises to heaven while waving good-bye, clinging to the treasured monogrammed sheets of the comically snobbish Fernanda (who proceeds to rave about her lost family linens). The rainstorm that lasts five years is blamed on the banana company and is thus only the latest if biggest outrage in a lengthy socioeconomic conflict. In these and many other such instances, magical events are recounted with a calm objectivity, "with a straight face" (one might say), as if what is being reported were merely one more item in what is an ongoing and endless series.

Magical realism is not solely the brainchild of García Márquez. Both the term and the practice have a long if scattered history dating back to early-twentieth-century literature, art, and criticism. The Colombian's accomplishment consists in his having taken a tangential, uncertain tradition, absorbing it, and giving it a strong profile and a key presence in his work. Among the precedents he most often cites is Kafka's *The Metamorphosis*, in which the protagonist Gregor Samsa's mysterious, horrific transformation into a gigantic dung-beetle is dealt with by him as a personal nuisance and by his uncomprehending next of kin as a family embarrassment.

Other sources of García Márquez's magical-realist imagination are of a local nature and thus are less known to non-Hispanic readers. Among such materials, one must mention the rich, popular culture of his native, Caribbean-coastal Colombia, a fascinating amalgam of African, indigenous, and Spanish-Galician lore. About its folk legends, home remedies, and far-flung superstitions the author wrote lovingly and frequently during his days as a greenhorn journalist. Another, more bookish inspiration came from the Mexican writer Juan Rulfo, whose remarkable novel *Pedro Páramo* takes place in a literal and figurative ghost town, populated largely by phantoms, two of which actually converse in the privacy of their adjacent tombs. The thirty-three-year old Colombian was thoroughly smitten with Rulfo's two brief, dense volumes, and he plunged assiduously into the study of *Pedro Páramo* shortly after his arrival in Mexico City in 1961 (Saldívar, 410–412). García Márquez's complex narrative vision hence synthesizes Euro-American and Latin American elements, oral and written both.

The wide diffusion of *One Hundred Years of Solitude* has helped open the way to a vastly newer and broader range of storytelling procedures for imaginative writers everywhere. In the United States, for instance, the distinguished novelists Toni Morrison, John Nichols, William Kennedy, Paul Theroux, Alice Walker, Anne Tyler, and Robert Coover have learned from and, in some cases, publicly expressed their debt to the Colombian author (see Bell-Villada 1990, pp. 204–208). Few are the books that end up altering the ways in which writers write and readers read; García Márquez's fictive chronicle of a mythic small town in the tropics stands as an outstanding instance of such an original, and originating, literary text.

And now for our critics.

Deciding on which eight to ten essays to include in an Oxford University Press casebook has been far from a simple task. In my searching and choosing, I've been guided by a number of distinct criteria, some of them mutually contradictory. First and foremost—and in keeping with the series guidelines—was accessibility. A volume of this sort, after all, is intended primarily for an audience of undergraduates, many of whom are still learning about the special language, methods, and issues of literary criticism. I thus felt compelled to seek essays that showed maximum lucidity and transparency in their expression and that foregrounded their theoretical apparatus and lexicon as little as possible. Hence, to my regret, many a serious, thoughtful piece that might have proved opaque and tough going for still-developing literary minds had to be ruled out. Conversely, a high proportion of critics from Great Britain is represented here. This is not by design but rather happened because English academics still excel at producing the kind of readable, direct, even chatty critical discourse that, on the U.S. scene, has become less prized and indeed is often discouraged, spurned as "amateurish."[2]

A casebook, by definition, tries to provide some sampling of the *history* of the criticism of a work. The objective, then, is not to allow any single critical "school" to predominate. However, certain essays on *One Hundred Years of Solitude* have become small classics in their own right, irrespective of their approach, and their inclusion in a volume of this sort is simply unavoidable. Such is the case with the two otherwise markedly different texts by the Mexican novelist Carlos Fuentes and the Puerto Rican critic Iris Zavala.

Other unique factors have both determined and inhibited the range of editorial choices. This anthology is the first Oxford University Press case-book to focus on a "multicultural" masterpiece that is of non-Anglophone origin. Dilemmas and constraints inevitably arise. As is only natural, much of the abundant scholarship on *One Hundred Years of Solitude*—some of it quite fine—has come out in Spanish, a fact that poses certain logistical prob-lems. Translation, for starters, would be necessary, a process requiring a fair amount of labor time, not to mention translator's fees. These re-sources, alas, are in short supply. Moreover, because such critical writing was originally aimed at Hispanic audiences, its prose cadences and echoes and its cultural frames of reference could seem alien or at best incompre-hensible to college students shaped by North American traditions. Its defining virtues would hence have been lost on many of the very readers for whom the volume is conceived.

As an example, I would have liked to include an item, any item, on Gar-cía Márquez from the pen of the great Uruguayan critic Angel Rama. In my experience, however, Rama's luxuriant prose, subtle allusiveness, easy-going cosmopolitanism, and intense commitment to Latin America's his-tory of social struggles all add up to a unique mix that does not travel well into U.S. English. After some digging around and careful perusing of his work, I saw no option—sadly—but to leave out Rama's special beauties from this collection.[3]

The ten articles gathered here are grouped in "clusters," rather than in chronological or strictly thematic sequence. The first two, by Fuentes and Higgins, share in common their traits and purposes as general, introduc-tory sorts of essays. The next three, by Griffin, Roses, and Wood, touch on specific aspects of *One Hundred Years of Solitude*—humor, women, and a major character, respectively. There follows another set of three, these by Franco, Zavala, and Bell-Villada, all of which deal with issues of Western imperial expansion and the fresh, imaginative means deployed by the Colombian author in responding to and engaging with this vast subject. Finally, Con-niff and Rincón bring to their analyses a postmodern, postcolonial focus, reading *One Hundred Years of Solitude* via theoretical concerns that link knowl-edge with power or that place the book within the global diffusion of cul-ture in our age of ever-proliferating mass media.

In the immediate wake of the publication of *One Hundred Years of Soli-tude*, there appeared a good many highly memorable appreciations of the novel by eminent as well as emerging writers, notably Rama, Rodríguez-Monegal, Arenas, Dorfman, and Carlos Fuentes (see the selected bibliogra-phy). I have settled on the relevant chapter from Fuentes's book-length study, *La nueva novela hispanoamericana* (The new Spanish-American novel; 1969).

When Fuentes's volume came out, García Márquez's great work had been just two years in print. The "boom" novelists, their allies, and some key precursors, moreover, were still alive and active. It was an era that seemed to offer an infinity of possibilities for narrative invention in Latin America, and these timely, inspired reflections by Mexico's leading novelist vividly capture and bespeak the literary excitement of that time. Luminously written and aglow with the special, sympathetic insights of a fellow creative artist, Fuentes's succinct contribution posits the "mythic imagination" as a means of recovering freedom. From among the narrative categories of Utopia, Epic, and Myth, the last is adjudged by Fuentes to best encompass all human times, all verbal tenses.[4] For Fuentes, *One Hundred Years of Solitude* is literally a foundational work that, with its distilled prose and myths, helps identify an entire people. In a concluding passage that has often since been cited, Fuentes evokes the central Latin American truths inscribed in García Márquez's landmark text, truths that official chroniclers and legislators, court historians, and realist novelists in the past could not or would not tell, eliding or concealing such truths, instead.

Of the many essay-length introductions to García Márquez and his novel published in English, James Higgins's piece, entitled simply "Gabriel García Márquez: *Cien años de soledad*," is perhaps the most thorough and complete. Following a useful biographical sketch, it examines Macondo's long story through such issues as magical realism, the tensions between oral and written traditions, the moral (in the widest sense of the word) perspective, the internal conflicts, the relationship to foreign capital, and the various roles played by egoism and incest. The attractions of "progress" and the human condition of existential angst are both touched upon. Higgins deftly reminds us that García Márquez's fictional chronicle is both comic and tragic in its effects—an essential if complex fact too often passed over in academic discussions of the book.

Indeed, although few novels are as funny as *One Hundred Years of Solitude*, this aspect of the book tends customarily to be scanted. But then humor is a notoriously difficult topic to discuss without falling into platitude and pedantry. Hearing jokes "explained" can hurt as well as help a jocular occasion. Few, moreover, are the great or even reputable theorists of laughter; Umberto Eco's *The Name of the Rose* dramatizes the subversive and threatening side that comedy can pose to the solemn powers that be. Clive Griffin's "The Humor of *One Hundred Years of Solitude*" gracefully avoids such pitfalls in its revealing look at "the wide range of different types of humor" found in García Márquez's masterwork. The high incidence of sexual and lavatorial jokes and the general irreverence toward all sorts of pomp and stuffiness are inevitably brought to our attention. Griffin notes García Márquez's more specifically linguistic jests involving colloquialisms, metaphors, and narrative conventions. The Colombian's celebrated skill at exaggeration and his sense of wonderment and surprise also come in for review. As an added bonus, some of the key local references in the novel are elucidated by Griffin in the course of his essay.

The special spaces occupied by women in García Márquez's world had been noted even before the publication of his greatest book. Lorraine Elena Roses's "The Sacred Harlots of *One Hundred Years of Solitude*" ably highlights a complex continuum, an ongoing dialectic between women of the social elite and the more "transgressive" females at the margins (Pilar Ternera, Petra Cotes), whose role is primarily sexual. Focusing on the latter personality type and their kinds of knowledge and power, Roses links them to certain ancient cults that assigned to female deities a sacred place and function related to fertility, nature, harvesting, and the well-being of the human body. She reminds us of the once wider, more inclusive semantic field of the noun "virgin," brings in the subject of women's legal rights in pre-Christian times, and connects the richness of García Márquez's novel to its traces and evocations of pagan religion. She caps her performance by noting an affinity between these issues and the underlying utopian side in the experience of literature.

Entire essays could well concentrate exclusively on any of the characters, major as well as minor, that inhabit García Márquez's populous pages. (This in spite of the fact that *One Hundred Years of Solitude* is the farthest thing possible from a psychological novel, with well-rounded characters of the nineteenth-century type.) "Aureliano's Smile," by Michael Wood, eloquently singles out the one male Buendía figure whose deeds attain heroic proportions and whose existence spans more than half the book. Wood's essay (actually a chapter from his excellent introductory volume, now out of print) captures the mysterious and elusive quality of the larger-than-life Colonel. The younger Aureliano's moral and principled response to political events is contrasted with his eventual corruption and his chill "inability to mourn." Significantly, few personages in *One Hundred Years of Solitude* are assigned physical, visual attributes, and the recurrent smile of Aureliano Buendía is here examined for all its shifting, polyvalent ironies.

Comparing García Márquez's novel with other books both old and new is a stock-in-trade of literary study, whether at learned conferences or in course syllabi. (Among the books I have seen chosen for such comparisons:

the Bible, Faulkner's *Absalom, Absalom!*, Vonnegut's *Cat's Cradle*, Rushdie's *Midnight's Children*, and Grass's *The Tin Drum*.) In her essay "The Limits of the Liberal Imagination: *One Hundred Years of Solitude* and *Nostromo*," the eminent British scholar Jean Franco juxtaposes Conrad's now-classic depiction of overseas, European-imperialist intrigues with the Colombian's updated and transformed representation of such skulduggery from the viewpoint of the colonized. Conrad's narrative, based on real-life figures, gives us the standard, comic-opera perception of Latin politicos and rebels that was the prevailing norm in Europe and the United States during his time (and that endured well into the mid-twentieth century). García Márquez, by contrast, frees himself from mimetic concerns and creates instead a "privileged space" in which "gratuitousness," "festivity," and "play" are more crucial—the vision of a more "archaic storyteller." Franco's pioneering early essay lays the basis for future contrastive studies between Eurocentric accounts of colonialism and those by "the natives," who reimagine their past history and, in Edward Said's term, are "writing back" (by analogy with "talking back") to Empire.

Of the many scholarly articles that appeared shortly after publication of García Márquez's landmark work, Iris M. Zavala's essay "*One Hundred Years of Solitude* as Chronicle of the Indies" stands out for its thorough grounding in "hard" researches and bibliographical information, as well as for its historic sweep. With its monumental range of source materials and of captivating small details, it remains remarkably fresh today. Zavala relates García Márquez's novel to two major discursive practices from centuries past. The first and most obvious of these is the European chronicles of "discovery" and exploration, with their fabulous, mythic tone and contents. The issue of the roundness of the Earth, the alleged fascination of the natives with the white newcomers' gadgets, and the exaggerated scale of the phenomena reported on to readers back in Europe are beautifully evoked in Zavala's grand survey—and are then shown to be revived intertextually by García Márquez. The other tradition she examines is that of the inspired and infamous novels of chivalry, which had been read by the more literate explorers and which in turn served as models for emulation when Iberian adventurers or scribes went on to narrate those bewildering experiences. Itself an invaluable source, Zavala's essay is encyclopedic in its scope, touching on a profusion of topics in less than twenty pages.

The Banana Company episodes are among the most forceful and dramatic in the entire saga of Macondo. Curiously, over the course of more than three decades of García Márquez criticism, little work has focused on that key section. Bell-Villada's "Banana Strike and Military Massacre: *One*

Hundred Years of Solitude and What Happened in 1928" examines the historical basis of those suspenseful scenes of work stoppage and repression, showing the remarkable degree to which García Márquez built his narrative around real-life facts and sources. In addition, the essay examines the formal structuring of those conflict-filled chapters and argues that the labor actions, as well as the official reprisals, are presented as merely one set of events among a host of others; García Márquez thereby avoids the fatal trap of insisting inordinately on class struggles. Rather, the banana events intermingle with accounts of romance, dissipation, natural death, the arrival of new Buendías, and the comical ascension of Remedios, the Beauty. Tall-tale techniques of exaggeration are put into play in depicting the social clashes, along with some subtle defamiliarization in the portrayal of the encroaching yet distant "gringos." Finally, magic is artfully deployed by García Márquez in the aftermath of the horrific events, precisely as a means of steering attention away from them.

The term "magical realism," as I noted previously, can fall prey to modish and formulaic overuse, as once tended to happen with equally worthy critical notions on the order of "archetype," "écriture," "logocentric," and "carnivalesque." The beauty of Brian Conniff's essay ("The Dark Side of Magical Realism: Science, Oppression, and Apocalypse in *One Hundred Years of Solitude*") is that it goes beyond the received limits of that handy set phrase and links the larger concept with issues of power and progress, science and exploration. The complex interplay between these diverse forces as developed by García Márquez's imaginings is such that—in the critic's own words—it makes "apocalypse appear not only credible but inevitable." Along the way Conniff provides an illuminating historical sketch of Colombia's railroad system. And throughout his essay he weaves a general argument that is singular and compact, sans extraneous matters or loose ends.

It is a truth sometimes acknowledged that García Márquez's novel has emerged as an unexpected leading actor in numerous odd corners of the world's big stage. Carlos Rincón's essay "Streams Out of Control: The Latin American Plot" is probably the first scholarly attempt at tracing this fascinating instance of planetary, literary transculturation. Citing examples of the presence of *One Hundred Years of Solitude* in the United States, the Near East, the erstwhile Soviet domains, mainland China, and Japan, he offers a bird's-eye glimpse of the remarkable appropriation of García Márquez's art by narrative modes and practices across our global village. What is especially new in this case, though, is not just the South-to-North flow but, more important, the South-to-*South* transfer of García Márquez's storytelling in the third world. Rincón then relates this dynamic to larger-scale trends such as urbanization, "deterritorialization," the rise of Latinos as a political force in the United States, and the integration of *cultura popular* into ordinary people's everyday life via the mass media. He ends his grand tour with a look at the all but universal reach of the *telenovela* (television soap opera) genre and its hungry, omnivorous fusion of traditional and modern, and rural and urban, elements. The grand odyssey experienced by *One Hundred Years of Solitude* thus becomes part of the even vaster movements of Ibero-American cultural capital in our time.

The Oxford Casebook series customarily includes an interview with the author under study. To this purpose I have retrieved my own conversation with the author, conducted in June 1982 and published the following year. The criterion for the choice, once again, was the ready availability of the item in English (it had originally run in British and U.S. periodicals) and also its not being tied to any specific occasion or ad hoc agenda. The interview, moreover, brings in some thorny political subjects that are central to the author's life and work, as well as relevant to most of the essays collected here. Finally, it is one of few such published encounters that touches on the geography and history of García Márquez's native land and on the man's plebeian side and his love of street life, aspects that are crucial to understanding and—indeed—sympathizing with this great novelist's distinctive art and vision.

Every book is, in some sense, a collaborative effort, and even more so in producing a volume of this sort. I wish to thank the series editor, Professor William Andrews, of the University of North Carolina, for inviting me to put together a casebook on *One Hundred Years of Solitude* and for his necessary support and guidance at various stages of its preparation. At Oxford University Press, Elissa Morris has been generous with her encouragement and advice, and Richard Nash-Siedlicki offered procedural suggestions on obtaining some of the more problematical permissions. Thanks to Jean Franco, Iris Zavala, Clive Griffin, and Michael Wood, for giving me their individual go-aheads to reproduce their respective out-of-print items; to Lorraine Elena Roses, for taking on the job of Englishing and formatting her manuscript essay; to the Carmen Balcells Literary Agency, for authorizing me to translate and publish several pages from Carlos Fuentes's book; and to Bruce Wheat and Christine Ménard, for helping me track down some film facts. More general thanks, finally, to Ronald Christ and to my wife, Audrey, for their early and later counsel in dealing with this project.

Notes

1. For one of the best examinations of this subject, see Tzvetan Todorov, *The Fantastic: A Structural Approach to a Literary Genre,* trans. Richard Howard (Ithaca, N.Y.: Cornell University Press, 1975).

2. Pablo Neruda, in his very funny "Oda a la crítica" (Ode to criticism), gently mocks all his critics, be they monarchists, Marxists, or those who are "ingleses, sencillamente ingleses" (English, simply English). ("Oda a la crítica" was published in Neruda's *Odas elementales* [Buenos Aires: Losada, 1958], pp. 50–53.) "Simply English," a literary voice going back to the early eighteenth-century essayists and their coffee-house public, still endures as a distinctive prose medium among quality journalistic and academic circles in Great Britain.

3. Rama met a terrible fate as an indirect result of U.S. immigration laws dating back to the McCarthy era. After an extended stint as a visiting professor at the University of Maryland, Rama was essentially deported by the Reagan State Department on vague, unspecified charges of a subversive past. He and his wife, Marta Traba (herself a novelist and art critic), died in the 1983 Avianca airplane crash outside Madrid.

4. For further investigation into the mythic aspect of *One Hundred Years of Solitude,* see the excellent article by Luis Beltrán Almería, "La revuelta del Futuro: Mito e historia en *Cien años de soledad,*" *Cuadernos Hispanoamericanos* 535 (January 1995): 23–28. Reading García Márquez's novel via the critical lens of the great Russian scholar Mikhail Bakhtin, Beltrán brings into comparable relief those topics of myth-time, historical-time, and Utopia raised by Fuentes. To these larger reflections Beltrán adds such "Bakhtinian" concerns as popular folklore, the Rabelaisian aesthetic, the parodic stance, and (in a striking insight) the interplay between the sense of smell and some of the most treasured realms of human experience, as portrayed by García Márquez.

A Conversation with
Gabriel García Márquez

GENE H. BELL-VILLADA

◆　◆　◆

T HE FOLLOWING CHAT with García Márquez took place in his
home on Calle Fuego, in the Pedregal section of Mexico City. It was
June 1982. His wife, Mercedes—as beautiful and as warmly engaging as rumors say—had opened the front door for me, smiled, and then pointed toward the inside driveway.

"There he is," she said. "There's García Márquez."

As I looked left, I saw *el señor* (as he is sometimes informally referred to)
in his BMW, attaching a compass to the dashboard.

"The compass of Melquíades," he joshed.

Doña Mercedes (the original inspiration, incidentally, for Mercedes the
mysterious pharmacist, encountered by Aureliano Babilonia during the
last days of Macondo) explained that her husband often got hopelessly lost
in the Mexican megalopolis, despite his twenty years' residence there.
Hence the compass.

Curly-haired and compact (about 5′ 6″ or 1 m. 66 cm.), García Márquez
now emerged from the car wearing blue one-piece overalls with a front
zipper—his morning writing gear, as it turns out. At this point their son
Gonzalo, a very Mexican twenty-year-old, showed up with a shy, taciturn
girlfriend.

The in-family banter grew lively. In contrast to Gonzalo's Mexican-

17

inflected speech, the novelist's soft voice and dropped s's immediately re-called to me the Caribbean accent of the northern Colombian coast where he had been born and raised.

Even before García Márquez received the Nobel Prize later that year, the Hispanic press had regularly besieged him with an attention normally reserved for movie stars and football heroes. My meeting with him, conse-quently, was obtained only after my first having negotiated countless ob-stacles. I'd first arrived in Mexico City solely with the intention of chatting with local members of his circle, as part of the preliminary researches for my projected book on him. However, a friend of mine, the writer Jorge Aguilar Mora, informed me that *el señor* had just returned from serving on the jury of the Cannes Film Festival and that it might be worth my while to reach the man himself.

So my friend telephoned Alva Rojo—the wife of a well-known Mexi-can painter—and gave me the receiver, whereupon I explained my busi-ness to her. She in turn gave me the phone number of Luis Vicens, whom I called directly and who invited me to drop by for a visit that evening.

Mr. Vicens, an expatriate Catalan bookseller and an elder buddy of Gar-cía Márquez from the 1950s, greeted me with his Colombian wife. We pro-ceeded to have a spirited conversation about the author's work and na-tional roots, among other topics. After about two hours, the fellow gave me a scrap of paper and said, "Well, look, here's Gabo's phone number. Why not give him a call?"

It would dawn on me only some days later that I was being tested and that for some reason I had passed the test.

Later that same evening I called the number. A female voice answered; I stated my business, and she passed me on to Gonzalo, who listened politely to my speech and then said, Well, Papá isn't in, but could I please call back Thursday at one o'clock?

Next day I got several busy signals before reaching the first female voice, who seemed to remember me. She gave the phone to Gonzalo, who then passed it on to Señora García, who in turn listened to my speech and, after noting that her husband was out with friends, suggested I call back Satur-day morning at 8 A.M.

Seventeen nervous hours later, I dialed. For the next thirty minutes, there were nonstop busy signals. At first I feared that the receiver had been intentionally kept off the hook. Eventually, however, the phone rang, and I spoke to the first female voice, then with Gonzalo, and finally with doña Mercedes, who said García Márquez was busy writing but could see me at 1 P.M. that day, for exactly ninety minutes, since he had a 2:30 date.

After all the delays and uncertainties I was almost taken aback by the precise nature of her instructions. But indeed the interview would take place shortly after I arrived at the scheduled hour. The author and Gonzalo soon led me across the backyard to the novelist's office, a separate bungalow equipped with special climatization (the author still could not take the morning chill in Mexico City), thousands of stereo LPs, various encyclopedias and other reference books, paintings by Latin American artists, and, on the coffee table, a Rubik's Cube. The remaining furnishings included a simple desk and chair and a matched sofa and armchair set, where our interview was held over beers.

García Márquez asked me not to use a tape recorder, presumably out of concern that I would try to sell the conversation to the media, and so the following is based on notes that I took and then transcribed shortly thereafter. We talked about numerous subjects, including politics, literature, foreign languages, and modern classical music (he loves Stravinsky but dislikes Schoenberg). Throughout our chat, son Gonzalo would drop in to offer a second and third bottle of beer. The following is a distillation of the more pertinent aspects of our interview.

Global fame notwithstanding, García Márquez remains a gentle and unassuming, indeed, an admirably balanced and normal sort of man. Throughout our conversation I found it easy to imagine him in a downtown café, sipping drinks with the TV repairman or trading stories with the tacomakers. He loves to chat; were it not for the cautious screening process set up by his friends and family, he could easily spend his entire day talking instead of writing.

Four months after our encounter, the Swedish Academy announced his Nobel Prize. One may speculate as to the additional obstacles that eventually were to become necessary in the wake of such an honor.

Gene Bell-Villada (*GB-V*): How many languages has *One Hundred Years of Solitude* been translated into?

Gabriel García Márquez (*GGM*): Thirty-seven at my wife's latest count.

GB-V: How did the Japanese version fare? Did readers understand it?

GGM: It caught on fast. Not only did they understand the book, they thought of me as Japanese! But then I've always been a devoted follower of Japanese literature.

GB-V: Outside of Spanish, which language has it sold best in?

GGM: It's hard to track down. The first Russian edition sold a million copies, in their foreign literature magazine. Apparently they're preparing translations into other Soviet languages, too. The Italian version has sold well, I believe. There are also pirated editions in Greek and Farsi—oh, and in Arabic. Arab readers seem to like the book. I hear those pirated translations aren't very good, though.

GB-V: There's a very famous strike scene in *One Hundred Years of Solitude*. Was it much trouble for you to get it right?

GGM: That sequence sticks closely to the facts of the United Fruit strike of 1928, which dates from my childhood; I was born that year.[1] The only exaggeration is in the number of dead, although it does fit the proportions of the novel. So, instead of hundreds dead, I upped it to thousands. But it's strange, a Colombian journalist the other day referred in passing to "the thousands who died in the 1928 strike." As my Patriarch says, it doesn't matter if it's true, because with enough time it *will* be!

GB-V: You maintain a certain lightness of tone in that scene.

GGM: The Yankees are depicted the way the local people saw them, hence the caricature with Virginia hams and blue pills. You see, some of my relatives back then had defended the Americans and blamed the strikers for "sabotaging prosperity" and all that, so this was my reply. Of course, my own view of Americans is a lot more complex, and I attempted to convey those events without any hate. United States may be our enemy, but it's a formidable adversary.

GB-V: Your *One Hundred Years of Solitude* is required reading in many history and political science courses in the United States. There's a sense that it's the best general introduction to Latin America. How have you felt about that?

GGM: I wasn't aware of that fact in particular, but I've had some interesting experiences along those lines. René Dumont, the French economist, recently published a lengthy academic study of Latin America. Well, right there in his bibliography, listed amid all the scholarly monographs and statistical analysis, was *One Hundred Years of Solitude*! On another occasion a sociologist from Austin, Texas, came to see me because he'd grown dissatisfied with his methods, found them arid, insufficient. So he asked me what my own method was. I told him I didn't have a method. All I do is read a lot, think a lot, and rewrite constantly. It's not a scientific thing.

GB-V: Some left-wing critics take you to task for not furnishing a more positive vision of Latin America. How do you answer them?

GGM: Yes, that happened to me in Cuba a while ago, where some critics gave *One Hundred Years of Solitude* high praise and then found fault with it for not offering a solution. I told them it's not the job of novels to furnish solutions.

GB-V: So what was your aim in *The Autumn of the Patriarch*?

GGM: I've always been interested in the figure of the Caribbean dictator, who's probably our one and only mythic personage. Where other countries have their saints, martyrs, or conquistadors, we have our dictators. I feel that the dictator is a product of ourselves, of our Caribbean culture, and in that book I tried to achieve a serene vision. I don't condemn him. Of course, I portray an earlier sort of dictator, unlike the ones today, who're propped up by a technological apparatus. They're technocrats, whereas those older dictators were often anti-imperialists, like Juan Vicente Gómez, who declared war on England and Germany.

GB-V: What about the technique in that book?

GGM: Since I wanted to create a synthesis, a composite character, I had to resort to a new narrative method. A lot of people thought the book hard going, but more and more readers now find it perfectly normal. Children today can read through much of *The Autumn of the Patriarch*. I'm not equating myself with Picasso, but it's a bit like his Cubist and other techniques, which seemed forbidding at first, yet soon became just another way of putting things together.

GB-V: Did you read *The Emperor Jones*? Or *The Comedians*?

GGM: I had *The Emperor Jones* in mind, together with a lot of other stuff. For ten years I devoured material dealing with Latin American dictators, and also studies of power, such as Suetonius. And afterward I tried to forget it all! I first read everything by O'Neill when I was in high school, though, whereas Greene taught me to evoke the heat of the tropics. It's interesting, my basic literary background consists of Golden Age poetry and twentieth-century U.S. fiction. But then the North American part is obvious. [*He laughs.*]

GB-V: You've said on occasions that Béla Bartók is a prime influence on your work. Is it the way he combined folklore with classical art?

GGM: That, and his sense of structure. Bartók is one of my favorite composers. I've learned a great deal from him. My novels are filled with symmetries of the kind Bartók has in his string quartets. (People think I'm a spontaneous writer, but I plan very carefully.) Although I've no technical knowledge of music, I can appreciate Bartók's sense of form, his architecture. Bartók also had a profound feeling for his people and for their music. His iconography is amazing, too. There's a beautiful photo of Bartók out in the field, turning the crank on a gramophone for a peasant woman to sing into it. He worked hard, you can see.

GB-V: Where is your short novel *Innocent Eréndira* set?

GGM: It takes place on the peninsula of La Guajira, which borders with

Venezuela and juts out into the Atlantic, like this. [*He sketches a rough map of La Guajira on a piece of paper.*]

GB-V: You're a writer with a very intimate knowledge of street life and plebeian ways. What do you owe it to?

GGM: [*He reflects for a moment.*] It's in my origins; it's my vocation, too. It's the life I know best, and I've deliberately cultivated it.

GB-V: Those smugglers in *Innocent Eréndira*, for instance. How did you get informed about them?

GGM: Oh, I grew up with smugglers! They were relatives of mine, uncles and cousins, operating on the Guajira peninsula, the setting for that story. Much of that contraband is gone today. The stuff they smuggled now gets stocked in duty-free shops; the rest has become internationalized and Mafia-controlled.

GB-V: With fame, is it hard, keeping up with your popular roots?

GGM: It's tough, but not as much as you'd think. I can go to a local café, and at most one person will request an autograph. What's nice is that they treat me like one of their own, especially in hotels up in the States, where they'll feel good just meeting a Latin American and sharing their gripes about the United States. But I never lose sight of the fact that I owe those experiences to the many readers of *One Hundred Years of Solitude*.

Where it does get difficult is at public events—literary cocktails, government functions, the like. The minute I walk through the door, I find myself surrounded by people who want to talk with me. My biggest struggle is leading my private life, so I'm always with old friends, who shield me from the crowds.

GB-V: How has being a journalist influenced your writing?

GGM: Journalism keeps you in contact with reality. I write a weekly syndicated column for ten newspapers and a magazine. And it helps, it's like a pitcher keeping his arm warmed up. You know, literary people have a tendency to get off on all sorts of unreality. Besides, if you stick to writing only books, you're always starting from scratch all over again.

On weekends I head out for my place in Cuernavaca and go through all kinds of magazines, clipping things from *Nouvel Observateur, Le Point*, and I used to read *Time* but have since shifted to *Newsweek*. [*He laughs.*]

GB-V: Can you, a Latin American leftist, really stand reading *Time*?

GGM: Well, I admire the techniques of U.S. journalism, the carefulness with facts, for example. Of course, it's all manipulated to fit a point of view, but that's another problem. There are also excellent non-Marxist leftists in the States, like the *Nation* people. I always pay a visit to my friend Victor Navasky when I'm in New York.

GB-V: You're on the U.S. Immigration blacklist. What's the story?

GGM: It's an odd situation. In the early 1960s I was New York correspondent for the Cuban press agency, Prensa Latina. Then, in 1961, I resigned over political disagreements and left for Mexico. I was denied entry into the United States for ten years after that. But, in 1971, Columbia University gave me an honorary doctorate, and a one-shot visa came through. Later, the Immigration people decided that if I do something that benefits the United States, such as deliver a lecture, they'd let me in. So Frank Mac-Shane[2] at Columbia was finding me lecture invitations. Eventually a secret pact took shape between the authorities and myself. They don't want the media making an issue over this thing, so if I show them an official document asking me to talk, they'll give me a visa.

At any rate, I've never really understood why they've got me in their black book—or yellow book, to be precise. My political views are clear. They may resemble the views of many a Communist Party man—but I've never belonged to a party. As far as I know, you can't deny people entry just on the basis of their ideas.[3]

[Gonzalo now stepped in, said quietly, "They're here," and stuck around to pick up our beer bottles and glasses. García Márquez and I rounded off a couple of other topics, and he asked if I had any more questions. I quickly searched in my notebook for an appropriate finale.]

GB-V: And which of your books is your favorite?

GGM: It's always the latest, so right now it's *Chronicle of a Death Foretold*. Of course, there are always differences with readers, and every book is a process. I'm particularly fond of *No One Writes to the Colonel*, but then that book led me to *One Hundred Years of Solitude*.

GARCÍA MÁRQUEZ REMAINED his amiable self, and, as we strolled through the garden, the three of us made small talk about Mexican taxis, American leftists, life in Paris, and also Harvard College, where the author's older son, Rodrigo, is a senior majoring in history. At the garden gate we shook hands; Gonzalo cordially offered a ride to the nearest taxi stand, and my conversation with the great novelist ended the way it had begun—with the youngest member of the family.

Notes

1. There had long been some controversy as to the exact year of García Márquez's birth. Dasso Saldívar, in his magisterial biography of the author, confirms that the author was actually born a year earlier, in 1927.

2. Frank MacShane was director of the Creative Writing program at Columbia University from the late 1960s to the 1980s and is the author of several literary biographies.

3. In the 1990s, the administration of President Bill Clinton lifted the long-standing ban on U.S. travel for García Márquez.

García Márquez:
On Second Reading

CARLOS FUENTES

◆　　◆　　◆

IN LATIN AMERICA, EVERYTHING IS LANGUAGE: Power and Freedom, Domination and Hope. But if the language of "barbarism" seeks to subject us all to the linear determinism of time, the language of the imagination seeks to break with that inevitability by liberating simultaneous spaces of the real. Perhaps the time has come to change the dichotomy posed by Sarmiento—Civilization or Barbarism?—for the one seemingly indicated to us by Alejo Carpentier and by the best artists of our part of the world: namely Imagination or Barbarism?

That liberation, via the imagination, of the simultaneous spaces of the real is, for me, the central fact of Gabriel García Márquez's great novel, *One Hundred Years of Solitude*. For if the enormous Latin American popularity of this work could be explained, at first glance, by the immediate shock of recognition, its comparable international success makes us think that there's something more here than a joyful discovery of identity (or even of several identities: within the genealogy of Macondo, what reader hasn't re-encountered a brother or a nanny, a girlfriend or a grandma?) and that, without a doubt, *One Hundred Years of Solitude* is one of the most entertaining books ever written in Latin America. Still, the self-recognition and the sheer fun of that first reading hardly exhaust the book's significance. Rather, they call for a second reading that corresponds to the true reading.

Such a requirement is the secret that lies at the core of this mythic and simultaneous novel: *One Hundred Years of Solitude* implies two readings because it also implies two writings. The initial reading coincides with a writing that we suppose to be true: a writer named Gabriel García Márquez is recounting, in linear and chronological fashion, the *history* of the genealogies of Macondo, with biblical and Rabelaisian hyperbole: Aureliano son of José Arcadio son of Aureliano son of José Arcadio. The second reading starts out the moment the first one ends: the chronicle of Macondo was already written down on the papers of a thaumaturgical gypsy, Melquíades, whose first apparition as character, a hundred years earlier, proves to be identical to his revelation to us as narrator, a hundred years hence. At that instant, two things occur: the book starts out all over again, yet this time the chronological history has been revealed as a historicity that is mythic, simultaneous. I say historicity and myth: the second reading of *One Hundred Years* fuses, in a true and fantastical way, the order of what happened (chronicle) with the order of what is probable (imagination). As a result, the fateful plot is liberated by the latter desire. Each historic act of the Buendías in Macondo is like an axle around which there spin all possibilities unknown to external chronicle and that, nonetheless, are as real as the dreams, the fears, the madness, and the imagination of the actors in its history.

In speaking of Carpentier I have discussed the trajectory from a foundational Utopia to a bastardized epic that degrades the former, should the mythical imagination not intervene in order to interrupt fate and recover freedom. One of the extraordinary aspects of García Márquez's novel is that its structure corresponds to that deep historicity of Spanish America—the tension between Utopia, Epic, and Myth. The New World was conceived of as the Utopia. When losing the geocentric illusion, destroyed by Copernicus, Europe needed to create a new space that would confirm the extent of the known world. Giuseppe Cocchiara has suggested that America and the American aborigines, before being discovered, were invented. That is to say: they were desired, were needed. America is above all the renewed possibility of an Arcadia, of a new beginning of history whose ancient presuppositions had been destroyed by the Copernican revolution. Thomas More's *Utopia* was embodied in the settlements of Christian missionaries, from California to Paraguay. Yet this dream—at heart, a representation of Innocence—was denied, immediately, by Epic, proof of historical necessity. Cortés and Pizarro corrupted the dream by subjecting it to the abstract demands of Spain's imperial mandate—Plus Ultra—and by the concrete demands of the hunger of individual will: that of the *homo faber* of the Renaissance. Utopia, in this way, was only an illusory bridge between Medieval geocentrism and Renaissance anthropocentrism.

It seems to me not accidental that the first two parts of *One Hundred Years of Solitude* correspond to that opposition of origins. The founding of Macondo is the founding of Utopia. José Arcadio Buendía and his family have wandered like pilgrims in the jungle, going around in circles, until they find, precisely, the place where they can found the new Arcadia, the promised land of origins: "The men on the expedition felt overwhelmed by their most ancient memories in that paradise of dampness and silence, going back to before original sin. . . ." As with More's Utopia, Macondo is an island of the imagination: José Arcadio Buendía believes it to be surrounded by water. And from his island, José Arcadio Buendía invents the world; he points at things with his finger, then learns to name them and, finally, to forget them. But—in a significant fact—at the very moment that Buendía the founder becomes aware of "the infinite possibilities of a loss of memory," he has to resort, for the first time, to writing. He hangs signs on objects. He discovers reflexive knowledge, which he understood previously as *divination*. And he feels obligated to dominate the world through science. What once he'd known quite naturally he will now know thanks only to the help of maps, magnets, and magnifying glasses. The Utopian founders were like fortune-tellers. They could recognize the hidden yet pre-established language of the world. They felt no need to create a second language. It sufficed for them to open themselves up to the language of what there was.

Michel Foucault states, in *The Order of Things*, that modern knowledge breaks with its former kinship with divinity. It ceases to *divine*. Divinity presupposes signs that are prior to itself. In the modern episteme, the sign signifies only within knowledge itself, and the drama of this break forces us to look eagerly for the extensions that can put us into contact once again with the world that predates us. Foucault cites as examples Malebranche's sensibility and Berkeley's sensation. Later on, and until today, those bridges will be History and Psychoanalysis.

However, José Arcadio Buendía—even as he abandons divination for science and moves from sacred knowledge to rational hypothesis—will open the doors to the second part of the novel: the Epic, an historical passage in which the utopian foundation of Macondo is negated by the active needs of linear time. This part occurs—basically and significantly—amid the thirty-two armed uprisings of Colonel Aureliano Buendía, the fever of banana exploitation and the final abandonment of Macondo, the Utopia of foundation exploited, degraded, and, finally, murdered by the Epic of history, action, commercialism, crime. The deluge—the punishment—leaves behind it a "Macondo forgotten even by the birds, where heat and dust had become so strong that breathing was a chore."

The survivors remain there, Aureliano and Amaranta Úrsula, "secluded by solitude and love and by the solitude of love in a house where it was almost impossible to sleep because of the noise of the red ants." And here begins the unfolding of the third space in the book, the Mythic, whose simultaneous and renewable quality will not be clarified until the final long paragraph, when we find out that that entire history had already been written by the gypsy Melquíades, the fortune teller who accompanied Macondo at its foundation and who, to keep it alive, must resort to José Arcadio Buendía's chief ruse: writing. Hence the profound paradox of the second reading of *One Hundred Years of Solitude*: everything was known, long before it happened, by the sacred, utopian, mythic, foundational divinations of Melquíades. Yet nothing would be known had Melquíades not registered it via writing. As did Cervantes, García Márquez establishes the frontiers of reality within a book and the frontiers of a book within reality. The symbiosis is perfect. And once it is realized, we begin the mythic reading of this beautiful, joyous, melancholy book, about an inclusive town that proliferates, as if by parthenogenesis, with the richness of a South American Yoknapatawpha.

As in Faulkner, in García Márquez the novel is self-generating. Every creation is a magical spell, an androgynous fertilization by the creator and consequently a myth, a fundamental act—the representation of the foundational act. *One Hundred Years of Solitude*, at the mythic level, is above all a permanent question: What does Macondo know about itself? That is to say: what does Macondo know about its creation? The novel constitutes a totalizing answer: in order to know, Macondo has to tell itself all of its history, both "real" and "fictive," all the proofs of the notaries, and all of the rumors, legends, slanders, pious lies, exaggerations, and fables written down by no one but that oldsters have passed on to youngsters, gossips have told priests, witch doctors have invoked in the middle of the night, and charlatans have represented in the middle of the square. The saga of Macondo and the Buendías includes the entirety of the oral and legendary past, in order to inform us that we cannot be satisfied with history as officially documented—that history is also all the Good and Evil dreamt, imagined, and desired by men for their self-preservation and self-destruction.

As with any faculty of memory that is mythic, ab-original, that of Macondo is creation and re-creation at a single instant. Time in this novel is simultaneity; we realize it only on second reading, at which point meaning is achieved in the primordial fact that one day José Arcadio Buendía decides it will always henceforth be Monday, or in the final fact that Úrsula says, "It's as if time had turned around and we were back at the beginning." Memories repeat the models, the matrixes of the origin, in the same way that, time and again, Colonel Buendía crafts little gold fishes, which he melts again in order that . . . that he may be continually reborn and ensure with severe, intimate, ritual acts the permanence of the cosmos. Such mythifying is not gratuitous. Through their imaginations, men defend themselves against the encompassing chaos, the jungles and rivers of the immense, devouring magma of South America. Nature has its domains. Men have their demons; they are bedeviled, as is the race of the Buendías—founders and usurpers, creators and destroyers, Sartorises and Snopeses within a single lineage.

An authentic revision of utopia, epic, and myth in Spanish America, *One Hundred Years of Solitude* dominates—by demonizing it—the dead time past of historiography in order to enter, metaphorically, mythically, simultaneously, into the total time of the present. A Spanish galleon lies stranded on the mountain; men tattoo their sex organs; a railroad wagon filled with peasants murdered by the banana company crosses the jungle and the corpses are hurled into the ocean; a grandfather ties himself forever onto a tree until he becomes an emblematic trunk, shaman-like, fashioned by rain, wind, and dust; flowers rain from the same sky into which Remedios, the Beauty, will ascend. In each of these fictive acts we shall see perish both the positivistic time of Epic (this really happened) and the nostalgic time of Utopia (this could have happened), and what is born is the absolute present time of Myth: this is happening.

But all the same there is here something simpler, clearer, and deeper. Lévi-Strauss has indicated that the purpose of a mythic system is to establish relations of homology between natural and social conditions. And it is at this level that *One Hundred Years of Solitude* becomes a terrifying metaphor for man's sense of abandonment and fear on this earth—the abandonment and fear of regressing to an anonymous, inhuman nature, the horror of engendering a child with the tail of a pig and embarking on the return to absolute origins: to nothingness. An Edenic couple, the first cousins José Arcadio and Úrsula are pilgrims who flee the original world of their sin and their terror to found a second paradise in Macondo. But the founding—of a town or a lineage—presupposes the repetition of the same act of coupling, of consummation, of incest, with land or flesh. Lévi-Strauss adds that matrimonial exchange serves as a mediator between Nature and Culture, these normally in mutual opposition. Marriage creates a second Nature, mediated, which man can influence. Hence those numerous myths about coupling between man and animal, about marriages between woman and beast, double metaphors for the natural sphere and the incest prohibition, for violation and sin. Such metaphors are nonetheless the condition for a synonymy expressed by the Yoruba word for *marriage*, which just as readily denotes *food, possession, merit, gain,* or *acquisition.* I believe that via this route we can approach the profound significance of *One Hundred Years of Solitude*: this novel is a long metaphor—extended over a long century of occurrences—that only designates the instantaneous act of carnal love between the first man and the first woman, José Arcadio and Ursula, who fornicate in fear that the fruit of their incest might be a child with the tail of a pig but who also fornicate so that the world will sustain itself, will eat, possess, and acquire, will merit, dream, and be.

Does myth—as Philip Rahv insisted—deny history? Yes, a deadening, oppressive, factitious history, which García Márquez leaves behind in order to situate, within a novel, the triple encounter of Latin American time. The encounter with the living, original, creative past, which is the tradition of risk and rupture: each generation of the Buendías will experience a son dead in a revolution—an epic—that never ends. The encounter with the longed-for future: ice arrives for the first time in the torrid jungle of Macondo amid wonder at the supernatural—magic and usefulness will remain inseparable. The encounter with the absolute present in which we remember and desire: a novel lived as the lengthy chronicle of a century of solitude in Colombia but read as the fable precariously registered within the peripatetic papers of Melquíades. Macondo's secular document consists of the instant pages of a mythomaniacal sorcerer who mixes indelibly the relations of life as it is lived with the relations of life as it is written.

Through this doubling process, *One Hundred Years of Solitude* becomes the *Quixote* of Latin American literature. As happens with the Knight of the Sorrowful Countenance, the men and women of Macondo can turn only to a novel—this novel—in order to prove that they exist. The creation of a novelistic language, then, as proof of being. The novel as certificate of birth, as negation of the false documents of civil status that, until recently, had concealed our reality. Language-fiction-truth versus lexicon-oratory-falsehood: *One Hundred Years of Solitude* against the conquistadors' arrogant letters to the crown, against the monarchs' unfulfilled Laws of the Indies, against the nineteenth-century liberators' violated Constitutions, against the oppressors' humiliating letters of an alliance for progress. Against all the texts that disguise us there stands a novelistic sign that indelibly identifies us, like those Ash Wednesday crosses that are never to be erased from the foreheads of the seventeen natural sons of Aureliano Buendía: the cross of a scorched earth, the black sign of baptism and also the target of death for the guns of dictatorships and oligarchies that—thanks to a fleshly cross—will always succeed in recognizing, and assassinating, the rebel, bastard sons of the patriarch.

Against invisible crimes, against anonymous criminals, García Márquez erects, in our name, a word and a place. He baptizes—as does the first Buendía, as did Carpentier—all the nameless things of a continent. And he fashions a place. The site of the myth is Macondo. García Márquez, fabulist, knows that presence dissolves in a site (a locus of resistances) that will be all sites: place that contains them all, that contains us all: the seat of time, the consecration of all times, the appointed place of memory and desire, a common present where everything may start again: a temple, a book. *One Hundred Years of Solitude* re-initiates, re-updates, re-orders—makes contemporary—all present times of a part of the Spanish American imagination that for too long seemed lost to letters and subject to the tyrannical weight of folklore, naturalistic testimony, and naive denunciation. Not among the least of García Márquez's virtues is that in his book he transforms evil into beauty and humor. The darker side of Latin American history had previously emerged—in the old novels of Rómulo Gallegos, José Eustasio Rivera, and Jorge Icaza—as the embodiment of an evil that was isolated, impenetrable, crudely realistic, and so alien and defined as to be ultimately ridiculous. García Márquez realizes that our history is not merely inevitable; in some obscure way, we have also desired it. Moreover, he makes evil into humor because evil desired is not an abstraction that is alien to our lives; it is the other, that which we can see outside ourselves but also as part of ourselves, reduced to its ironic, proportional, chance encounter with our everyday weaknesses and our imaginary representations.

Freshly dissolving those false polemics and dilemmas concerning realism versus fantasy, art *engagé* versus art for art's sake, national literature versus cosmopolitan literature, García Márquez's book destroys those idiotic a prioris in order to proclaim and conquer the right to an imagination that nonetheless can distinguish between *mystifications*—in which a dead past wishes to pass as living present—and *mythifications*—in which a living present recaptures, also, the life of the past.

Note

This essay was translated by Gene H. Bell-Villada.

Gabriel García Márquez

Cien años de soledad

JAMES HIGGINS

◆　　◆　　◆

BORN IN 1928, Gabriel García Márquez spent the formative years of his childhood in Aracataca, a small town in the tropical Caribbean region on Colombia's north coast. In the early years of the century the North American United Fruit Company had moved into the area to exploit its banana-producing potential and in the 1910s Aracataca became something of a boom town. By the time of the author's birth the boom had passed, but it was still a bustling, prosperous little community. However, following United Fruit's withdrawal from Colombia in 1941, the economy of the region collapsed, and a few years later, when the writer and his mother returned to arrange for the sale of his grandparent's house, they were to find that the once thriving Aracataca had become a dilapidated ghost town.

Because of the unusual circumstances of his upbringing, García Márquez was to experience solitude from an early age. His mother, Luisa, the daughter of one of the region's long-established families, had married a humble telegraphist, Gabriel Eligio García, against her parents' wishes, but to placate them she returned home for the birth of her first child and left the boy behind to be brought up by them. In his grandparents' large, rambling house, shared by three aunts, he grew up as a solitary little boy among elderly adults. Later experiences were to reinforce the deep-rooted sense of solitude that runs through all his writing.

Nonetheless, his childhood was a happy one in which he enjoyed a particularly close relationship with his grandfather, and he was raised in a storytelling environment in that the elders were constantly reliving the past and recounting anecdotes about the history of the family and the town. His grandfather Colonel Nicolás Márquez had fought on the Liberal side against the ruling Conservatives in the Thousand Days' War (1899–1902), the last of a succession of civil wars that had rent Colombia, and would often reminisce about those stirring times. For their part, his grandmother and aunts were credulous, superstitious women who believed in the supernatural and recounted all sorts of magical happenings as if they were everyday events, and the author has often claimed that it was from his grandmother that he learned his narrative manner. That childhood world was to come to an end, however, with the death of his grandfather in 1936, and García Márquez has frequently stated that no other period in his life has matched his first eight years for richness of experience.

García Márquez spent most of the next ten years as a boarder at a school in Zipaquirá, near Bogota, and in 1947 he entered the National University in the capital to study law. Coming as he did from the Caribbean region, he never felt at home in the alien environment of the Andean highlands, whose cold climate and formal, traditionalist atmosphere proved uncongenial to him. He found solace in books, among which he singles out Kafka's *Metamorphosis* as exercising a profound influence on him, and himself began writing short stories. In 1948 he abandoned his studies and returned to the north coast, where he worked as a journalist, first in Cartagena and then, from 1950, in Barranquilla. The latter city was to have a decisive influence on his literary development, for there he took up with a group of bohemian literati, who introduced him to the work of modern Anglo-Saxon writers, especially Joyce, Virginia Woolf, and William Faulkner. Later he was to render homage to this so-called Barranquilla Group by portraying them in the latter pages of *Cien años de soledad.*

It was in Barranquilla that he wrote most of his early short stories and his first novel, *La hojarasca,* writing at night and in his spare time. The novel was eventually published in 1955, but he encountered difficulty in establishing himself as a novelist and was, in fact, achieving greater success as a reporter. In 1954 he had joined the staff of *El Espectador* in Bogotá and soon became one of Colombia's best-known journalists, boosting the paper's circulation with articles such as "Relato de un náufrago," a serialized account of the ordeal of a shipwrecked sailor.

Like his fellow Colombians, García Márquez was deeply affected by the years of political violence unleashed by the assassination in 1948 of the Liberal presidential candidate, Jorge Eliécer Gaitán, violence that claimed 2000,000–300,000 lives in the period from 1949 to 1962 and led to the dictatorship of General Gustavo Rojas Pinilla (1953–1957). An indication of his own political leanings is that in 1955 he was briefly a member of the Communist Party. As a child he had come under the influence of his grandfather's radical liberalism, a lasting impression was made on him by accounts of the massacre of striking United Fruit Company workers in Ciénaga in the year of his birth,[1] and at school in Zipaquirá he had been introduced to Marxist thought by leftist teachers. His flirtation with the Communist Party was transitory, and he has always rejected hard-line Marxist dogmatism, but he has consistently championed left-wing causes and has always maintained that the future of the world lies with socialism

In 1955 García Márquez was sent to Europe by *El Espectador* as a foreign correspondent, only to discover shortly after his arrival in Paris that the paper had been closed down by the government, and for several months he endured the struggles and hardships of the impecunious artist. In 1957 he moved to Caracas, working there as a journalist for almost two years, and in 1959, following the Cuban Revolution, he joined the Cuban news agency Prensa Latina, first in Bogotá and then in Cuba and New York. In 1961 he resigned in protest against the manoeuvers of the Communist Party hard-liners and with his wife—he had married in 1958—moved to Mexico City, where he continued his journalistic career, worked for a public relations firm, and wrote film scripts. In the meantime, he had persevered with his writing and achieved modest success with the novella *El coronel no tiene quien le escriba* (1961), the novel *La mala hora* (1962), and a collection of short stories, *Los funerales de la Mamá Grande* (1962), and in 1967 he was to win an international reputation almost overnight with the publication of his masterpiece, *Cien años de soledad*.[2]

While considerable works in their own right, García Márquez's early writings are also stages in the maturation of *Cien años*. *La hojarasca* and several of the short stories introduce us to Macondo, the fictional representation of the world in which the author grew up. The former shows the effects of the short-lived "banana boom" and the subsequent depression on that small rural community, while "Los funerales de la Mamá Grande" portrays the traditional dominance of the land-owning oligarchy through the mythical story of the legendary matriarch who ruled over the region from time immemorial. *El coronel no tiene quien le escriba* and *La mala hora* recreate the climate of political violence that prevailed in the Colombian countryside in the 1950s, the former linking it to a long tradition of such violence and the latter depicting its corrosive effect on the community. Many of the characters of these early narratives are also forerunners of the Buendías of *Cien años de soledad* in that they are lonely, isolated individuals leading a solitary existence With regard to style, "Los funerales de la Mamá Grande" marks a major evolution. In all of his fiction, García Márquez endeavors to achieve a poetic transposition of reality, but in most of his early work he does so in a style that by and large is still essentially realistic. However, in this story he was to hit on the narrative manner best suited to give literary expression to the world he had known as a child. Here the narrator introduces himself as someone who sits down at his front door to tell a tale as a kind of spokesman for the community. The story, in effect, has the character of popular oral narrative, privileging the legendary and depicting the world in larger-than-life terms, but at the same time its "magical realism" is counterbalanced by an ironic, irreverent tone that subverts the very legend it is propagating. In *Cien años* García Márquez was to perfect that narrative manner and to create an all-encompassing fictional world which incorporates the principal themes treated separately in his earlier work.

Following his success with *Cien años,* García Márquez went on to consolidate his reputation with a number of other books, notably *La increíble y triste historia de la cándida Eréndida y de su abuela desalmada* (1972), *El otoño del patriarca* (1975), *Crónica de una muerte anunciada* (1981), and *El amor en los tiempos del cólera* (1985). His status as one of the world's great novelists was recognized by the award of the Nobel Prize for Literature in 1982.

Cien años narrates the history of the town of Macondo and of its founding family, the Buendías. Following his killing of a neighbor who insulted his honor, José Arcadio Buendía, his wife, Úrsula, and a group of friends abandon their native town and set out in search of a new home, settling eventually in an isolated region in the swamplands. For some time Macondo lives in a state of primeval innocence, its only contact with the outside world coming through the occasional visits of a tribe of gypsies, led by Melquíades, who introduce the inhabitants to wondrous inventions such as false teeth, ice, and the magnet and arouse in José Arcadio the thirst for scientific experiment and the ambition to see the town enjoy the benefits of technological progress. In the course of time, progress does come to Macondo as it gradually emerges from its isolation, but, although it brings relative prosperity, it does not turn the town into the Utopia envisaged by its founder. A magistrate is sent by the central government to assume authority over the district, and, as it is drawn into the sphere of national politics, the town becomes embroiled in a series of bloody civil wars. The establishment of a railway link paves the way for the commercial exploitation of the region's natural resources by the North American Banana Company, and overnight Macondo is transformed into a boom town; disgruntled by their low wages and poor working conditions, the workers declare a strike and are shot down by government troops; subsequently, torrential rain destroys the plantations, the Banana Company withdraws, and Macondo declines into a ghost town. The history of the Buendías began with an "original sin" in that José Arcadio and Úrsula were first cousins, and succeeding generations likewise betray a propensity to incest, and throughout the novel the family is haunted by the fear of punishment in the form of the birth of a monstrous child with a pig's tail. That fear is eventually realized when the love affair between the last remaining Buendías, Aureliano Babilonia and his aunt Amaranta Úrsula, produces the dreaded monstrosity. Shortly afterward, when Aureliano finally succeeds in making sense of the puzzling manuscript written by Melquíades decades earlier and which over the generations various members of the family have vainly attempted to decipher, he discovers that it is a prophetic account of the history of Macondo and that the Buendías and their world will come to an end when he reads the last sentence.

Cien años is a novel that maintains a tension or dialectic between different perspectives. It is, first of all, a comic novel, an entertainment, which adopts an irreverent attitude toward literature—"the best plaything ever invented for making fun of people" (p. 462)—as something not to be taken seriously.[3] Yet, at the same time, it is a deeply serious and highly ambitious book that sets out to rewrite the history of Latin America and to offer a view of the human condition. Again, it proclaims its fictionality when, on the closing page, Aureliano Babilonia discovers that, in effect, the Buendías are no more than creatures of Melquíades's imagination with no existence outside the pages of his manuscript, an ending which serves, among other things, to warn the reader that the novel is "a fictive construct, a creation, and not a mirror that meticulously reflects reality."[4] Lurking behind the book is the ontological uncertainty of our times, as is revealed by an earlier episode when the same Aureliano, trying to persuade others of the truth of his version of Macondo's history, runs up against the skepticism of the local priest, who, ironically, is conspicuously lacking in the certainties that he is supposed to embody:

> El párroco lo midió con una mirada de lástima.
> —Ay, hijo—suspiró—. A mí me bastaría con estar seguro de que tu y yo existimos en este momento. (p. 484)

Unable to share traditional realist fiction's confident assumption of man's ability to understand and describe the world, García Márquez effectively waives any claim to be "telling it the way it is." And yet, despite his awareness of the limitations of literature, he nonetheless endeavors to do what novelists have always sought to do: to depict the world around him. Paradoxically, he attempts to translate reality into words while casting doubt on the feasibility of such an undertaking.

García Márquez has stated that his primary aim in writing *Cien años* was to recreate the lost world of his childhood.[5] He does so through the vehicle of a so-called magical realism that eschews the documentary approach of realist fiction and instead gives expression to the worldview of a rural people living in remote isolation from the modern developed world. It should be stressed that the magical realism of *Cien años* does not imply that Latin American reality is somehow inherently magical, though the novel does highlight the prodigious dimensions of the natural environment and the excesses of political life. Nor does the much-bandied term "fantasy" have much meaning in relation to *Cien años,* since every event described, no matter how fantastic it might appear, has a perfectly logical explanation. What the novel does is to present events, not as they actually occurred but as they were perceived and interpreted by the local people. Thus, for example, the narrative points to the real explanation of Remedios's disappearance by recording that outsiders were of the opinion that she had run off with a man and that the story put about by her family was an invention designed to cover up the scandal, but it is the family's version—that she ascended into heaven—which the text privileges and recounts in full and plausible detail, since it was the one that was widely accepted in the community (pp. 313–314). Likewise, the systematic use of hyperbole—José Arcadio's prodigious virility, Colonel Aureliano's thirty-two armed uprisings, the seventy-two schoolgirls queuing up to empty seventy-two chamberpots, to cite but a few examples—corresponds to the way in which the popular collective memory blows events up to larger-than-life proportions. The narrative, too, has an Old Testament ring to it—there is an original sin, an exodus, the discovery of an (un)promised land, a plague, a deluge, an apocalypse—that is a reflection both of the cultural environment and of the myth-making tendency of popular history. In effect, *Cien años* transmits the history of Macondo as it was recorded and elaborated over the generations by popular oral tradition, and, by so doing, it permits a rural society to give expression to itself in terms of its own cultural experience.

Yet *Cien años* is a written text, and a story that gives the impression of being an oral narrative turns out on the final pages to be recorded in Melquíades's manuscript.[6] Another layer of tension informing the novel, therefore, is that between the oral and the written. By incorporating popular oral history into literature to convey a third-world experience, García Márquez accords it the status and prestige associated with the written word. He also highlights the relativity of all worldviews, for events that appear fantastic to the sophisticated reader—Remedios's ascent into heaven, trips on flying carpets, the parish priesnt's feats of levitation—are accepted as everyday realities in the cultural environment of Macondo, and, by contrast, the modern technology that the sophisticated reader takes for granted—ice cubes, false teeth, the locomotive—is greeted with awe as something wonderful and magical. *Cien años* thus not only challenges conventional assumptions as to what constitutes reality but subverts the novelistic genre's conventional Eurocentrism and, indeed, the whole rationalist cultural tradition of the West. At the same time, though, the narrator writes in an ironic, tongue-in-cheek manner that distances him from the oral history that he is transmitting. Thus, for example, in the episode discussed earlier, the story of Remedios's ascent into heaven is recounted straightfaced but is undermined by insinuation of the real, more prosaic explanation of the facts. In effect, if *Cien años* sets out to subvert Eurocentric attitudes, it also simultaneously subverts Latin Americans' perceptions of their own history.

As has already been implied, García Márquez is writing against the Western novelistic tradition, and *Cien años* demands a reading which eschewing the kind of narrow Eurocentrism that disguises itself as universalism, approaches the novel in terms of its own specificity. However, at the same time, the novel draws heavily on literary sources, and, if Borges would seem to be the main influence, it should be remembered that behind the latter lies the whole corpus of Western culture.[7] It is significant that in the provincial environment of Macondo a privileged space should be allotted to Melquíades's room, representing the timeless world of literature, and significant, too, that, having had his horizons broadened by the Catalan bibliophile, the younger writer Gabriel should leave Macondo for Paris. For, while challenging the Western novelistic tradition, García Márquez is also writing within it, and in *Cien años* he has set out not only to portray a Latin American reality but also to express the universal through the local.

In giving a literary depiction of the world of his childhood, García Márquez has also created in the fictional community of Macondo a microcosm of a larger world. The story of Macondo, in fact, reflects the general pattern of Latin America's history. It is founded by settlers fleeing a homeland haunted by the specter of violence and is born of a utopian dream, being built on the spot where José Arcadio has a vision of a luminous city of houses walled with mirrors (p. 97). By the final page, however, the city of mirrors has become a city of mirages. Macondo thus represents the dream of a brave new world that America seemed to promise and that was cruelly proved illusory by the subsequent course of history. *Cien años,* in effect, is a demystifying rewriting of the history of the subcontinent. The ruling establishment's tradition of manipulating history is exposed in the latter part of the novel, when the authorities hush up the massacre of the striking banana workers and the roundup and disappearance of all potential subversives, claiming that Macondo is a peaceful and contented community where social harmony reigns (p. 383). Later, young Aureliano, brought up by his uncle to regard Macondo as the victim of the Banana Company's imperialist exploitation, discovers that the school history books portray the company as a benefactor which brought prosperity and progress (pp. 422–423). *Cien años* sets out to debunk the official myths by offering an alternative history. In part, this is a popular view of a local community subjected to domination by outside forces. At the same time, however, it is the view of a privileged class, since the dominant perspective is that of the Buendías, the local provincial elite, and their version of history is undermined in its turn by the narrator's ironic distancing of himself from it.

While in strictly chronological terms the events of the novel roughly span the century from the years after Independence to around 1930, the early phase of Macondo's history evokes Latin America's colonial period, when communities lived isolated from one another and the viceroyalties themselves had little contact with the distant metropolis. Latin America's isolation from intellectual developments in Europe is hilariously brought out when José Arcadio's researches lead him to the discovery that the earth is round (p. 75), and colonial underdevelopment is reflected in his acute awareness of Macondo's backwardness in relation to the outside world:

> "En el mundo están ocurriendo cosas increíbles," le decía a Úrsula. "Ahí mismo, al otro lado del río, hay toda clase de aparatos mágicos, mientras nosotros seguimos viviendo como los burros." (p. 79)

The novel thus ironically debunks Spain's claim to have bequeathed to America the benefits of European civilization. Indeed, the Conquest itself is parodied, in a passage reminiscent of the chronicles (pp. 82–83),[8] by the expedition in which the men of Macondo re-enact the ordeals of the Spanish explorers and conquistadores in order to make contact with the civilization that Spain allegedly spread to its colonies.

Furthermore, the Spanish colonial heritage is identified as one of the principal factors in Latin America's continuing underdevelopment. Significantly, the Macondo men's expedition fails to make contact with civilization and succeeds only in finding the hulk of an old Spanish galleon, stranded on dry land and overgrown with vegetation (p. 83), symbol of a heritage that is anachronistic, out of context and ill equipped to tackle the awesome American environment. Above all, that heritage takes the form of a mentality, personified in the novel by Fernanda del Carpio. An incomer from the capital, she embodies the Castilian traditionalism of the *cachacos,* the inhabitants of the cities of the Colombian *altiplano,* and, beyond that, a whole set of values and attitudes that Latin America has inherited from Spain. Nursing aristocratic pretensions that are reflected in her name—an echo of that of Bernardo del Carpio, a legendary Spanish hero of medieval times—she lives the illusion of a grandeur that no longer exists and clings to antiquated customs in a world that no longer has any use for them; and, as Macondo falls into the hands of the Banana Company and is invaded by lower-class upstarts, she comforts herself with the belief that she is spiritually superior to the vulgar tradesmen who have taken over the world, an attitude that echoes the response of Spanish American intellectuals of the Arielist generation to North American expansionism.[9] The heirlooms that she receives from her father as Christmas presents are ironically described by her husband as a family cemetery, and, as though to confirm the truth of his words, the last present turns out to be a box containing the father's corpse (pp. 289–290). What they symbolize, in fact, is an outmoded, traditionalist mentality that prevents Latin America from coming to terms with the modern world.

The advent of the republican era is marked by the arrival of Don Apolinar Moscote to assume authority over the town as representative of the central government. Reversing the conventional wisdom that has traditionally attributed the political instability of the nineteenth century to the "barbaric" countryside, whose backwardness and lawlessness supposedly hindered the "civilized' cities" efforts to lead the subcontinent toward order and progress,[10] the novel identifies government intervention in local affairs as the origin of Macondo's troubles. Till then it had always been a well-ordered community, and, far from bringing law and order, the new magistrate immediately stirs up unrest by decreeing that all houses are to be painted blue (pp. 133–134), the color of the ruling Conservative party, an act symptomatic of the autocratic and insensitive impositions of central government. Moreover, if Don Apolinar introduces Macondo to parliamentary democracy, he also introduces it to the cynical manipulation of democratic institutions, the first elections being rigged to ensure the victory of the government party (p. 173). And as Macondo is incorporated into the national political system, it becomes caught up in the civil violence engendered by that tainted system.

For much of the novel, Macondo is afflicted by the civil wars between Liberals and Conservatives that were a feature of the nineteenth century in Colombia and other Latin American countries. The futility of that bloodshed is conveyed by the progressive disillusionment of Colonel Aureliano Buendía, the champion of the Liberal cause. A principal cause of his disenchantment is the ideological fanaticism typified by the agitator Dr. Alirio Noguera, who conceives a plan for liquidating Conservatism by a coordinated nationwide campaign of assassination (p. 175). While such fanaticism leads extremists on both sides to forget their common humanity, Aureliano establishes a friendship with General Moncada across the ideological divide, and at one point the two men consider the possibility of breaking with their respective parties and joining forces to establish a humanitarian regime that would combine the best features of the warring doctrines (p. 223). Yet he later has Moncada executed, for he himself falls prey to the same fanaticism and is ready to sacrifice even his friends to achieve his political objectives, and before his death his old friend warns him that his obsessive hatred of his political enemies has dehumanized him (p. 235). Fortunately, Aureliano is sensitive enough to realize what is happening to him, and his subsequent determination to bring the war to an end is born in part of the wish to save himself as a human being.

The irony is that, despite their ideological differences, both parties are dominated by the same privileged elite, and in practice the distinction between them ultimately becomes blurred, just as the houses in Macondo take on an indeterminate color as a result of being constantly repainted red or blue according to which group is in control (p. 201). In power the Liberals commit the same abuses as the Conservatives. As Governor, Arcadio Buendía behaves like a petty dictator, and the deal that he strikes with the second José Arcadio, whereby he legalizes the latter's right to lands that he has usurped in exchange for the right to levy taxes (pp. 190–191), exemplifies and reinforces the traditional pattern of oligarchic domination and, significantly, is later ratified by the Conservatives. Committed to a program of radical reform, Colonel Aureliano finds himself not only fighting the Conservatives but at odds with his own party. The Liberal landowners react to the threat to their property by entering into secret alliances with the Conservatives, financial backing is withdrawn, and eventually the party strategists drop all radical policies from their program in order to broaden their support (p. 244). At this point, Aureliano comes to realize that they have been fighting not for change but for power, for access to office and the spoils that go with it, and, disillusioned, he brings the war to an end and withdraws from political life. In the end a compromise is reached whereby the two parties share power, a solution that restores peace but that leaves the socioeconomic status quo intact. Liberals and Conservatives are thus exposed as ultimately representing the same class interests.

As peace and stability return to Macondo, the region enters a period of neocolonial domination. Early in the novel José Arcadio articulates the dream of a world transformed by scientific and technological progress:

> Trató de seducirla con . . . la promesa de un mundo prodigioso donde bastaba con echar unos líquidos mágicos en la tierra para que las plantas dieran frutos a voluntad del hombre, y donde se vendían a precio de baratillo toda clase de aparatos para el dolor. (p. 86)

What he is voicing, in effect, is a constant of Latin American thought since Independence, the aspiration to "modernize" on the model of the advanced industrial nations in order to achieve a similar level of development. In the event, Macondo does come to enjoy a period of economic growth. However, "modernization" does not come about as the result of internal development but is imported from the outside, and hence José Arcadio's original dream of a city of mirrors takes on an ironic significance in that Macondo's role becomes that of reflecting the developed world. And, though Macondo does undoubtedly prosper and progress, it continues to trail behind the rest of the world, and, furthermore, it finds itself the victim of foreign economic and cultural imperialism.

In fact, the story of the later Macondo illustrates Latin America's neo-colonial status as an economic dependency of international capital, particularly North American. No sooner had Macondo embarked on a phase of autonomous economic development than it falls under the domination of North American capital and, incorporated into the world economy as a source of primary products, becomes subject to cycles of boom and recession determined by the fluctuations of the international market. Aureliano Segundo accumulates a fantastic fortune quite fortuitously, thanks to the astonishing fertility of his livestock (p. 267), and the whole community enjoys an equally fortuitous prosperity generated by the banana boom. Macondo's experience of prosperity is thus due not to any real economic development but to the amazing richness of the region's natural resources and to international demand for those resources. Hence it is defenseless against sudden slumps in the market. Symbol of such slumps is the great deluge that ruins Aureliano Segundo by killing his stock and that halts banana production and leads to the departure of the company, turning Macondo into a ghost town. The extent to which the Latin American economy is manipulated by foreign capital is indicated by the suggestion that the crisis was deliberately engineered by the company, whose directors were so powerful that they were able to control the weather (p. 422). In the wake of his ruin, Aureliano Segundo is reduced to running a lottery to make ends meet and is nicknamed Don Divina Providencia. He comes, in fact, to personify Latin America, whose economic role in the world is passively to wait for the stroke of good fortune that will bring it another period of prosperity.

Furthermore, such progress and prosperity as are brought to Macondo by foreign capital are achieved at a price. The Banana Company exploits its workforce quite cynically, as is indicated by the list of complaints presented by the workers (p. 372), and Macondo effectively becomes a colony, a company town run by company men backed up by armed thugs dressed as policemen. And such is the power exercised by the company that when the workers take strike action, the authorities send in troops to break the strike by force, massacring the strikers and liquidating the union leaders. The dominant influence exerted by foreign capital in Latin America is thus seen to extend beyond the economic to the political sphere.

The patrician Buendías represent that oligarchy that has traditionally ruled Latin America. Macondo's founding family, they develop into a landowning class, the process by which the latifundia system was established being encapsulated in the episode in which the second José Arcadio makes use of his enormous physical strength to appropriate the best lands in the district (p. 190), and subsequently they evolve into an entrepreneurial bourgeoisie by branching into business. The solitude that is their dominant family trait is directly related to their egoism: living exclusively for themselves, they are incapable of loving, of sharing, of giving themselves to others. Perhaps the most extreme examples are the introverted Aureliano, who lives in a private world of his own that no one is allowed to enter, and Amaranta, who ruins the lives of four men by arousing their passion without being able to bring herself to satisfy it, but their egocentric attitude is shared by the whole family, for everyone in the Buendía household is too wrapped up in his own affairs to think of anyone else: "nadie se daba cuenta de nada mientras no se gritara en el corredor, porque los afanes de la panadería, los sobresaltos de la guerra, el cuidado de los niños, no dejaban tiempo para pensar en la felicidad ajena" (p. 432).

Relating to that egoism is the family's propensity to incest. The Buendía dynasty originates with an incestuous marriage, and successive generations become involved in more or less incestuous relationships. Their phobia about the monstrous child with a pig's tail ironically highlights their blindness to their failings, for the apparently normal Buendías are, in fact, deformed by their monstrous egoism, as Úrsula glimpses on more than one occasion (pp. 98, 245). García Márquez himself has pointed out that, as the negation of solidarity, solitude has political implications.[11] The solitude of the Buendías, in effect, is a reflection of the egoistic, individualistic values by which they live. And their propensity to incest mirrors the selfish, inward-looking attitude of a privileged oligarchy jealously defending its class interests against other sectors of society.

Yet, contrary to the view of many critics, there is in the novel a notable progression that seems to offer a way out of the vicious circle in which Macondo/Latin America is caught. For, as the Buendías fall on hard times in the wake of Macondo's economic decline, adversity teaches them how to love. The once frivolous Aureliano Segundo and Petra Cotes not only discover a sense of mutual solidarity but take pleasure in making sacrifices to help others in need. The same pattern is repeated with Aureliano Babilonia and Amaranta Úrsula, and the latter is convinced that the child born of their love will represent a fresh start for the Buendías (p. 486). In the event, he turns out to be the long-feared monster with the pig's tail whose birth marks the end of the line. For the emergence of love in the novel to displace the traditional egoism of the Buendías reflects the emergence of socialist values as a political force in Latin America, a force that will sweep away the Buendías and the order they represent.

The ending of the novel reflects, at least on the sociopolitical level, the optimism generated throughout Latin America in the 1960s by the triumph of the Cuban Revolution. The sense of the ending is clarified by an early episode where Melquíades comes across a prophecy of Nostradamus which he interprets as predicting a future Macondo that will be the luminous city of José Arcadio's dream but where there will be no trace of the Buendías (p. 130). In effect, what Aureliano Babilonia reads in Melquíades's manuscript is the imminent demise of his own class. The Buendías' attempts to make sense of the manuscripts can be interpreted as a metaphor of Latin Americans' attempts to understand their history, and it is no accident that it should be Aureliano who finally succeeds where all others in the family have failed.[12] Not only is he one of a new breed of Buendías who have learned to love, but also he has been educated by his uncle José Arcadio Segundo, a union activist, who has taught him history from a working-class viewpoint. Aureliano, in other words, has broken out of the narrow perspective of his own privileged class and developed a social awareness. That awareness enables him to arrive at an understanding of Macondo's history and to see that it must culminate in a new socialist ethos that will do away with the old oligarchic and neocolonial order.

First and foremost, then, *Cien años* is a novel that has to be read in its own Latin American context. But it is also a novel about the human condition, and the story of the Buendías is susceptible to being read as a Latin American version of the history of Western man. Despite its humor, the novel presents an essentially pessimistic view of man's condition. The novel's central theme, highlighted by the title, is human isolation. If, as we have seen, the solitude of the Buendías is directly linked to their egoism, it is so only in part, for it is too pervasive to be explained away so easily and appears, in fact, as an existential condition. Disfigured "forever and from the beginning of the world by the pox of solitude" (p. 469) that prevents all communication with others, the Buendías share a common condition that, paradoxically, isolates them from one another: "the unfathomable solitude which separated and united them at the same time" (p. 448). Rather than a family, the Buendías are a group of solitary individuals living together as strangers in the same house. As such, they personify the predicament of the human race.

The story of the Buendías also reveals the limited nature of the individual's control of his own destiny. Experience teaches Pilar Ternera that "the history of the family was a mechanism of irreversible repetitions" (p. 470), while Úrsula observes that "time wasn't passing . . . but going round in circles" (p. 409). These insights are sparked off by the perception that the same character traits are passed on from generation to generation (p. 258) and that each new generation engages in activities that echo those of its predecessors. Thus, Aureliano Triste's sketch of the railroad is "a direct descendant of the diagrams with which José Arcadio Buendía illustrated his scheme for solar warfare" (p. 297), and when José Arcadio Segundo, following the precedent of other members of the family, shuts himself away to study Melquíades's manuscript, his face reflects "the irreparable fate of his great-grandfather" (p. 387). Implied here is not merely that the human personality is largely shaped by heredity and environment, but also that individual life is subject to generic laws in that, since all men live out a limited range of experiences, every human existence corresponds to an archetypal pattern.

The world that the Buendías inhabit is one that fails to come up to the level of man's expectations, and their history is a catalog of "lost dreams"

(p. 438) and "numerous frustrated enterprises" (p. 452). Again and again the characters find fulfillment denied them: the only crown that Fernanda gets to wear—that of a Carnival Queen—makes a mockery of her regal pretensions; Pilar Ternera wastes her life away waiting for the lover who never comes; the virginity that Amaranta preserves to her death is an emblem of her sterile life. José Arcadio re-enacts man's perennial striving to surmount the limitations of his condition, first when he attempts to break out of Macondo's narrow confines and reach the utopian land of the great inventions, and later when he endeavors to realize the alchemists' dream of converting base metals into gold, but in the former case he finds himself hemmed in by the sea and in the latter he succeeds only in reducing gold to a molten mess that reminds his son of dog shit (p. 102). Not only are the Buendías' hopes and aspirations thwarted by life, but also misfortunes arbitrarily befall them, as when Colonel Aureliano sees first his wife die and later his sons or when Rebeca and Meme tragically lose the men who brought them happiness, and the unexplained murder of the second José Arcadio stands as a metaphor for the inexplicable mystery of evil and suffering. For many of the characters, indeed, life becomes synonymous with suffering, and a recurring motif is withdrawal from the world in a symbolic retreat to the refuge of the womb. In *Cien años,* peace of mind is achieved only when the Buendías opt out of active emotional involvement in life.

The character with the acutest sense of life's futility is the disillusioned Colonel Aureliano. After undertaking thirty-two armed uprisings, he comes to the conclusion that he has squandered twenty years of his life to no purpose and withdraws to his workshop, where he devotes himself to making the same little golden ornaments over and over again. This routine represents a recognition of the vanity of all human enterprises: it is completely senseless, but for the Colonel it is no more absurd than his previous activities, and it is a means of filling in the time while he waits for death. A few moments before he dies, a circus parades down the street, and in it he sees a tableau of his own life, a showy, rediculous spectacle that has given way to an emptiness as bleak as the deserted street (p. 342).

If the story of Macondo reflects the general pattern of Latin America's history, it also reflects the evolution of Western civilization and the progressive alienation of Western man. The mythical account of its history depicts Macondo's early years as a Golden Age and the town itself as an earthly paradise where men lived in happy innocence, in harmony with their world. The Fall comes with its incorporation into the modern age, and, as Macondo keeps changing around her, Úrsula feels reality becoming too complicated for her to cope with: "'Los años de ahora ya no vienen como los de antes,' solía decir sintiendo que la realidad cotidiana se le escapaba de las manos" (p. 321). In a local version of a universal myth that attributes man's alienation to his development of reason as a tool for dominating the world, the expulsion from paradise is depicted as a punishment for the sin of acquiring forbidden knowledge. The mysterious gypsy Melquíades appears as a personification of the intellectual curiosity that impels man to pursue knowledge and progress. It is Melquíades's tribe that brings the first scientific advances to Macondo, but the tribe is punished with extinction "for exceeding the limits of human knowledge" (p. 113). However, Melquíades himself survives and, like the serpent in the Christian myth of the Fall, plays the role of the tempter, inviting men to partake of the fruit of knowledge, and at one point Úrsula identifies the odor of his experiments with the Devil (p. 77). Under his influence, José Arcadio is seduced by the fascination of science and feverishly devotes himself to all kinds of experiments, but his passionate pursuit of knowledge distances him more and more from reality and brings him to a state of madness that leaves him completely alienated. Disoriented in a world turned chaotic, he vents his rage by destroying the laboratory and the apparatus that have brought him to this sad condition and, like Prometheus chained to his mountainside, lives out the rest of his days bound to a tree (the tree of knowledge?).

Moreover, when the progress so desired by José Arcadio reaches Macondo, it brings with it a general alienation as the town suffers a plague of insomnia that causes loss of memory. Lapsing into a kind of idiocy in which they cease to know the function of things and the identity of people and are no longer aware even of their own being, the inhabitants of Macondo are cast adrift in a world bereft of order and coherence. To counter the effects of the plague, they identify things with labels, and in the main street they erect a banner proclaiming the existence of God. This represents a desperate attempt to preserve the old values that gave life a meaning, to cling to a coherent vision of an ordered world, but elusive, shifting reality slips away from them as they forget the written word (p. 123). Reality, in other words, refuses to adapt itself to the old molds, no longer conforms to the old concepts or order, and its meaning becomes increasingly inaccessible. And, although the town apparently returns to normality after Melquíades restores its memory, things are never quite the same again, and, indeed, the memory-restoring potion would seem to be a metaphor of the process whereby men become conditioned to change after the first traumatic impact of progress.

Various members of the Buendía family have the image of Melquíades imprinted in their mind as a hereditary memory (p. 77), and several of them devote themselves to the task of deciphering his manuscript. That image would seem to represent the human urge for knowledge, and the study of the manuscript is a metaphor of man's attempts to discover the secret of existence. For most of the novel, the manuscript, like life, remains an incomprehensible enigma, and it is ironically implied that the search for truth is a useless activity when Melquíades's room is converted into a storeroom for chamberpots. When Aureliano Babilonia finally succeeds in decoding the manuscript in a denouement reminiscent of Unamuno's *Niebla* and Borges's "Las ruinas circulares," the truth he comes face to face with is a disheartening one. For what he discovers is that the Buendías are no more than fictions created by Melquíades's imagination, that life is a dream, an illusion, that ultimately existence has no meaning. It is significant that that truth should be arrived at by the last of the Buendías, for it is, in effect, the worldview of the last representative of a worn-out, declining society whose perception of life becomes more and more disillusioned as its world collapses around it. The novel's ending, therefore, can be seen as an expression of the existential anguish of twentieth-century Western man.

Given the narrator's ironic distancing of himself from the version of Macondo's history that he is transmitting, it would seem that to some extent he is dissociating himself from the worldview conveyed by the novel and identifying bourgeois individualism as one of the root causes of Western man's existential anguish. Nonetheless, the novel also communicates a sense of the ultimately tragic nature of life, one that goes beyond the subjective perceptions of the characters and resists explanation as the consequence of human failings, and the dénouement would appear to express a view of the world held by the author himself. Such a pessimistic worldview does not seem to me to be incompatible with faith in social progress, as Shaw suggests.[13] Other writers, such as the Peruvian poet César Vallejo, have managed to balance both attitudes, and the ambivalence of the dénouement and of Aureliano Babilonia as a character epitomizes the way in which the novel maintains a tension between differing perspectives, playing off against each other a passionate social commitment and a belief that in the long run nothing has any meaning. Furthermore, it has to be stressed that García Márquez's pessimism with regard to life is tempered by a number of factors. The first of these is his conviction that the advent of socialism will create a healthier and more harmonious world. Then again, the image of humanity projected in the novel is far from being entirely negative, for, despite their many failings, the Buendías come across as sympathetic characters and possess optimism-inspiring virtues: José Arcadio's heroic striving to triumph over circumstances; the tireless tenacity with which Úrsula struggles to keep the family going; Colonel Aureliano's stubborn refusal to be beaten, exemplified by his dying on his feet after urinating on the tree of life (p. 342). Last but not least, *Cien años*'s exuberant humor conveys a sense that, if life is tragic, it is also a great joke.

Notes

1. This incident is incorporated into *Cien años de soledad.* See L. I. Mena, "La huelga de la compañía bananera como expresión de lo 'real maravilloso' americano en *Cien años de soledad,*" *Bulletin Hispanique,* vol. 74 (1972), pp. 379–405.

2. See G. García Márquez, *Cien años de soledad,* ed. Jacques Joset (Cátedra, Madrid, 1984). All references are to this edition. Henceforth the abbreviation *Cien años* will be used. Certain quotations incorporated into the body of this text have been rendered into English.

3. See C. Griffin, "The Humor of *One Hundred Years of Solitude,*" in B. McGuirk and R. Cardwell (eds.), *Gabriel García Márquez: New Readings* (Cambridge University Press, Cambridge, 1987), pp. 81–94.

4. D. P. Gallagher, *Modern Latin American Literature* (Oxford University Press, Oxford, 1973), p. 88.

5. P. A. Mendoza, *The Fragrance of Guava,* trans. A. Wright (Verso, London, 1983), p. 72.

6. It does not follow, of course, that the novel replicates Melquíades's manuscript. In his previously mentioned edition of the text, J. Joset argues that the narrator is an unknown person who rescued Melquíades's manuscript from oblivion by transcribing the translation, using the key discovered by Aureliano Babilonia (p. 44). He further points out that *Cien años* includes elements that could not possibly have been contained in Melquíades's manuscript (p. 491, n. 42).

7. On the influence of Borges see R. González Echevarría, "With Borges in Macondo," *Diacritics,* vol. 2, no. 1 (1972), pp. 57–60.

8. On García Márquez's use of the chronicles as a source, see I. M. Zavala, "*Cien años de soledad,* crónica de Indias," *Ínsula,* no. 286 (1970), pp. 3, 11.

9. The most influential expression of that response was the Uruguayan José E. Rodó's essay *Ariel* (1900). See J. Franco, *The Modern Culture of Latin America: Society and the Artist* (Pall Mall Press, London, 1967), pp. 49–53.

10. This view, essentially that of the Europeanized urban elites, was given its clearest fromulation in Argentina by Domingo F. Sarmiento in *Facundo* (1845) but was widely held throughout Latin America.

11. See E. González Bermejo, "Gabriel García Márquez: ahora doscientos años de soledad," *Casa de las Américas,* vol. 10, no. 63 (1970), p. 164.

12. See G. Martin. "On 'Magical" and Social Realism in García Márquez," in McGuirk and Cardwell (eds.), *Gabriel García Márquez: New Readings,* pp. 95–116.

13. D. L. Shaw, "Concerning the Interpretation of *Cien años de soldedad,*" *Ibero-Amerikanisches Archiv,* vol. 3, no. 1 (1977), p. 321.

The Humor of
One Hundred Years of Solitude

CLIVE GRIFFIN

◆　　◆　　◆

IT IS THE FATE of fine comic writers to be taken seriously. Masters of entertainment like Cervantes and Molière have been woefully misused by those who consider humor and the spinning of a good tale to be worthy of a distinguished artist only when a vehicle for something else. Reappraisals of these two writers have, however, helped to rescue them from critics intent on extracting complex philosophies or literary theories from their comic works.[1] Such reappraisals suggest that García Márquez might similarly be examined with profit first and foremost as a humorist, for there are already clear signs that he is not to escape the fate of his predecessors. *One Hundred Years of Solitude,* the novel that brought him fame and on which his reputation still largely rests, has been called a work of "deep pessimism," "an interpretative meditation" upon the literature of the subcontinent, or an analysis of "the failure of Latin-American history."[2] Isolated passages of the novel could, at a pinch, be made to support such assertions, but these interpretations will not help us to understand it as a whole or to account for its remarkable popularity among a heterogeneous readership that has scant knowledge of the history of Colombia or of the recent literary production of Spanish America. Humor, however, can cut across cultural and even linguistic boundaries, appealing to the least and most sophisticated and knowledgeable readers.

To assert from the outset that *One Hundred Years* is funny is, perhaps, to beg the question. Nevertheless, there is ample evidence in the novel that the characters themselves find each other's antics and statements comical as they "roar with laughter" or "choke back guffaws"; incidentally, the author also appears to have found the novel's composition a source of considerable amusement.[3] To claim that *One Hundred Years* is humorous is not to sell the novel short, nor is it to deny that it may contain passages that are not funny; indeed, one of García Márquez's strengths is his ability to capture the poignant or even sentimental moment. Rather, it is to recognize that, as Cervantes himself maintained, comic writing can be as difficult to accomplish and as worthwhile to read as any other, and to oblige the literary critic to examine the author's skill as a humorist.

I would maintain that the novel's appeal is largely due to the wide range of different types of humor employed by its author. At one end of the spectrum we have the "eternal comic situations: beatings, disguises, mistaken identity, wit, buffoonery, indecency" appreciated by readers regardless of their cultural background and literary experience;[4] then there are other kinds of humor that find an echo only among those with particular knowledge of Colombia or of the literature of the subcontinent; and, at the other end of the spectrum, we are treated to the Shandyism and novelistic self-awareness so beloved of modern critics. Nevertheless, however observant the reader, he will inevitably miss, at the very end of this range, the "in-jokes" that the author claims were inserted for the benefit of a few friends.[5] Europeans and those obliged to read the work in translation will, of course, miss even more. In this essay I shall give an account of this broad spectrum of subjects and techniques that provoke laughter.

Some theoreticians of humor concentrate on the sort of subjects that are "inherently comical," maintaining, for example, that one universal source of laughter in Western societies is the violation of taboos. The commonest of these subjects concern sexual or other bodily functions. *One Hundred Years* abounds with such scenes. José Arcadio's Herculean strength and stature may be funny enough in itself, but even more so is his minutely described and "incredible member, covered with a maze of blue and red tattoos written in several languages" (p. 84),[6] a fitting forebear of Aureliano Babilonia's equally astonishing appendage on which, at the end of the novel, he balances a bottle of beer as he cavorts drunkenly around one of Macondo's brothels. Scenes of sexual intercourse cause us to smile either because of their exuberant eroticism, like the seismic orgasms enjoyed by José Arcadio and Rebeca, or because of some of the female characters' ridiculous prudery: Úrsula is reluctant to remove her chastity belt and consummate her marriage, and Fernanda obeys a calendar of "prohibited days" on which she refuses to grant the husband whom she later describes as her "rightful despoiler" even the frigid submission that characterizes their physical relationship. Deviation provides even more fun: José Arcadio Segundo and the local verger have a penchant for she-asses; Amaranta is a maiden aunt who, even when old, is the object of incestuous fantasies for generations of Buendías; not only is the effete Pietro Crespi thought to be a homosexual,[7] but also Catarino is known to be one; there is even a dog in the "zoological brothel" that is described as "a gentle pederast who, nevertheless, serviced bitches to earn his keep" (p. 333). Similarly, García Márquez employs lavatorial jokes, describing the complexities of entertaining sixty-eight schoolgirls and four nuns in a house with only one toilet or the pungency of José Arcadio's flatulence, which makes flowers wither on the spot.

Taboos are not limited to bodily functions. Death and religion are a source of jokes in most societies, the latter being even more piquant in as conservatively Catholic a country as Colombia In *One Hundred Years,* most of the characters either fade away in old age (José Arcadio Buendía, the Colonel, Úrsula, Rebeca, and Melquíades), or else their deaths are treated with black humor. José Arcadio's corpse emits such an evil stench that his mourners decide in desperation to "season it with pepper, cumin and laurel leaves and boil it over a gentle heat for a whole day" (p. 118); the body of Fernanda's distinguished father—appropriately enough a Knight of the Order of the Holy Sepulchre—spent so long on its journey to Macondo that when the coffin was opened "the skin had erupted in stinking belches and was simmering in a bubbling, frothy stew' (p. 186); a drunken funeral party buries the twins. José Arcadio Segundo and Aureliano Segundo, in each other's graves, thus putting the final touch to the running joke about their muddled identities.

Fernanda's stuffy religiosity makes her the butt of numerous comic scenes, but, more subtly and with nice irony, the narrator claims that the indelible cross worn by all of the Colonel's campaign sons will guarantee their safety, yet, in the end, their murderers recognize them precisely by this sacred sign. A statue of St. Joseph revered by Úrsula turns out to be merely a hiding place for the gold that enables a renegade apprentice Pope to indulge in orgies with his potential catamites while obsessed by incestuous desires for his great-great-aunt.

The final taboo is a linguistic one, for the dialogue of *One Hundred Years* is a convincing representation of the expression of uncultured characters for whom expletives are part of everyday speech. These are frequently used comically to deflate scenes that are in danger of becoming oversentimental. For example, the amiable Gerineldo Márquez's grief at being rejected by Amaranta is reflected by a sympathetic Nature; he sends his comrade, the Colonel, a poignant message, "Aureliano, it is raining in Macondo," only to receive the reply, "Don't be a prick, Gerineldo. Of course it's raining; it's August" (p. 144).

The violation of these taboos is never prurient. The author treats sex, death, religion, and language with a light-hearted candor. Indeed, as Aureliano Segundo observes when he sees Fernanda's prim nightdress, which covers her from head to foot but has "a large, round, delicately trimmed hole over her lower stomach" (p. 182), it is prudishness that is really obscene. Similarly, euphemism leads only to pain and ridicule: Fernanda seeks a cure for her medical condition, but, as she cannot bring herself to describe the embarrassing symptoms openly, the invisible doctors are unable to diagnose her complaint, and she is condemned to a life of suffering.

Renaissance theorists of comedy, understandably enough, did not identify the contravention of such taboos as a source of humor; rather, they conjectured more abstractly that it was the provocation of wonderment and surprise in the reader or spectator that caused mirth.[8] Such wonderment lies at the heart of much of the laughter of *One Hundred Years,* where García Márquez has frequent recourse to exaggeration, fantasy, and the ridiculous. While we are willing to accept that José Arcadio returns from his travels a grown man, the exaggeration with which his exploits and appetites are recounted either leads the reader to reject the novel as nonsense or, as Forster has it, to pay the extra sixpence at the fair and revel in fantasy and hyperbole.[9] Just as he laughs at the reaction of the naive inhabitants of Macondo whose description of the first train to be seen in the town is of "a terrifying object like a kitchen pulling a village" (p. 192), so the reader is invited to laugh at his own reaction when his expectations of the narrative are challenged and he has to suspend his normal judgment about what is possible in reality and fiction and what is not. It is with wonderment that he learns of a fantastic character like Melquíades, who frequently returns from the land of the dead but who grows old there just as people do in the land of the living, of the appearance of the Duke of Marlborough (the "Mambru" of the traditional Spanish nursery rhyme) at the Colonel's side in the civil war, or of other equally fantastic situations, often described in absurdly precise detail, such as the lovemaking of Petra Cotes and Aureliano Segundo, which increases the numbers of their livestock overnight. Although the fantasy is often an extension of, or a metaphor for, reality, such wonderment provokes laughter. A situation, and event, or a character may start out as entirely credible, but by a logical development ad absurdum they become comical. Thus, we understand that Fernanda and Úrsula, following a well-established tradition among upper-crust Colombian families, should wish José Arcadio, their only legitimate son and great-great-grandson, to enter the church; their ambition only becomes humorous because they are determined that he should not be just any sort of priest and set about grooming him from childhood for the job of Pope. On other occasions, however, the comedy resides in astonishing us by gratuitous details—José Arcadio Buendía can increase his weight at will—or by a challenge to our notions of cause and effect either through the events of the novel or the illogicality of the characters' reasoning: thus, for instance, Francis Drake comes to Riohacha exclusively to set in motion the events of the novel that will eventually lead to the birth of a baby with a pig's tail; when Melquíades's breath begins to smell, he is given a bath.

García Márquez surprises the reader by a constant switching of tone, which, like the expletives mentioned earlier, serves humorously to deflate a carefully constructed mood of seriousness or foreboding. Pietro Crespi is described as the perfect suitor for Amaranta: he is infatuated in a way, it is implied, that only romantic Italians can be; love makes his business prosper; he is loved, in turn, by the whole family. All augurs well for their marriage and happiness. Yet, after this long build-up, his passionate proposal is met with her "Don't be a fool, Crespi, I'd rather die than marry you" (p. 98). Similarly, the author carefully creates suspense about the Colonel's reaction to the signing of the Treaty of Neerlandia. We have all the traditional clues that Aureliano will do the honorable thing after surrendering to the government: The Colonel ensures that he has a single bullet in his pistol, he asks his doctor with apparent casualness in what part of his chest his heart is located, he destroys all his papers, and his mother bids him farewell, making him promise that his last thought will be of her. As we had feared, he does indeed shoot himself, and, the narrator assures us, Úrsula realizes with her extraordinary powers of intuition that Aureliano has been killed. It then transpires that he is not dead at all but, rather, consumed with anger: the doctor had tricked him and the bullet missed his heart; in a trice he is planning to lead a new rebellion against the government.

Here it is the unexpected, and this often means the incongruous, that causes wonderment and therefore humor. It has already been observed that poignant scenes are frequently undermined by an incongruous expletive, an inappropriate statement, or a bathetic conclusion to an episode. In other ways, surprise is created by exaggeration, by the narrator's ingenuous throw-away comment, or by bizarre reactions to events. The power of the Banana Company to decree that it should rain in Macondo for four years, eleven months, and two days is funny because it is an exaggerated and absurdly precise extension of the real power of the multinationals in the third world. The narrator's comment coming after his detailed account of José Arcadio's popularity with Macondo's whores, his sexual prowess, riotous living, and barbarous manners that "he didn't manage to settle down in the family" (p. 84) is comical because it is a laconic understatement of the disparity between family life and José Arcadio's behavior. The detail that Fernanda's only concern after Remedios, the Beautiful, had been assumed into the heavens while hanging out the washing was that her sheets had disappeared is humorous because it is such an inappropriately mundane reaction to a supernatural event with Christian undertones.

Just as linguistic taboos are violated, so the author causes wonderment in the reader by his use of language. This is often the result of concrete and almost poetic metaphors that are employed to describe abstract moods in an expressive but decidedly off-key fashion, such as "the mangrove-swamp of delirium" (p. 63), "the eggplant-patch of her memories" (p. 236), "the perfumed and worm-eaten guava-grove of love" (p. 237), "a quagmire of anguish" (p. 246), and "a bog of concupiscence" (p. 311), or the telling zeugma like Patricia Brown's "nights of intolerance and pickled cucumbers in Prattville, Alabama" (p. 340). In a different way, inappropriate words are used for comic effect: when he foresees José Arcadio Buendía's death, Cataure, an uneducated Indian servant, returns to Macondo for, as he puts it, "the king's exequies" (p. 125). The reader is further surprised by the way in which clichés are treated literally and have unforeseen results. Úrsula refuses to be photographed because "she didn't want to become a laughing-stock for her grandchildren" (p. 49): yet later she becomes quite literally a plaything for her great-great-grandchildren. We are used, at least in fiction, to hearing infatuated men protest to their sweethearts that they will die if their love is not requited: Remedios, the Beautiful, really does have lethal powers and deals painful deaths of her admirers; and Úrsula gives up trying to domesticate Remedios, trusting that "sooner or later some miracle would happen" (p. 204) in the shape of a suitor who would rid the family of her, only for a real miracle to solve the problem when Remedios is assumed into heaven.

However, not all the funny elements in the novel can be neatly accounted for by being categorized as taboo subjects or as the cause of the wonderment Renaissance writers believed to lie at the roots of laughter.

Irony is all-pervasive, and García Márquez mixes it with straightforward comedy of situation, character, and language. José Arcadio Buendía strips down and rebuilds a pianola in such a way that the long-awaited party to celebrate the extension of the family home is accompanied, in a scene of high farce, not by Pietro Crespi's melodious waltzes but by a musical cacophony. The traditional exposure of hypocrisy provides comedy of character especially when the butt is somebody as unpleasant as Fernanda. Her first reaction to the news of the birth of her illegitimate grandson is to think of murdering the innocent nun who brought the baby to the family home; she subsequently lies about his origins, sacrilegiously rehearsing the story of Moses found among the bulrushes. It is a nice irony that it is this grandson who will decipher the prophesies about the history of his people. Language is itself a source of humor, from the simple play on words by José Arcadio Buendía "we need no judge [*corregidor*: literally corrector] in Macondo, because there is nothing in need of correction here" (p. 55) and the constant repetition of epithets until they become absurd: the oriental traders are always referred to as "the Arabs who exchange trinkets for parrots" (pp. 69, 281, etc.) to the inversion of a set-phrase: the authorities come to Macondo to "establish disorder" (p. 55) and the playful alliteration of gobbledegook such as "quién iba a saber qué pendejo menjunje de jarapellinosos genios jerosolimitanos [literally God knew what bloody concoction of syrupy Hierosolymitan geniuses]" (p. 193). As is traditional in the theater, accent and verbal pomposity are used to comic effect: so Fernanda speaks a travesty of the language of the Colombian highlands that is ridiculed as an imitation of peninsular Spanish and contrasts markedly with the earthy and laconic Caribbean speech of the narrator and the other inhabitants of Macondo. It is no coincidence that two of Fernanda's surnames are Argote and Carpio, for her "unnatural" Spanish, as well as her anachronistic education, aspirations, and religiosity, identifies her as a descendant of two of Spain's greatest Golden Age practitioners of elaborate literary styles, Luis de Góngora y Argote and Lope de Vega Carpio. Her language is frequently incomprehensible to the other characters and, it is implied, moribund—her childhood occupation in her cold ancestral home was, appropriately enough, the manufacture of funeral wreaths. On one occasion she describes herself as "goddaughter to the Duke of Alba, and a gentlewoman of such pure pedigree that she caused presidents' wives greate envy, a noble ladie of the bloode, entitled to sign herselfe with the eleven surnames which graced her Spanish forbears" (p. 274).

These elements of humor would appeal to most readers of *One Hundred Years*. However, many of the novel's scenes depend for a fuller appreciation of their darker and more ironic humor upon a broad acquaintance with the Latin American past and present, and a more specific knowledge of Colombia with its violent history of internal struggles and the extraordinary isolation of its village communities rich in folklore. Characters from this folklore, such as Francisco el Hombre, are amusingly incorporated into the novel, while true episodes from Colombian history are fused with the fictional narrative. Indeed, the story of the strike of banana workers and their subsequent massacre is, paradoxically, less funny to a reader who realizes how close it is to the real events that took place in Ciénaga in 1928 and 1929 and who recognizes the names of real participants in those events than it would be for a reader who sees it merely as another exaggerated scene from a "typical" episode in Latin American history.[10] Yet the employment of a reductio ad absurdum of local political issues is elsewhere more comical. It is true that Colombian liberals had fought at the turn of the century for, among other things, the recognition of civil marriage; but in *One Hundred Years* a liberal soldier claims that "we're waging this war against the priests so that we can marry our own mothers" (p. 132). More indirect are the ironic references to the Cuban Revolution, which was still the most important political event in the subcontinent when *One Hundred Years* was written. The choice of a character called General Moncada, to whom Úrsula talks after receiving a message from Santiago de Cuba, is not fortuitous, for the Revolution could reasonably be said to have started with Fidel Castro's unsuccessful attack on the Moncada barracks in Santiago de Cuba in 1953. Subsequent events in the novel lead to General Moncada's insight that so much fighting against the military has made Colonel Aureliano Buendía indistinguishable from them. The irony of this comment would not be missed by readers accustomed to seeing Castro, the erstwhile guerrilla, dressed in military uniform and constantly reviewing one of the most powerful armies in the subcontinent. Neither would he miss Moncada's deflation of a typical example of Castro's rhetoric in the scene in which the Colonel visits the General in his cell on the eve of his execution:

> "Remember, Moncada, it is not I who is having you shot, but the Revolution."
>
> General Moncada did not even bother to get up from his bed when he saw the Colonel come in.
>
> "Fuck off, Buendía," he replied. (p. 140)

There is also much in *One Hundred Years* for the more experienced reader of novels with whom García Márquez plays, constantly undermining his expectations. The first sentence of the book is an example of this playfulness:

> Many years later, as he faced the firing squad, Colonel Aureliano Buendía would recall that distant afternoon on which his father took him to see what ice was. (p. 9)

Apart from the reader's surprise that one can be taken to "discover" something as commonplace as ice, this introductory sentence contains two important implications about the subsequent story. First, the Colonel will be executed by firing squad, and, second, as is traditional in novels where a condemned or drowning man's life rushes before his eyes at the moment of death, the Colonel relives the experiences of his infancy. The novel is, then, going to be the life story of this character, beginning in early childhood and ending with his execution. This assumption is carefully reinforced by the author throughout the first few chapters of the novel. We read, for example, that "many years later, a second before the regular army officer gave the firing squad the order to shoot, Colonel Buendía relived that warm March afternoon" (p. 21 [see also pp. 50, 75, and 87]). A measure of doubt is later cast on the assumption that he is to die in this manner when we hear that "he lived to old age by making little gold fishes which he manufactured in his workshop in Macondo" (p. 94) and that he survived at least one firing squad, but, as this is accompanied by the statement that he never allowed himself to be photographed and we already know this to be untrue (p. 50), we have learnt by this point in the novel to treat such details with healthy skepticism. Our expectations are further confirmed by the fate of his nephew, Arcadio. We are told that "Years later, when he was facing the firing squad, Arcadio would recall . . ." (p. 68); "She was the last person Arcadio thought of, a few years later, when he faced the firing squad" (p. 82); and "A few months later, when he faced the firing squad, Arcadio would relive . . ." (p. 101). As in this case the foreshadowing turns out to be accurate and Arcadio does, indeed, meet his end in such an execution, the reader's belief that the Colonel will do so also is confirmed. It is, then, with not a little consternation that when the Colonel's frequently announced "execution" does occur—not at the end of the novel as expected but less than halfway through—the reader discovers that he is not even killed. In a humorously bathetic scene, the Colonel is rescued at the eleventh hour, much to the relief of the squad, who immediately join him in a new rebellion. The first sentence of the novel and its deceptive implications thus teach the reader that the narrator is not to be trusted. Sometimes he (or, possibly, García Márquez himself) is merely muddled: when Aureliano Segundo is said to dream of dying in a night of passion with Fernanda, he surely means Petra Cotes;[11] when he says that the Colonel's seventeen campaign sons are all murdered in a single evening (p. 94), he overlooks Aureliano Amador who escapes, only to be shot in Macondo many years later (p. 317); when he casually mentions that Arcadio and his mistress, Santa Sofía de la Piedad, transfer their lovemaking to the room at the back of her shop after the school where Arcadio had lived until then was stormed by the government soldiers (p. 102), he misleads the reader yet again, for the lovers never meet after the troops enter Macondo; and when he prefaces his stories with the phrase "many years later" or "a few months earlier," he omits to give any clue that would help the reader to discover before or after exactly what these events are meant to have occurred. These examples could be attributed to the forgetfulness of a narrator who is characterized as a spinner of yarns, but, on other occasions, as has been seen in the first sentence of the novel, it is clear that the reader is the victim of more willful deception.

In *Don Quixote,* Cervantes had invented a certain Cide Hamete Benengeli who, he playfully told the reader, was the "author" of the work, the original version of which was written in Arabic; in *One Hundred Years,* García Márquez equates his novel with the manuscripts written in Sanskrit by one of its characters, Melquíades. Just as Cide Hamete is at the same time both "a most truthful historian" and a "lying Moor," so Melquíades is said to be "an honest man" (p. 9) but, as we realize from the very first page, is a gypsy and a charlatan: he there explains to the villagers who are astonished by the effects of magnets upon metal that "objects have a life of their own; it's just a question of arousing their spirit." García Márquez, like Cervantes before him, deliberately lays false trails. For example, the experienced reader will pick up small details about the Colonel's only surviving son: like his brothers, his fate is to be killed before he is thirty-five years old, and he bears an indelible cross on his forehead; not only do his age and the cross suggest Christian symbolism, but also he is called Aureliano Amador ("Lover") and he is by profession a carpenter. He returns to his father's house only to be rejected in his hour of need by those who claim not to recognize him, one of whom is, ironically enough, the apprentice Pope, that spurious descendant of Peter the denier of Christ. The experienced reader of fiction, then, spots a symbol, his expectations are raised, and then Amador is killed and the carpet is pulled from under the reader's feet as the character in question simply disappears from the novel, never to be mentioned again. García Márquez is aware of his readers and sets out to dupe them, just as he later claimed, possibly with some measure of truthfulness, to have planted banana skins in *One Hundred Years* for the critics whom he so despises to slip on.[12]

Not only are the reader's expectations dashed, but also the author proves willing to poke fun at himself and his own devices. *One Hundred Years* is built upon predictions of what will happen to the characters in the future: indeed, the phrase "había de" (he was to) is one of the most frequent in the book. This is a convention often encountered in novels or stories, but in *One Hundred Years* the narrator's predictions are no more reliable than is Pilar Ternera's cartomancy. Thus, the Colonel does not suffer the fate that, according to the first sentence of the novel, awaited him, while Aureliano José, whose destiny was to have seven children by Carmelita Montiel and to die as an old man in her arms, is murdered even before he can meet her. Like an oral spinner of a good yarn, the narrator of *One Hundred Years* is digressive; we do not have a linear narrative of the history of Macondo, let alone of the life of a single character. One may react with anger and frustration to this mockery of the novel's conventions and of the reader's good faith, as the narrator tells what amounts to a shaggy-dog story; yet the popularity of the novel is clear proof of the capacity of readers to treat such inventiveness and mockery with wonderment and laughter.

At the other end of the spectrum of humor from the sexual and lavatorial jokes are the sly references to other Spanish American writers. These would, of course, be appreciated only by a minority of readers familiar with the works concerned. Critics have drawn our attention to the author's predilection for referring to characters invented by other writers: there are Victor Hugues from the Cuban Alejo Carpentier, Artemio Cruz from the Mexican Carlos Fuentes, and Rocamadour from the Argentine Julio Cortázar.[13] The Mamá Grande is even borrowed from another of García Márquez's own works. More important than this mere list of names is the author's knowing wink to the initiated and the effect this has on his own novel. For example, Colonel Lorenzo Gavilán, who comes from Fuentes's *The Death of Artemio Cruz,* says in *One Hundred Years* that he witnessed Cruz's heroism during the Mexican Revolution. Yet the reader familiar with Fuentes's novel knows that Gavilán was duped by Cruz, who deserted during an engagement and then contrived to put a good face on his disappearance from the battlefield. García Márquez is careful to stress that Gavilán only *claimed* to have seen Cruz's bravery; this, then, is an "in-joke" for the reader of modern Spanish American fiction. García Márquez eventually kills off Gavilán during the slaughter of banana workers, but, even in the apparently grim episode in which José Arcadio Segundo identifies comrades in a train full of corpses speeding away from the scene of the massacre, García Márquez cannot resist lifting another detail straight from Fuentes's novel: the belt with a silver buckle that was worn by the un-named comrade whom Cruz could possibly have saved from death but whom he selfishly abandoned at a critical moment of the story.[14] In the second part of *Don Quixote,* "real" characters rub shoulders with self-confessed inventions, leading to a humorous, if bewildering, play of levels of fiction. This same game is played by García Márquez, who infuses with deflating comic ambiguity an episode that some have ingenuously re-garded as a straightforward denunciation of the United Fruit Company's machinations in the Colombia of the 1920s and 1930s.

Similar ambiguity resulting from literary games can be seen in the treatment of what we might expect to be other serious episodes in the novel, such as the death of one of its central characters. Colonel Aureliano Buendía. Just as we saw earlier that an incongruous statement or an exple-tive might be introduced to puncture a sentimental mood, so here the death scene is undermined by the author's decision to narrate it in a style that is a close parody of that employed in story entitled "The Aleph," by the influential Argentine writer Jorge Luis Borges. Similarly, he had already deflated the execution of Arcadio by a clear literary allusion, this time to another of Borges's stories. "The Secret Miracle."[15] This practice is not a systematic "meditation upon" Spanish American literature, as some would assert. Rather, it has the important consequence of undermining any serious involvement with characters or situations that the novel might otherwise have possessed. *One Hundred Years* thus becomes a cornucopia of adventure and laughter on many levels, but one that, like all great comic works, resists and ridicules any attempt to extract from it a clear message or meaning, and we are tempted as a result to take at face value the au-thor's statement that "*One Hundred Years of Solitude* is completely devoid of seriousness."[16]

Readers of Borges or of the *nouvelle critique* will have appreciated the pass-ing references to the novel's self-awareness as a fictional work in the course of construction: when José Arcadio Buendía "looked through the window and saw two barefooted children in the sunny garden, and had the impres-sion that they had come into existence at just that instant" (p. 20), he is of course correct, for this is the first time that the children are focused upon by the narrator. The final joke in *One Hundred Years,* however, comically de-flates not just an episode or a character but the whole novel. At the end of the last chapter, Aureliano Babilonia discovers that Melquíades's manu-scripts are an account of the history of Macondo, including the moment at which Aureliano Babilonia discovers this fact. It is suggested that the novel is, in some way, merely a transcript of Melquíades's predictions, although, typically enough, García Márquez does not attempt to wrestle with the logical problems presented by the author's being a character in his own work. The implication is that the reader should ask himself how serious a work can be which is written by a liar, which is a self-confessed piece of fiction—Macondo is constructed of "mirrors (or reflections)" (p. 351), and its characters suspect that they are unreal (p. 345)—and whose rightful destiny is to be stored away like the manuscripts among disused chamber-pots. In the end Macondo is destroyed by a literary wind which recalls that in *Strong Wind,* a novel by the Guatemalan writer Miguel Angel Asturias. Márquez's novelistic world does not exist after the reader has finished the book. The novel is a way of passing time; it is the spinning out of a yarn—a process already seen in miniature in the cyclical tale of the capon that the villagers tell one another to while away nights of insomnia (p. 46). *One Hundred Years* is an entertainment that does not transcend the enjoyment of reading it, and it does not pose serious questions upon which the reader is invited to meditate at length. On the contrary, it is a kaleidoscope, or spectrum, of comic narration in which the overearnest reader or critic is the final butt of the author's jokes, for, as Aureliano Babilonia discovers, "literature was the best toy which had ever been invented to pull people's legs" (p. 327). To take it all too seriously would be about as fruitful as a discussion of "the various mediaeval techniques for killing cockroaches" (p. 327).

Notes

EO = Plinio Apuleyo Mendoza, *El olor de la guayaba* (Barcelona, 1982)

1. For example. W. G. Moore, *Molière: A New Criticism* (Oxford, 1949); P. F. Russell, "Don Quixote as a Funny Book," *Modern Language Review* 64 (1969), 312–326, and the latter's *Cervantes* (Oxford and New York, 1985), passim.

2. Donald L. Shaw, *Nueva narrativa hispanoamericana* (Madrid, 1981), p. 215; David Gallagher, *Modern Latin American Literature* (London, 1973), pp. 147 and 162.

3. *EO,* p. 111.

4. Moore, *Molière,* p. 99.

5. *EO,* p. 104.

6. All page references are to the Editorial Sudamericana 1975 edition. The translations are my own.

7. Pietro Crespi is also given a comically inappropriate name: it recalls Pedro Crespo, one of the best-known figures from Spanish drama of the seventeenth century, where he is the major character in Pedro Calderón de la Barca's *El alcalde de*

Zalamea; Crespo, far from being an effete Italian, was a forceful and cunning Spanish peasant.

8. Russell, "Don Quixote," p. 321.

9. E. M. Forster, *Aspects of the Novel* (Harmondsworth, 1977), pp. 103–104.

10. Mario Vargas Llosa, *García Márquez: Historia de un deicidio* (Barcelona, 1971), pp. 16, 20. Regina Janes, *Gabriel García Márquez: Revolutions in Wonderland* (Columbia and London, 1981), pp. 11, 12.

11. P. 166; the English translation, *One Hundred Years of Solitude,* translated by Gregory Rabassa (London, 1978), p. 159, "corrects" this slip.

12. *EO,* p. 104.

13. Gallagher, *Modern Latin American Literature,* p. 146.

14. Carlos Fuentes, *La muerte de Artemio Cruz* (Mexico City, 1973), pp 73–79. Originally published in 1962.

15. Compare *Cien años de soledad,* p. 229, with Jorge Luis Borges, "El aleph," in *El aleph* (Buenos Aires, 1952), pp. 151–152; compare *Cien años,* pp. 107–108 with Borges, "El milagro secreto" in *Ficciones* (Buenos Aires, 1971), pp. 165–167.

16. *EO,* p. 104.

The Sacred Harlots of
One Hundred Years of Solitude

LORRAINE ELENA ROSES

◆　◆　◆

L ITERARY CRITIQUES OF Gabriel García Márquez's *One Hundred Years of Solitude* frequently describe a dynamic between visionary male and industrious female characters, highlighting an interplay in which men and women pursue distinct objectives within their separate realms: the former live by futuristic dreams, and the latter struggle to keep body and soul together. Mario Vargas Llosa painted a picture early on (1971) of the [Buendía] man as "lord and master of the world" and the woman as "lady and mistress of the hearth," subservient to her husband and exerting "limited authority over the children" (Vargas Llosa, 505).[1] Males lay claim to the prerogatives and requisite spaces for engaging in imaginative, scientific, and sexual pursuits, while female possibilities of self-actualization are circumscribed within the confines of the domestic sphere, as conveyed by Úrsula's "surrender" to conjugal sex. As a result of this dichotomy, Vargas Llosa continues, the male characters drive the novel's argument, embodying at once the grandeur and the woes of Latin American history and, by implication, those of humankind. Such a reading is circular in that it reproduces and reinforces a nineteenth-century ideology dubbed the "cult of domesticity," in which a value was placed on everything associated with homes, leaving domesticity and sentimentality as the only avenues through which women could define themselves.

At the outset, the mythical village of Macondo is conceived as an egalitarian utopia, a realm unto itself: José Arcadio Buendía, its founder, "had set up the placement of the houses in such a way that from all of them one could reach the river and draw water with the same effort . . . " and that "no house got more sun than another during the hot time of day" (García Márquez, 9). Originally, females' work capacity was the same as that of males (García Márquez, 9), and José Arcadio owns no more than Úrsula— on the contrary, she holds a hidden stash of Spanish gold. But Úrsula and her female descendants compromise their position of equality by subordinating themselves to male endeavors. By assuming limited, one-dimensional roles, such as the self-sacrificing mother and wife or the concubine, women support and enhance men's self-advancement and hegemony at the expense of their own.

Many other critics have established a similar Manichaean typology of García Márquez's female characters, ultimately coming to the conclusion that women cannot transcend the limited space assigned to them in the novel. I will cite some prominent examples: Ernesto Volkening, a distinguished champion of Gabriel García Márquez, states that the female characters are "privadas del don de deslizarse a fanásticas regiones," that is, devoid of the ability to [ascend] to imaginative and inventive heights (Volkening, 161); it is women's inherent limitations that prevent them from actively engaging in the creative, global visionary projects pursued by the Buendía men.

Margaret Sayers Peden also elaborates on the dichotomous scheme distinguishing between the positive female characters—Úrsula Buendía, Remedios, the Beauty, Amaranta Buendía, and Fernanda del Carpio de Buendía, all marked by pretensions to high morality, familial loyalty, and boundless self-abnegation—and the "bad"—Pilar Ternera, Rebeca Buendía, Santa Sofía de la Piedad, Petra Cotes, Meme Buendía, and Amaranta Úrsula Buendía, all branded by transgressive eroticism and social marginalization (Peden, passim). Such critiques all coincide in the questionable proposition that women witness the novel's most important endeavors, rather than participating in them—nowhere do women figure in the imaginative, philosophic quest for knowledge and the search for a social utopia.

Alternatively, Peden offers the important insight that *One Hundred Years of Solitude* portrays women not naturalistically but mythically, deploying archetypal representations of women as Mother, Nature, Pride, and Concubine. Antonio Benítez Rojo and Hilda O. Benítez have since established that Márquez's work ("the great majority of his texts") is propitious for an archetypal Jungian analysis (Benítez Rojo and Benítez, 198).[2] Taken together, these insights open the door, as I hope to show, to a more nuanced reading of García Márquez's female figures. A third contribution, by Struebig, is the point that García Márquez, himself deconstructing bipolar notions, "makes absolutely clear his positive assessment of the qualities of the common woman" (Struebig, 60).

First, I propose that the dichotomy between the "good" and the "bad" women should be dismantled and reconfigured as a dialectic and a progression in which the socially elite women struggle to wield social power over the transgressive or abject members of their sex, while simultaneously being challenged and influenced by them. For instance, Úrsula's superior social position as the wife of the patriarch contrasts with the subaltern position of Pilar Ternera, a free agent active in the transgressive sphere of sex work. These characters at the subaltern end of the continuum move in and out of the Buendía household. By sharing physical space and by sustaining sexual bonds with the Buendía men, the marginal women evince qualities repressed by institutionalized propriety and assert a connection to those who paradoxically depend on them. The elite women (such as Úrsula), though they provide stability, strength, and productivity, have been socialized in such a way that they cannot supply the sensuality and eroticism sought by their Buendía consorts. As a result and through these subtle interconnections, both classes of women inhabit a continuum of defining characteristics that mutually reinforce, rather than oppose, each other. A fine example is Pilar, to whom Úrsula's sons turn for sexual initiation and through whom they procreate the next generation of Buendías.

The trajectory of the female characters throughout the novel and the agency exercised by them reveal a pattern of symbiosis. The entrepreneurial and self-sacrificing pillars of the Buendía family are portrayed throughout as sanctimonious and rigid; their puritanical primness, spiritual shortcomings, and pretensions to grandeur are inscribed in the text with deeply ironic negativity. The tendency that begins in Úrsula as an incapacity to accept the marriage of her son to his foster sister gradually morphs into the murderous intolerance of Fernanda, with the resultant maiming of her transgressive daughter's lover, Mauricio Babilonia, and the exile of this daughter to a convent in Cracow. Remedios, la Bella, another socially elite woman, is metonymically connected to death, for the sight of her causes men to lose consciousness or die in the attempt to be with her, such as the young man who climbs onto a shaky roof to view her in the bath; yet a third Buendía woman, Remedios's Aunt Amaranta, drives her refined Italian suitor to suicide.

The hard-working and emotionally vibrant Pilar, by contrast, perpetuates the Buendía lineage, while radiating a compassionate tenderness, an
erotic enthusiasm, and a stamina absent in the characters of Úrsula and
Fernanda. She endures past the age of 145, still stationed at the door of
her sexual "paradise" (García Márquez, 404). The characteristics of Petra
Cotes—fertility, eroticism, and clairvoyance—highlight, by the same
token, a dimension of female power previously unexplored by literary critiques of *One Hundred Years of Solitude.*

It should be clear that the socially marginal, abject women occupy, *alongside the elites,* a privileged space in the novel. Absent Pilar Ternera and her ilk,
the Buendía men would falter in their cognitive and philosophical mission.
These women enable the male search for knowledge of their origins, the
very intellectual and spiritual quest that drives the narrative. Rather than
merely serving as a foil for the legitimate Buendía women—their alleged
opposites in the "good/bad" dichotomy—transgressive women hold a powerful position intrinsically related to the principles that govern the novel.
Although these women do not directly participate in the intellectual adventure of deciphering Melquíades's manuscript, nor do they receive the
tutelage of the semidivine gypsy, they follow the path to knowledge in a
transcendent sense, one of mythic and quasi-biblical dimensions. With a
sustaining immanent wisdom complementary to that stored in the manuscripts of Melquíades, these female characters, down the generations, illuminate a path toward possible redemption through love.

Pilar Ternera's character embodies the paradigm that illustrates this
point. Of all the characters in the novel, only she is present throughout—
even the critics who regard her as but a "grotesque replica of Ursula" (Deveny and Marcos, 86) have noted her pervasive presence during the narrative. She arrives in the Buendía household to "help with the domestic
tasks" (García Márquez, 29) and progresses from managing kitchen chores
to initiating (on her own terrain) the Buendía sons into manhood and pro-
creation. In that she also has the power to heal and to read the future in
the tarot, her knowledge clearly transcends the cult of domesticity. During the family's plague of forgetfulness and insomnia, Pilar inverts her art,
"when she conceived the trick of reading the past in the cards as she had
read the future before" (García Márquez, 49). Úrsula, Rebeca, and Meme
continue to seek out Pilar and her cards, as do the men during times of
doubt or crisis. Clearly, Pilar, as the character who possesses the primordial
traits of fertility and memory, occupies a primary and critical space in the
novel—a position of power that previous critiques have erroneously over-
looked or obscured.

Pilar ages alone, yet the loss of her youth only enhances her knowledge and generosity. Described as a "sorceress" and "prophetess," Pilar and her potent spirit call to the Buendías generation after generation, and it is she who gives birth to first offspring of the Buendía men born in Macondo. At the interruption of the repeated cycling of time, Pilar remains the clairvoyant, the counselor, the first in a chain of characters who procreate with and comfort the Buendía males, sustain them, and act to enable the decoding of the revelatory manuscripts. Pilar's fundamental and pivotal functions reveal that her character, far from being incidental, is necessary to the novel. How, then, to read the re-creation of such a role in at least three more women, including Petra Cotes, Santa Sofía de la Piedad, and Nigromanta?

There exists a vast body of research that seeks to illuminate sexual roles in ancient societies. Innumerable and diverse studies (e.g., Frazer, Graves, James, Ochshorn, and Stone) have suggested that, during a millennium of human history, religion was feminocentric and based on a system of beliefs associated with fertility and nature. In the ancient world, some scholars argue, a pantheon often presumed to be exclusively male in fact included female goddesses, who played a pivotal religious role. Those asserting that the veneration of the female deity occurred transnationally and transculturally take the most extreme position: in Sumeria as Inanna, in Babylon as Ishtar, in Greece as Aphrodite, and in Persia as Anahita. The Canaanites, the Hebrews, and the Phoenicians prostrated themselves before the altar of Anat, also known as Astarté or Ashtart (Qualls-Corbett, 57). Cross-cultural inference links her in Lydia to Cybeles and in Rome, Venus. Sir James Frazer, in *The Golden Bough,* was among the first contemporaries to set out the argument for a female monotheism in the ancient world:

> If we survey the whole of the evidence on this subject . . . we may conclude that a great Mother Goddess, the personification of all the reproductive energies of nature, was worshipped under different names but with a substantial similarity of myth and ritual by many people of Western Asia. (Frazer, 39)

In addition, the cult of the Goddess included so-called virgins—women pure in the sense of integrity and honor, not physically untouched. These "virtual" virgins simultaneously represented a sexual and a spiritual essence. Living in the sacred complex, they also acted as lovers, uniting with those who came to the temple to venerate the Goddess. Frazer further points out the earthly counterpart of the Goddess in ritualized sexual activities:

> Associated with her was a lover, or rather a series of lovers, divine yet mortal, with whom she mated year by year, their commerce being deemed essential to the propagation of animals and plants . . . and further, that the fabulous union of the divine pair was simulated and, as it were, multiplied on earth by the real, though temporary, union of the human sexes at the sanctuary of the Goddess for the sake of thereby ensuring the fruitfulness of the ground and the increase of man and beast. (Frazer, 39)

Those who follow in Frazer's footsteps reiterate that the sacred bond of marriage or "hieros gamos" was seen as propitiating the harvest and the well-being of the human body (Stone, 154); we note that Pilar ravishes the Buendía men on the site of a granary. Again, these women were virgins, not in the sense of lacking sexual experience but in the sense of not belonging to one man and, like Pilar, having a heart still "intact." Very different from the profane prostitute (or *hetaira*), the sacred woman may have enjoyed respect and social status. In temples of sacred prostitution, such as the temples of Aphrodite in Corinth, "sexuality, fertility and spirituality were not radically distinguished" (Bell, 200). In ancient Mesopotamia, the gods were considered to actually inhabit the temples, and the concern for fertility led to the formation of a class of women who offered their sexual services to the gods within the temple (Walker, 809).

Another argument advanced in this direction is a distinction between the concepts of *virgin* and *prostitute*. *Virgo* in Latin signifies "single or unattached woman," while *virgo intacta* denotes "lack of sexual experience." By contrast, prostitute (derived from *prostituere* [*pro* indicating public, and *statuere* meaning "to place"]) translates as "to be exposed in public" (Corominas). Therefore, describing the sacred prostitutes as virgins evokes not a contradiction but a mythic tradition in which ancient societies elevated, rather than feared or circumscribed, women's sexuality. The advent of Christianity (and, previously, Judaism) eliminated the place of the single, untouched woman in religious practices, paving the way for the previously described dichotomy between women: morally superior intact virgins on one side and immoral, inferior, and unclean whores on the other. In other words: "Together, the Virgin and the Magdalene form a diptych of Christian patriarchy's idea of woman. There is no place in the conceptual architecture of Christian society for a single woman who is neither a virgin or a whore" (Warner, 235). Such is the burden of the Western tradition, which García Márquez seeks to ironize, parody, and deconstruct in one novel after another (Benítez Rojo and Benítez; Peñuel). Nor is "machismo," the cult of male superiority, exempt from his parodic pen.

It is significant that the omniscient narrator in *One Hundred Years of Solitude* abstains from the label "prostitute" when referring to Pilar Ternera. Even occasional references to "bad women" lack a forceful connotation, the exception being Arcadio, who is unaware that Pilar is his mother and directs this epithet at her for rejecting him sexually: "Don't pretend to be a saint. The whole world knows that you are a whore" (García Márquez, 104). Only then does a challenge emerge to the quasi-sanctity of Pilar. The mythic dimension of the character fades, and the reality of her social position intrudes. Put another way, utopia yields to dystopia. The word "whore" (as hetaira) appears again, used by Colonel Aureliano when he refuses to receive a delegation from his political party: "Take them to the whores" (García Márquez, 161). One critic seized upon this naturalistic moment to assert that "for all García Márquez's [*sic*] leftist aspirations, his work perpetuates the confinement of women to the roles ascribed to them by male fantasy, namely mothering and prostitution. They have no access to public life" (Solomon, 192). Such a simplistic assessment misses the metaphorical textures of utopia and dystopia in the Márquezian literary world .

Once again, the "goddess" critics explain the transition (or perhaps descent) from spiritual matriarchy to patriarchy as motivated by economic and political ends, that is to say, the destruction (in legal terms) of the "maternal right" to land and political power (Briffault; Stone). Some argue that during the Neolithic period the matriarchal system and maternal law prevailed in most places: the most ancient Egyptian writings describe woman's total dominion over her body and habitat and show that property was passed from mother to daughter. The transition from matriarchy to patriarchy took place in classical Greece, while in other parts of the world the matriarchal system survived until much later (e.g., for certain British tribes, until the ninth century). During the Christian era, woman was totally stripped of the right to own property. While the matriarchal religious system prevailed, the sacred, or sacred harlot, occupied a privileged position as representative of the goddess. During the transitional phase, woman was displaced from ritual religious life in order to implant a male Trinity. The Virgin Mary then could be venerated but not worshiped, in order to impede her becoming an avenue through which to re-establish the old cult of the divine female—a theological issue that continues to be thorny today. Beginning with Saint Paul, according to this train of thought, the feminine ceased to be considered a source of physical pleasure and spiritual ecstasy. The negative attitude became predominant, and so did the concept of the mundane woman as a witch. In the Puritanical and

Victorian periods, so the argument runs, the collective attitude was one of degradation of sexual activity and marginalization of women. We can see the appeal of a theory that offers a global explanation for the otherwise inexplicable gender imbalances of the Western world, especially at a time when gender roles are fiercely debated and contested.

Attractive as this position may be, it has been and continues to be contested on archaeological and historical grounds (v. Frymer-Kensky). In short, the idea of an original Mother Goddess in prehistory is surrounded by an intense controversy in which new approaches—cognitive, contextual, and feminist archaeology among them—contend (Goodison and Morris, 6). This seductive panorama, where religiosity, spirituality, and eroticism meet, is evocative of the utopian yearnings and visions that have endured in Western culture, from Plato, More, Shakespeare, and Montaigne to Charlotte Perkins Gilman's *Herland*. Even as attempted utopias vanish or turn dystopic over time, *there is no renunciation of the vision itself*—and therein lies the key to understanding Márquez and to deciphering his female characters.

Returning to Pilar Ternera, I propose that she is the first in a chain of signifiers to evoke the sacred harlot, since she, like Melquíades, is a sexualized source of knowledge and inspiration to the Buendías. This characteristic removes her from the realm of the common prostitute, populated by women like the ones in Catarino's drinking establishment, and distinguishes her from the women that "do it for food," out of hunger. Instead, Pilar belongs to a sacred zone proximate to the location of the mysterious manuscripts left undeciphered by Melquíades. One could also explore the notion that Pilar corresponds, together with Melquíades, to the definition of the Jungian archetype of the wise man (and also of the animal), but I will not pursue that direction. Still, I am drawn once more to emphasize the role of ancient pagan belief. Remember that Pilar is juxtaposed to "a grain storage room" next to the kitchen, a site for lovemaking, thus linking with the goddess of corn and cereals. At the same time, the "smell of smoke" on Pilar associates her with the sensuality of sacrificial bonfires lit at the altars of ancient deities.

It is true that by the end Pilar runs a brothel and charges money for her services, but only when the hourglass of time has almost run out. Earlier, at the peak of her powers, she lent out rooms and never charged for her favors. When the textual space between Pilar's actions and her death runs out, her powers are transferred to Petra Cotes. Petra, in turn, is explicitly associated with fertility through her amazing capability of making her and her partner Aureliano Segundo's livestock procreate.

Subsequently, her aura is transmitted to a younger female, Santa Sofía de la Piedad, who is referred to as "virgin"—this woman procreates with Arcadio Remedios la Bella, an exquisite creature of marianistic attributes who is so pure she is "not of this world," and must depart by ascension to the heavens. And later, despite her being the most submissive and silent of the lineage, it is Santa Sofía de la Piedad who purchases for Aureliano the Sanskrit primer that leads to the eventual decoding of the manuscripts.

The mantle passes to Nigromanta, "a big black woman, with sturdy bones, mare's hips and tits like living melons," who consoles and sustains Aureliano, at first only in a nonsexual role and then in an erotic one. The proper names of these women sustain our argument: let us recall that Sofía means wisdom and Nigromanta connotes necromancy, an alternate path in the quest for knowledge. But Nigromanta also is Black, suggesting the presence of Afro-Colombia, submerged in the narrative as it is in national discourses, to this day. These names, therefore, are almost always more than mere coincidence and indicative of Márquezian semantics.[3] In the case of all these women, it is made explicit that they possess, each in a different way, a depth of understanding and a spirit lacking in their Buendía female counterparts. Without material belongings or property, these women (in descending order of sacralization) possess the secret to survival and to life lived with reverent enthusiasm and vitality.

Going a step farther, the sacred harlot is not an isolated element but rather belongs to the vaster context of García Márquez's mythical search for origins and renewal of the spirit. In *One Hundred Years of Solitude*, the primitive religions of the Near East, Palestine, and Mesopotamia, where civilization is said to have begun, are evoked in a meaningful way. Márquez signals his search for the historical and mythic origins of humanity most prominently through paralleling his novel to Scriptures (Roses). The studies of proper names in *One Hundred Years of Solitude* reveal this intention geographically. Mauricio Babilonia, for example, is the male character who infuses the decadent Buendía family with new blood, as the father of Aureliano, decipherer of the manuscripts. The appearance of Babilonia is not coincidental but can be related to the fact that in ancient Babylon (now Iraq), writing and urban civilization appeared for the first time. The mention of a "Babylonian matriarch" in Macondo also calls the reader's attention to the ideal of shared male-female hierarchies of those times (as well as to the phrase "whores of Babylon"). If, on the one hand, young Babilonia's name takes us to the Near East, the same applies to Petra, whose name can be identified with an ancient city carved in stone whose ruins lie near Amman, in present-day Jordan. Added to this associative chain, there appear in Macondo during carnival time soldiers dressed as "false Bedouins" that once again make us think of that seminal region and of archaeological traces of incipient civilizations.

Let us remember the ties between *One Hundred Years of Solitude* and the Scriptures of the Occident. Let us widen the links and relate them to the foundational inquiries that deeply concern our author. Seen this way, both the biblical references and the ones that evoke ancient pagan societies join, pointing in a very specific direction—the desire to move away from repressive orders and toward others consonant with the enduring utopian projects of humankind.

In the semidivine female figure, represented in the text by the appearance of Pilar Ternera and her successors, Petra, Santa Sofía, and Nigromanta, I have located a system of coded allusion to cults and beliefs that some believe to be superior to ours, especially in balancing the claims of gender and sexuality. Through this code, we are urged to recommence the mythical voyage to reclaim our pristine essence, our roots and our common humanity, and then advance to the creation of social utopia on earth.

Why does *One Hundred Years of Solitude* emphasize so strongly the lost or unrealized powers of women? I believe that one answer lies in Márquez's constant preoccupation with the tenure of political power by vested interests, a preoccupation that implicates women because their subalternity is a factor detracting from (gender) justice in the history of the world, even as a preponderance of male power has led to intense bellicosity. García Márquez's utopian, as well as his dystopian, discourses thus take on added significance for current debates surrounding these issues.

I have tried to show that the "other" woman in *One Hundred Years of Solitude*, far from being a distorted reflection of the protagonist, Úrsula, a generalized Earth Mother, or the stock figure of a concubine, can be read as an avatar of the female deities and sacred harlots of pre–Judeo-Christian antiquity that populate the visionary utopias of feminist thought. Textual evidence abounds in the presence of a fertility cult, repeated references to Babylon and other regions of the Near East, and the assignment of symbolic names to key characters. I believe that an analysis applied to mythical figures would further advance the link between utopian ideas and the thesis proposed in this work. Furthermore, the utopian impulse blends with the biblical intertexualities of the novel. Not only does this approach explain the key functions of the female characters, but it also valorizes the transhistorical and transcultural complexity of García Márquez's works. Finally, it reinforces the novel's transcendence as it becomes the history of humankind, with its thwarted dreams of freedom and equality.

Márquez elucidates what is manifest: that technology has advanced, but human beings often cannot do so without personal experience. Ontology recapitulates philogeny, and human beings still struggle with the same tragedies and devastating conflicts between reality and desire, repression and libido, matter and spirit.

Notes

For Julia Skelly

1. All translations from Spanish originals are mine, except for *One Hundred Years of Solitude*, translated by Gregory Rabassa.

2. The Benítezes think that traditional Jungian analysis has definite shortcomings; they deploy its nomenclature and method for hermeneutical reasons and also to show that it "explodes" itself at its origin.

3. See John C. Miller, "Onomatology of Male Characters in the *One Hundred Years of Solitude* of Gabriel García Márquez," *Literary Onomastic Studies* 1 (1974), 66–73.

Works Cited

Bell, Shannon. "Tomb of the Sacred Prostitute: The Symposium." In *Shadow of Spirit: Postmodernism and Religion*, ed. Philippa Berry and Andrew Wernick. London: Routledge, 1992. 198–210.

Benítez Rojo, Antonio, and Hilda O. Benítez. "Eréndira liberada, o la liberación del macho occidental." *Revista Iberoamericana* 50, nos. 128–129 (July–December 1984), 1057–1075.

Briffault, Robert. *The Mothers: A Study of the Origins of Sentiments and Institutions.* New York: Macmillan, 1927.

Corominas, Joan. *Breve diccionario etimológico de la lengua castellana.* Madrid: Gredos, 1980.

Deveny, John J., Jr., and Juan Manuel Marcos. "García Márquez III: Women and Society in *One Hundred Years of Solitude.*" *Journal of Popular Culture* 22, no. 1 (Summer 1988), 83–90.

Frazer, Sir James G. *The Golden Bough*, Book I. New York: Macmillan, 1937.

Frymer-Kensky, Tikva. *In the Wake of the Goddesses: Women, Culture, and the Biblical Transformation of Pagan Myth.* New York: Free Press, 1992.

García Márquez, Gabriel. *One Hundred Years of Solitude,* trans. Gregory Rabassa. New York: Harper and Row, 1970.

Goodison, Lucy, and Christine Morris. *Ancient Goddesses: The Myths and the Evidence.* Madison: University of Wisconsin Press, 1999.

Graves, Robert. *The White Goddess: A Historical Grammar of Poetic Myth.* New York: Creative Age Press, 1948.

James, Edwin Oliver. *The Cult of the Mother Goddess*. New York: Barnes and Noble, 1961.

Ochshorn, Judith. *The Female Experience and the Nature of the Divine*. Bloomington: Indiana University Press, 1981.

Peden, Margaret Sayers. "Las buenas y las malas mujeres de Macondo." In *Explicación de Cien años de soledad* 4, no. supp. 1, ed. Francisco De Porrata. San Jose, Calif.: Porrata y Avendaño, 1976. 313–327.

Peñuel, Arnold M. "The Sleep of Vital Reason in García Márquez' *Chronicle of a Death Foretold*," *Hispania* 68, no. 4 (December 1985), 753–766.

Qualls-Corbett, Nancy. *The Sacred Prostitute: Eternal Aspects of the Feminine*. San Francisco: Inner City Press, 1988.

Roses, Lorraine E. "A Code of Many Colors: Biblical Intertextualities in *One Hundred Years of Solitude*." In *Justina: Homenaje a Justina Ruiz de Conde*. ed. Elena Gascón-Vera and Joy Renjilian-Burgy. Madrid: Aldeu, 1992. 172–178.

Solomon, Irvin D. "Latin American Women in Literature and Reality: García Márquez's *One Hundred Years of Solitude*." *Midwest Quarterly* 34 (Winter 1993), 2, 14.

Stone, Merlin. *When God Was a Woman*. New York: Harcourt Brace Jovanovich, 1975.

Struebig, Patricia. "Nature and Natural Sexuality in Gabriel García Márquez' *One Hundred Years of Solitude*." *Selecta: Journal of the Pacific Northwest Conference on Foreign Languages* 15 (1994), 58–62.

Vargas Llosa, Mario. *García Márquez: Historia de un deicidio*. Barcelona: Barral, 1972.

Volkening, Ernesto. "Gabriel García Márquez, o el trópico desembrujado." In *9 Asedios a García Márquez*, ed. Mario Benedetti. Santiago de Chile: Ed. Universitaria, 1969. 147–163.

Walker, Barbara G. *Women's Encyclopedia of Myths and Secrets*, vol. 1. New York: Macmillan, 1999.

Warner, Marina. *Alone of All Her Sex: The Myth and the Cult of the Virgin Mary*. New York: Knopf, 1976.

Aureliano's Smile

MICHAEL WOOD

❖   ❖   ❖

"She cannot do without shooting, Gedali," I told the
old man, "because she is the Revolution."
                                                    —Isaac Babel

COLONEL AURELIANO BUENDÍA is the most complex and
haunting character in *One Hundred Years of Solitude*, although not the
most forceful or the most necessary to life in Macondo. We are in his mind
in the first sentence of the book, and worrying about his vanished political
legacy on the last pages. He is austere, distant, yet oddly appealing, and
seems to provoke in others an irresistible urge to simplify him—the others
including many critics, many readers, García Márquez himself, and Aureliano's mother, Úrsula. There is also at one point a sort of drift in the character, an uncertainty in the narrator's hold on him, which threatens
to take him quite out of focus, beyond simplification but also beyond
understanding.

A daguerrotype of Aureliano as a child is described—he is between
Amaranta and Rebeca, wears a black velvet suit, has "the same languor and
the same clairvoyant look that he was to have years later as he faced the
firing squad" (51: 56)—but he permitted no photographs during his military days or after. The Buendía children of a later generation are told that a
Tartar horseman in an encyclopedia is Aureliano because "in spite of his
strange outfit" he has "a familiar (or a family) air," "un aire familiar" (280:
297).[1] And of course this *is* a picture of Aureliano, of the kind this book af-
fords: his bony face and drooping moustache give him the oriental appear-

ance so common in Latin America, and his spells of tyranny suggest some Asiatic scourge. But the gag also insists that the only picture we have of him as an adult is a picture of someone else, and from half the world away at that—a joking metaphor for our need of metaphor.

There are pictures of Aureliano outside the text, since he is the one character with a particularly marked historical source. Clearly all the characters have sources—how could they not?—and García Márquez has spoken of making up "jigsaw puzzles of many different people and, naturally, bits of myself as well." But Aureliano is an allusion as well as a character. He has the rank attained by García Márquez's own grandfather in the Liberal Army in Colombia's War of the Thousand Days, but he has the power, career, and angular looks of General Rafael Uribe Uribe, leader of the liberal forces in the same war. Uribe fought in various insurrections all abortive, started as early as 1876; was elected to the House of Representatives; waged the long war; signed the Peace of Neerlandia; was assassinated in 1914—unlike Aureliano, who dies quietly at home on a day when the circus comes to town. The General was immensely popular, and, as Stephen Minta says, "perhaps the strangest aspect of Uribe Uribe's life and military career was the way in which he was able to preserve a glorious reputation unscathed through a wealth of defeats." Of course, it may be that failure is essential to such a reputation, that success would only wreck it, and that we can understand the historical Uribe through the fictional Aureliano; that Aureliano is a reading of Uribe as well as an allusion to him, an exploration of the legend. Lucila Inés Mena puts the matter very well:

> Colonel Aureliano Buendía embodies the whole of Liberal history in the period. He is a synthesis of the rebellion, with its leaders, its ideals and its failures. On the other hand, the colonel is the war . . .

He is the war. He is at first solitary decency dragged into war. He has very little grasp of the issues involved but a strong instinct for justice, and the political situation is evoked around him with a casual lucidity, an apparent offhandedness that is itself a form of commentary. The customary deadpan of the narrative tone here edges toward brilliant caricature.

Aureliano receives "schematic lessons" in current affairs from his father-in-law, the Conservative *corregidor.* The Liberals, Don Apolinar says, are

> freemasons, bad people, wanting to hang priests, to institute civil marriage and divorce, to recognize the rights of illegitimate children as equal to those

of legitimate ones, and to cut the country up into a federal system that would take power away from the supreme authority. The Conservatives, on the other hand, who had received their power directly from God, proposed the establishment of public order and family morality. They were the defenders of the faith of Christ, of the principle of authority, and were not prepared to permit the country to be broken down into autonomous entities. (90: 97)

Aureliano has an illegitimate son and leans to the Liberals for that reason. But he would lean to them, anyway, and his first insight into the electoral process confirms his preference. The election has been quite proper and well conducted, as far as the actual voting is concerned. Don Apolinar has the votes counted. They are very close, so he removes most of the Liberal ballots and makes up the numbers with Conservative ballots. "The Liberals will go to war," Aureliano says, amazed, but Don Apolinar says not: that is why a few Liberal ballots were left in the box. The next exchange is worthy of Stendhal on French electioneering:

> Aureliano understood the disadvantages of being in the opposition. "If I were a Liberal," he said, "I'd go to war because of those ballots." His father-in-law looked at him over his glasses.
>
> "Oh Aurelito," he said, "if you were a Liberal, even though you're my son-in-law, you wouldn't have seen the switching of the ballots." (91: 98)

Don Apolinar's "Ay" in "Ay, Aurelito" is really untranslatable: much wisdom and history and sadness in such *ays*.

But what takes Aureliano to war is not Conservative vote-fixing but government-supported violence. The war has started, the military has taken over from Don Apolinar, who retains only an ornamental jurisdiction in Macondo, and four soldiers brutally kill a woman who has been bitten by a rabid dog. Aureliano and his friends. armed with kitchen knives and sharpened bits of iron, capture the garrison and shoot the captain and the four offending soldiers. Aureliano's career has begun.

We should pause to note the movie logic here. Aureliano doesn't understand "how people arrived at the extreme of waging war over things that could not be touched with the hand" (91: 97). He is Gary Cooper or Humphrey Bogart, unmoved by abstractions but provoked by cruelty, by the sight of victimization. This is the way that American isolation, another long solitude, ends in film after film. We don't need to think about the movies themselves in any detail, only to see that Aureliano is behaving here like a legend, like a simplification. He *is* moved by abstractions when they are close enough, as the matter of the vote shows, and I don't mean to underestimate decency as a political motive, for from it. I do want to suggest that the purity of Aureliano's response allows an effect that William Empson would call pastoral: we don't disbelieve the simplification, but we do know the world is more complex, indeed the simplification itself seems to glance at what it leaves out.

In fact, Aureliano's position is not a political one at all but a moral response to a political world, and many ambiguities in the novel revolve around our feelings about this response. Is it haughty and unrealistic, for example, or a rare instance of honesty and dignity? The same questions can be asked, not coincidentally and with unusual frequency, about many gestures, past and present, in Latin American politics. At times, Aureliano seems blinkered or self-deluding, his strategy a form of solitude. At others, he seems to be taking the only untainted stance there is, and there are moments when his very failure seems to ensure his integrity, to be all that decency could ever expect.

In the midst of the civil wars he is busy losing, Aureliano appears to turn into a sort of Shakespearean tyrant, wishing a rival dead and then executing the eager lieutenant who anticipates his wish. He has a chalk circle drawn around him wherever he goes, and from its center he decides "the destiny of the world" (148: 159). He is "lost in the solitude of his immense power" (149: 160) and says things like "The best friend a person has is one who has just died" (149: 161). He comes close to executing his old comrade Gerineldo Márquez because they disagree about the terms of a peace, and his mother swears to kill him if he carries out the sentence, saying, "It's exactly what I would have done if you'd been born with a pig's tail" (152: 163). He is a monster, a "mythical warrior" (153: 165) who seems to be everywhere and whom no one can kill. He is told that his heart is "rotting alive" (148: 159), and he himself later thinks his affections have "rotted" (155: 167). He contracts an "inner coldness" (149: 160) that is never to leave him and that is a grim, displaced reflection of the ice that delighted him as a child.

The "destiny of the world" and the "immense power" are either delusions on Aureliano's part or verbal flourishes on García Márquez's. Aureliano has the power of life and death that any bandit or gangster has, but he really would need to win a battle or two to have the tremendous power this rhetoric suggests. We seem to be reading a trial run for the dictator-novel García Márquez was later to write as *Autumn of the Patriarch,* with its mingled horror and fascination for the loneliness and folly of men who actually do decide vast destinies. But then here, in *One Hundred Years of Solitude,*

García Márquez lets go of Aureliano the tyrant almost as soon as he has picked him up. "The intoxication of power began to fall apart in gusts of uneasiness ["ráfagas de desazón," literally gusts of insipidity, flavorlessness, barrenness, or discomfort]. . . . He felt scattered . . . and more solitary than ever" (149: 160–161). This is not the solitude of power; it is the solitude that neither power nor anything else can change, and another phrase takes us even closer to the problem. "Only he knew," we are told of Aureliano, "that his confused heart was condemned to uncertainty for ever": "su aturdido corazón," his confused or bewildered heart (148: 159). The coldness and the spoiling of the affections are a way of dealing with bewilderment, of freezing it.

However, if Aureliano is not an imperial tyrant, he is for a time a harsh military commander and an image of how loneliness can look like heartlessness. He has not become like his enemies through fighting them, as an intelligent opponent suggests (144: 154), because he is and remains the opposite of the ambitious and time-serving military. He is unbendingly honest and principled, willing to have this same opponent executed, although he likes and admires him, because "it's the Revolution" that is doing the shooting, and the other man would have done the same in his place (143: 153). But there is certainly a stoppage of feelings in Aureliano, and some self-deception: we are reading a fable about the corruption of incorruption. When Aureliano looks at José Raquel, the man he is about to have killed, he sees him "with his heart":

> He was startled to see how much he had aged, how his hands shook, and the rather routine air of acceptance ["la conformidad un poco rutinaria"] with which he awaited death, and then he felt a profound contempt for himself which he took for the beginnings of pity. (143–144; 154)

This is an extraordinary insight, but kept just beyond the reach of the character. Aureliano despises the depth of his own mistake. A man who didn't recognize abstractions is about to have an abstraction kill a man he would rather keep alive. But even now Aureliano himself doesn't understand his own response. He feels the self-contempt but thinks it is pity. His heart is in worse shape than he thinks.

As I have suggested, García Márquez loses sight of Aureliano at times, or rather wants him for too many jobs. But this slippage of interest (unintended, I take it) does mirror Aureliano's own central uncertainty. Among the five volumes of verse Aureliano has written is a poem about a man who went out into the rain and got lost, "el poema de hombre que se había extraviado en la lluvia" (115: 123). A similar misfortune occurs in "Isabel watching the rain in Macondo," except that the man gets lost in time, "se extravío en el tiempo," Aureliano—the word "extraviado" is used of him too (149: 160)—is a man who gets lost in time and the war, one of history's strays. And, in this rainy light, his recurring self-contempt must be less a justified verdict than an intense and tangled response to his own bewilderment, the raging of his confused heart. Guilt is at least better than helplessness, a tormenting alternative to freezing the feelings. Power for Aureliano is not the world of politics he despises or even the license to order life and death; it is everything he feels called upon to do singlehanded, his lonely mission against the world's wrongs: an expression of his altruism but also of his arrogance.

Aureliano tries, with some success, not to permit himself emotions. When his little bride, Remedios, dies, his reaction is not the "commotion he feared" but only a "dull feeling of rage that gradually dissolved into a solitary and passive frustration, similar to the one he had felt during the time when he had resigned himself to celibacy" (90: 97). "We see," Jacques Joset comments in his edition, "that Aureliano's feeling for Remedios was not exactly love." Is this what we see? Surely we see a man who is chronically afraid of feeling, romantically risks it, and retreats into cold fury when calamity occurs. Aureliano's response is the same when sixteen of his sons are massacred, a "dull anger," "una cólera sorda," which puts a frightening glint back into his eyes—of the kind that at other times made chairs move just because he looked at them (212: 226–227).

> As had happened with the death of his wife, as had happened to him so many times during the war with the deaths of his best friends, he did not have a feeling of sorrow but a blind and directionless rage, and extenuating impotence. (211: 226)

This looks less like an inability to love than an inability to mourn, abetted perhaps by a strangled regret, the belated, self-protecting thought that it would have been better to have felt nothing at all.

The dryness of Aureliano's heart, the coldness of his entrails that is said to be a source of vitality (141: 151), is both a mask and a desolate achievement—since the mask can no longer be lifted or distinguished from the face. Aureliano's defense against nostalgia, for example, is horribly secure. The past holds out "insidious traps" for him, shows him that his mother at least understands his unhappiness. He gazes at her face, her leathery skin, decayed teeth, faded hair, her dazed look; sees the scars and scratches that half a century of daily life has left on her; but cannot even feel pity. At this moment, we are told, Remedios is only the blurred image of someone who might have been his daughter, and his countless mistresses in the wars have left no trace in his feelings (154–155: 166–167). He has a gruesome memory that confirms rather than contradicts his immunity to nostalgia. One eleventh of October he woke in bed with a woman who was dead. He remembers the date because she had asked him about it an hour before, but he didn't know her name or see her face, because she came to him in the darkness, as so many women did. And he doesn't remember that she was drowning in tears and swore to love him till she died. Only the text, and Melquíades, remember for him and let us see the pathos of the woman's too quickly kept promise (231: 247).

Aureliano does have moments of what he would call weakness. "Caught at last in one of nostalgia's traps," he confusedly remembers the nameless girl who in a later García Márquez story was to be called Eréndira. Perhaps if he had married her he would have been "a man without war and without glory, a nameless artisan, a happy animal" (157: 168–169). Perhaps. The scenario is improbable, *only* nostalgic, but revealing all the same. Eréndira is a girl who accidentally caused a fire in her grandmother's house and is now brutally subject to prostitution until she has paid off the value of the property. She has already slept with seventy-three men the night the young Aureliano meets her and reckons she has about ten years to go, at seventy men a night, before her debt is canceled. Aureliano feels "an irresistible need to love her and protect her" (53: 58), but when he looks for her again she and her grandmother have moved on.

The victim to be protected is repeated in Remedios, the child-bride. There is fear and solitude in such a choice, of course; perhaps an incapacity for a love that would not flatter pride, would not look like a favor. But there is generosity too, the same spirit we have seen in Aureliano's political impulses, and something not felt at all by Eréndira's other seventy clients a night, or by most suitors of grown-up girls with nice dowries. Aureliano finds Remedios, we are told, not in any of the material places where he might seek her but "only in the image that saturated his private and terrible solitude" (64: 69). This is a Proustian passion, all in the obsessed mind, but the girl and her emerald eyes do exist, and Aureliano does marry her. The saturated solitude ends, and part of our distress at Remedios's sudden death must be distress *for* Aureliano, for the road that can now only lead back to loneliness.

Úrsula's theory about her son is harsher than this, more deeply rooted in magic and in her own guilt. Aureliano cried inside her before he was born, and she was sure this was the first indication that the child would have the dreaded pig's tail. She "begged God to let the child die in her womb" (218: 233). Later she sees, with what is called "the lucidity of decrepitude," that a baby's crying before birth is "an unequivocal sign of the inability to love." She also sees that

> Colonel Aureliano Buendía had not lost his love for the family because he had been hardened by the war, as she had thought before, but that he had never loved anyone, not even his wife Remedios or the countless one-night women who had passed through his life, and much less his sons. . . . He had not fought so many wars out of idealism, as everyone had thought, nor had he given up an imminent victory because of weariness, as everyone had thought, but had won and lost for one and the same reason, pure and sinful pride. (218: 233)

This is a comprehensive theory, not lightly to be dismissed. There is nothing in the text to distance the author from it and plenty outside the text to suggest that he agrees. And the theory must in large part be right. Aureliano himself suspects his own idealism and diagnoses pride.

> One night he asked Colonel Gerineldo Márquez:
> "Tell me something, old friend: why are you fighting?"
> "What other reason could there be, old friend?" Colonel Gerineldo Márquez answered. "For the great Liberal Party."
> "You're lucky you know," he answered. "As far as I'm concerned, I've only just realized that I'm fighting out of pride."
> "That's bad," Colonel Gerineldo Márquez said.
> Colonel Aureliano Buendía was amused at his alarm. "Naturally," he said. "But in any case, it's better than not knowing why you're fighting." He looked him in the eyes and added with a smile:
> "Or fighting, like you, for something that doesn't have any meaning for anyone." (124: 133)

What Úrsula can't see—the lucidity of decrepitude must be some way from omniscience—and what García Márquez has forgotten is Aureliano's irony, his amusement at Gerineldo's alarm, his smile as he puts his old friend on the spot. Aureliano's diagnosis of pride is correct but simplified, far from the whole story: another version of pastoral.

His smile is frequently mentioned in the text, and quite often perceptible even without a mention—implicit in the wit of what he says. It is a smile that in no way denies pain or disillusionment or solitude and is full of sadness. But I can't find any cynicism in it, only a bitter, balanced awareness of the grounds for despair and amusement. A man reads out a set of peace proposals that imply the abandonment of every principle the Liberals have stood for, to which Aureliano says, *smiling,* "You mean we're just fighting for power?" "These are tactical reforms," one of the delegates says, and we don't need to be told that Aureliano's smile remains or what it means (150–151: 162).

One day Aureliano finds his mother weeping in the courtyard of their house, in the company of his father's ghost which he has never seen and never will see:

> "What does he say?" he asked.
>
> "He's very sad," Úrsula answered, "because he thinks you are going to die."
>
> "Tell him," the colonel smiled, "that a person doesn't die when he should but when he can." (212: 227)

It must be hardness of heart and his attempted refusal of the past that prevent Aureliano from seeing his father's ghost, but there is a marvelously underplayed wisdom in his smiling epigram. At this moment he almost has the knowledge of Melquíades. He had premonitions as a child, knew when someone was coming, or when a pot was about to fall off a table. He can see the present and the immediate future, he reads minds, sees through his own and other people's illusions. He can picture, we are told, both sides of his thought (124: 133). He can't see the splintered, retarded time in Melquíades' room, the magical release from dust and decay, but when Melquíades finally vanishes and the room succumbs to change, it is eerily said to be the room Aureliano had *foreseen* (312: 331). Even his blindness is a form of sight: the problem is the misery of what he perceives, the wintry triumph of his lucidity. He is a writer, or has been, but is in this sense the exact opposite of our invisible novelist, who can't do without the past, who needs to see ghosts and to enlist the power of fiction to fight fictions. This is what Aureliano's smile seems to say: that truth is scarce and bleak and not enough, but that knowledge of helplessness is still a form of knowledge.

Aureliano's continuing life in the novel enacts precisely this insight. He does not become a ghost, like his father, like Melquíades, inventors both of them, men of the imagination. He becomes a disputed memory, a lost integrity, a historical question. He is the truth no one believes, and his only visible legacy is a street name. "Ah," Aureliano Babilonia says to a priest, "then you don't believe it either":

> "Believe what?"
>
> "That Colonel Aureliano Buendía fought thirty-two civil wars and lost

them all," Aureliano answered. "That the army hemmed in and machine-gunned three thousand workers and that their bodies were carried off on a train with two hundred coaches to be thrown into the sea."

The priest measured him with a pitying look.

"Oh, my son," he sighed. "It would be enough for me to be sure that you and I exist at this moment." (354: 376)

The complicated twist here is that Colonel Aureliano Buendía is a model for both types of thought: for the stubborn resistance to official untruth and for the habit of solitude that makes even one's own existence doubtful.

"Many years later, as he faced the firing squad, Colonel Aureliano Buendía was to remember that distant afternoon when his father took him to discover ice." Years later still, facing only an apparently interminable old age, he remembers the ice again, the bright miracle that for him has become only a melancholy metaphor. The memory is triggered by the sound of a brass band and the happy cries of children. A circus has come to town, as if to say goodbye to Aureliano on behalf of all the color and profusion of the life he has so austerely refused. He dies losing track of a thought:

> He saw a woman dressed in gold sitting on the back of an elephant. He saw a sad dromedary. He saw a bear dressed like a Dutch girl keeping time to the music with a soup spoon and a pan. He saw the clowns doing cartwheels at the end of the parade and once more he saw the face of his miserable solitude when everything had passed by and there was nothing but the bright expanse of the street and the air full of flying ants with a few onlookers peering into the precipice of uncertainty. Then he went to the chestnut tree, thinking about the circus, and while he urinated he tried to keep on thinking about the circus, but he could no longer find the memory. He pulled his head in between his shoulders like a baby chick and remained motionless with his forehead against the trunk of the chestnut tree. The family didn't find out until the next day. . . . (233–234: 250)

He couldn't find the memory, "ya no encontro el recuerdo." He can't remember, isn't remembered. He is not the most necessary character in the book, but he is the most missed, the one we most need to understand. He is the first human being to be born in Macondo, and his humanity, however tenuous and chilled, is important. He is the novel's dark conscience. No wonder García Márquez was reluctant to have him die and went upstairs trembling, he says, when he had written the words I have just quoted. His wife, Mercedes, knew at once what had happened. "The colonel's dead," she said, and García Márquez himself lay on his bed and cried for two hours. This is not a sentimental story, and there is no contradiction be-tween those tears and Aureliano's smile.

Note

1. I have used Gregory Rabassa's familiar and effective translation of *One Hundred Years of Solitude* whenever I could, which was most of the time. Where it wasn't accu-rate or didn't reflect the point I was after in the Spanish, I have either adapted it or offered my own wording entirely. Quotations are identified on the page, Spanish text first, for example [216: 231]. References are to the readily available editions by Editorial Sudamericana, 1967, and Avon, 1971.

The Limits of the
Liberal Imagination

One Hundred Years of
Solitude *and* Nostromo

JEAN FRANCO

✦   ✦   ✦

W HEN JOSEPH CONRAD'S NOVEL *Nostromo* appeared in 1904, British imperialism was at its self-confident height, for the Boer War had, if anything, increased nationalist fervor. Like all imperial powers, Britain had legitimized direct aggression and informal colonization by claiming a civilizing mission on the Roman model whose visible symbols were the statues of Victoria, orb in hand, presiding like Minerva over the neoclassical facades of banks and exchanges. Wars might rage in farflung outposts; but within the island, at least, there was relatively little interest in questioning the legitimacy of the *pax britannica*. Even those novelists who apparently dissented from the materialist goals of Victorian society usually turned a blind eye to empire. The colonies, when mentioned at all in fiction, were represented by Thackeray's nabobs, Dickens's Miss Fuzzy Wuzzy; or they were those mysterious "foreign parts" into which characters conveniently disappeared or out of which they returned with large, unexplained fortunes. Not until 1902, when J. A. Hobson published *Imperialism: A Study,* was there any detailed, theoretical critique of the economics of empire building; not until the appearance of Conrad's novels was there real awareness of the complexity of the effects of empire on the aggressors, as well as on the victims of neocolonialism, nor any novel that charted the national differences between European imperialist ideologies.

Nostromo is a penetrating study of European manipulation of the politics of a dependent country. Precisely because the drama focuses on Europeans whose activities transform the society of Sulaco, the novel presents us with the reverse side of Macondo in Gabriel García Márquez's *One Hundred Years of Solitude,* a place whose inhabitants never project their desires into durable institutions. The tragedy of Sulaco is conceived in terms of the Europeans who are corrupted because their ambitions are acted out upon the stage of a dependent nation. The tragedy of Macondo is that of a dependent population whose very imagination is no longer inviolate.

The two novels are *not,* of course, analogous projects. The constraint under which Conrad worked was that of verisimilitude, and contemporary critics tended to judge his work according to his ability to create plausible characters and situations. In *Nostromo,* however, he was up against a difficulty: no amount of verisimilitude would shake the British conviction that Latin America was a comic opera world. Even the sympathetic *Manchester Guardian* critic was intolerably patronizing on this score:

> Most of us have from time to time read idly of some crisis or revolution in a
> South American republic and perhaps dismissed idly the "farcical" episodes
> in the life of a community which seems to change its government with the
> weather. It is to one of these episodes in the separation of the "Occidental
> Republic" from "Costaguana" that Mr. Conrad has addressed himself. It
> need hardly be said that he does not lack the humorous perception of the
> events that he records, and in a corner of the world that is hardly worthy of
> our perfunctory and impatient regard that he finds a richness and variety of
> life that cannot be matched in our careful civilization.[1]

The apparently objective and universal standard of verisimilitude breaks down when the novel extends its scope to include peoples "hardly worthy" of the "perfunctory and impatient regard" of the European reader. By the time that García Márquez comes to write, the critical *desideratum* has changed; and it is the writer's ability to create "another reality" or a "total fiction" that is to be praised. The danger now is that implausibility, instead of having a liberating effect, may well reflect the separation of reality from the imagination that is ideologically given.

It is easy to see why Conrad, after writing of Africa and the Far East, should have wished to set a novel in "Latin America," where the complexity of forces could not be reduced to some simplistic novelized formula. The Hispanic ways of life (so contrary to the British ethic) and the developed superstructures of state organization and legal institutions called for a densely populated novel if verisimilitude was to be achieved.

The single figure of the lone trader as outcast of capitalism and bearer of its ideology no longer sufficed as protagonist. Nor, as Conrad discovered as he began to write, was his brief experience of Latin America enough "pour batir un roman dessus."[2] He therefore drew heavily on some of the dozens of travel books, many written by Britishers who felt themselves inspired by the patriotic urge to extend their country's hegemony over these once forbidden realms. The brothers Robertson in Paraguay, Francis Bond Head and Woodbine Parish in the Argentine, Basil Hall in Chile, among others, were not simply travel writers but emissaries of a civilization that considered local traditions obstacles to progress and the Catholic religion backward. Yet more than the well-attested influence of Masterman's *Seven Eventful Years in Paraguay* or Eastwick's *Venezuela* and other travel books, it is the sublime metropolitan self-confidence that is important to *Nostromo*.[3] Not that the travelers were entirely uncritical of their own civilization. Francis Bond Head, who rode across the Argentine pampa in the hope of taking over silver mines abandoned by the Spaniards, found his vision of the undiluted benefits of industrial civilization somewhat shaken as he compared the wizened appearance of Chilean miners to the healthy freedom of the gaucho.[4] What is merely a passing mood in Head's travels turns into fierce questioning in the work of W. H. Hudson and R. B. Cunninghame Graham, who were two of Conrad's closest friends.

Hudson had been brought up in the Plate Region, though his adult life was lived, for the most part, in Victorian London. In 1885, he published an autobiographical novel, *The Purple Land,* whose full title (later shortened) was *The Purple Land That England Lost*. Its protagonist, Richard Lamb, leaves Montevideo to seek his fortune in the interior of the Banda Oriental (as Uruguay was then called) and becomes, in the course of his wanderings, a true gaucho. His experiences make him lose faith in the undisputed superiority of the British way of life; and at the end of his journey he meditates on the "wild delightful flavor" that would certainly disappear with the material prosperity "resulting from Anglo-Saxon energy." Were this to happen, he writes:

> I must breathe the wish that this land may never know such prosperity. . . . We do not live by bread alone, and British occupation does not give to the heart all the things for which it craves. Blessings may even be curses when the gigantic power that bestows them on us scares from our midst the shy spirits of Beauty and Poesy.[5]

It is very much the attitude of Conrad's Mrs. Gould, who preserves the original beauty of the San Tomé ravine in her watercolor sketches but who, at the end of *Nostromo,* sees the silver mine as the spirit of evil, "feared, hated, wealthy, more soulless than any tyrant, more pitiless and autocratic than the worst government, ready to crush innumerable lives in the expansion of its greatness."[6] As for Conrad's other close friend, Cunninghame Graham, whose romantic rebelliousness was not altogether to Conrad's taste, something of his quixotic disdain for the material apparatus of "perfected civilization" with its obliteration of "the individuality of old town under the stereotyped conveniences of modern life" found its way into the novel.[7]

In his study, Hobson had suggested that imperialism encouraged perverted forms of nationalism, whether it be self-defensive nationalism or "the nationalism which glows with the animus of greed and self-aggrandisement at the expense of others."[8] Conrad, on the other hand, appears more concerned with the way that certain national ideals promote the neocolonialist venture while masking its true nature from the participants. His main interest is, therefore, in ideology. The fact that his Englishmen are entrepreneurs, his Americans financiers, his Italians railway workers, foremen, and innkeepers, and that his Frenchman is an intellectual underscores the historic role of these countries in Latin America. It is precisely the accuracy of his reconstruction of nineteenth-century Latin American politics during the period of transition from the colonial era to the era of financial and industrial dependency that gives weight to the criticism of the materialist goals implicit in the "fable."[9] To achieve this accuracy required both insight and recourse to historical data. To take one example: the dictator Guzmán Bento, who tyrannizes Costaguana shortly after its independence from Spain, is closely modeled on two Paraguayan dictators, President López and Dr. Francia. Indeed, so close is the resemblance that, like Dr. Francia, Guzmán Bento's body is spirited from the tomb soon after burial. But this "bricolage" of historical fact suggests, more than self indulgence, the existence of a problematic. For Conrad has to show the changes that come to Costaguana through the portrayal of specific individuals caught up in a political situation with which few of his readers were familiar. As it happened, however, painstaking and accurate detail were not enough to make Costaguana more than a comic opera setting in the eyes of the British readers; and Conrad himself was not able to transcend the ideological limitations of a liberal critique that, whatever its reservations about the materialism of the age, was not prepared to see the European domination of the underdeveloped world as anything other than inevitable.

The symbolic agents in the transformation of Sulaco are two: the railway and the Ocean Navigation Company, which opens up the port and hence allows silver to be exported. Conrad gives the company steamships classical names—Minerva, Juno, and Cerberus—as if these deities were intended to legitimize, in the name of civilization, a British imperial expansion based on trade rather than armed conquest. As raw material, the silver is useless without the British-owned railway and steamship line. Together they form the triad on which financial-industrial dependency is to be based. To protect them, Charles Gould and the other foreigners must become directly involved in the politics of Costaguana. It is they who support the benevolent civilian dictator, Ribeira, a figure closely modeled on those Latin American liberals who encouraged foreign investment in the name of a civilization that differentiated them from their more barbarous countrymen. The downfall of Ribeira after a coup that exploits antiforeign elements precipitates the civil war out of which the mining interests emerge strengthened by the declaration of Sulaco's independence from Costaguana. This final stroke (which opens up Sulaco to "development") was almost certainly suggested by Panama's declaration of independence, which was in the air precisely when Conrad was writing his novel.

There is, nevertheless, one curious limitation even in Conrad's impressive reconstruction of the course of nineteenth-century Latin American politics: in the depiction of character, Conrad loads the dice in favor those natives who are most amenable to European manipulation, and hence he reproduces the very liberal ideology that helped promote dependency. It was the cultivated and enlightened liberals of Argentina and Mexico, for example, who most eagerly welcomed railways and foreign investment as signs of progress, while ignoring or glossing over the structure of dependency that these implied. In sympathy with the Europeans are the more "civilized" inhabitants of Sulaco: the historian, Don José Avellanos, and his daughter, Antonia; the old independence fighter, Don Pepe; and, of course, the president of Costaguana, Don Vicente Ribeira, whom Conrad describes as a man of "delicate and melancholy mind." The weighting of forces in favor of civilization becomes even more blatant when even the noble "barbarians" are recruited to the European cause. Thus, the loyalist General Barrios is modeled on those "men on horseback" who terrorized post-Independence politics; yet, as Conrad depicts him, he is the perfect bourgeois whose one desire is to "convert our swords into ploughshares and grow rich. Even I, myself," he confides to Mrs. Gould, "as soon as this little business is settled, shall open a *fundacion* on some land I have on the Llanos and try to make a little money in peace and quietness." More surprisingly and even less probable from the point of view of historical verisimilitude, the Europeans recruit the primitive rebel, Hernández, who becomes the minister of war in independent Sulaco, and Father Corbalán, once an ascetic missionary among remote indian tribes and hence the epitome of the Hispanic disdain for material progress that the British found so inexplicable.

In contrast, the reader is given no opportunity to take the rebel side seriously. After all, Conrad was not really concerned with the conflict between civilization and barbarism as played out in Latin America but rather with what was going on in the European mind. His rebel general is dismissed as a sinister "vaquero." He has, it is hinted, Negro blood in his veins. The son of a lackey who had served a well-known European traveler and hence had received a smattering of education, General Montero is not civilized enough to play the European game. His brother, Pedro, is an even more interesting example of loaded characterization. Represented as an ambitious politician who has lived in Paris and conceived an admiration for the Duc de Mornay, his rise to power can only be ascribed to the backwardness of a people who, like the primitive peoples of the past, admire successful duplicity and "who went straighter to their aim and were more artless in their recognition of success as the only standard of morality." Pedro and all the other members of the rebel forces are distinguished by their need of immediate gratification and a corresponding inability to work for long-term or supranational goals. Commandante Sotillo, the rebel admiral, is, for instance, not only a drunkard but also a man obsessed with the desire to recover the silver. His obsession prevents him from joining up with Montero's forces, thus ruining the rebel cause. Pedro Montero's actions are also "usually determined by motives so improbable in themselves as to escape the penetration of a *rational* person" (my italics). And the Monterist revolution itself is "rooted in the political immaturity of the people, in the indolence of the upper classes and the mental darkness of the lower." Conrad's novel is thus based on the assumption that dependency is inevitable given the "immaturity" of Latin Americans.

The critical insights in *Nostromo* belong to the mature wisdom of the Artist and the Healer. Dr. Monygham is a survivor from the days of Guzmán Bento, under whose regime he suffered torture and solitary confinement, which had bound him "indissolubly" to Costaguana "like an awful procedure of naturalization." It was this experience that involved him deeply in national life "far deeper than any amount of success and honor could have done." Mrs. Gould, with her watercolors and her Hudson-like love of nature, is Monygham's natural ally. "Even here," she remarks at one point, "there are simple and picturesque things that one would like to preserve." But this conversation is with the railway magnate, who would certainly not allow those simple and picturesque things to stand in the way of progress. Although she is a woman of "endurance and compassion," her critique is contained by the limits which a paternalistic society puts on females. Thus, she is caught in the conflict between regretting change and supporting her husband, who is its instrument. In a telling phrase, moreover, Conrad reveals that even her charity is based on a sense of distance from the native peoples whose "flat, joyless faces . . . looked all alike" to her. Thus, the mature critique of the Artist and the Healer alters not at all the "inevitable" process of development. It is a critique that like the novel itself, at no point endangers the rules of "civilized" communication.[10]

Within these limitations, Conrad's novel is a devastating and perceptive account of the internalization of those nationalist drives that, as Hobson had shown, had been exacerbated by imperialism. Behind them all, shaping them all, is the "future" power of the United States. "We shall run the world's business whether the world likes it or not," promises Holroyd, whose company finances the mine. "The world can't help it—and neither can we, I guess." Once again, Conrad has underlined the inevitability of the process, hinting that this future will also see "more subtle, outwardly unmarked" changes that will affect "the minds and hearts of the workers." But of central importance in the novel are not these forces of the future so much as those of the present. In his Europeans, Conrad explores the hypostatization of certain values—honesty, honor, intellectual detachment, and romantic passion—that are, in reality, ideological masks hiding the drive for power. It is precisely because individuals act in the name of honesty or courage that they are effective in furthering the ends of neo-colonialism. And it is Conrad's particular genius to have shown the interconnection between moral values and ideology.

The British offer a particularly interesting example of the internalization of socially useful values, for their reliance on the apparently disinterested virtues of "good faith, order, honesty, peace" (to use the language of the railway magnate) is the element cementing the structures of the empire. These virtues formed the basis for carrying on trade, but, because they were defined by the metropolis, they were also double-edged. The benevolent dictator, Vicente Ribeira, is a man whose honesty is, in the British view, above reproach; yet his countrymen know he has sold them out to the foreigners. It is no accident then that the pivotal point of the action is Nostromo's theft of the silver that he was supposed to prevent from falling into the enemy's hands during the civil war. His theft, however, is trivial compared with the long-term exploitation of the natives in the mine and the "innumerable lives" that are sacrificed to it. Individuals might try to live according to "good faith" and with "honesty," yet, as the novel reveals, practiced within the dependency context, such virtues merely further a development whose main beneficiary was the metropolis. Bourgeois society divides the private from the public domain and encourages the belief that there can be an unviolated personal life. Nostromo shows the two to be inseparable. Neither the impeccable Charles Gould nor the incorruptible Nostromo escape the tainting influence of the silver, which contaminates precisely because of its role within the total system. Gould's conviction that he is working for the public good is thus a delusion. He believes that "once material interests get a firm footing. . . . they are bound to impose the conditions on which alone they can continue to exist. . . . A better justice will come afterwards." In this he shares the optimism of a Macauley, for whom the spread of railways would bring about "universal brotherhood and peace," or of a Spencer, who declared that "as surely as there is . . . any meaning in such terms as habit, custom, practice, so surely must evil and immorality disappear; so surely must man become perfect."[11] Yet Gould's final solitude is also the indication of how far Conrad himself was removed from this undiluted optimism.

The way in which Ducoud's intellectual (and secretly romantic) passion and the peculiarly Italian combination of abstract idealism (Viola) and manly virtues (Nostromo) also represent European ideologies is less obvious. The French, whose revolutionary tradition made that country a model for Latin America, were not above using intellectual prestige in the furtherance of economic interests and from early on exercised a spiritual hegemony through publishing houses and magazines, while also pursuing maximilianesque-like adventures. Ducoud's intellectual hubris—the fact that he is the self-appointed architect of Sulaco's independence, the founder of the newspaper *El Porvenir* and the passionate admirer of Antonia, for whom he is prepared to risk his life—not only constitutes a nice foil for British pragmatism but provides a specific example of French ideology at work. It is particularly interesting that this man who communicates through *writing* and has a certain intellectual detachment should be considered Conrad's mouthpiece by several critics.[12] They are, of course, betraying their own ideological preferences for the intellectual. Yet Conrad's irony should guard against such a reading, for Ducoud's fate parallels that of Gould and Nostromo. His intellectual detachment is just as much an ideological mask as Gould's practical involvement and Nostromo's incorruptibility.

The Italians do not reflect imperialist ideology (though Italy had just embarked on African ventures) as much as they reveal the attitudes of the immigrant who formed a major proportion of new settlers in the nineteenth-century Americas. They brought with them revolutionary ideals and were founders of anarchist and socialist movements; and they also engaged in Mafia-like activities. That is why, at the end of *Nostromo*, Conrad has the Sulaco Democratic Party depending "on these socialistic Italians . . . with their secret societies, camorras, and such like." The very nickname Nostromo (so reminiscent of today's *Cosa Nostra*) suggests the reciprocal bond of personal loyalty to a fearless leader that characterizes Nostromo's relationship with the harbor workers and which, in another context, produced the Mafia. Unlike the British emphasis on honesty for its own sake, the Mediterranean concept of honor depended very much on public recognition of manliness and generosity. That is why Nostromo hides out when he has no money to spend and why his incorruptibility depends on its public recognition as such. His friend, Viola, on the other hand, is the pure revolutionary, one whose abstract ideal is undiluted by practice. And—as was actually the case with many Italian immigrants to the Argentine—this idealism was not incompatible with racist distrust of the natives.

In *Nostromo*, the novelist can show what the historian can only conjecture: how the goals of capitalist society are internalized by individuals and how this in turn conceals the fact that relationships are mediated by money and based on exploitation. It is this contradiction between the sense of individual worth and the real forces of society that drives each one of the main characters to that solitary end just before which his values are seen to be illusory. Gould, reified by the mine, becomes remote from his wife and remains without an heir who might have made his work more meaningful. Ducoud, stranded on an island and thwarted in his heroic gesture, "entertains doubts as to his own individuality." His suicide by drowning is the supremely ironic negation of his life. Nostromo's theft turns him into two people, as if the public and the private aspects of his personality could no longer be made to fit together. To the public, he is the respectable trader, Captain Fidanza; in his own eyes, he is the furtive thief, Nostromo. His violent death when he is killed in mistake by his old friend Viola could not have happened but for this split in his personality, which is of the utmost symbolic significance in the overall meaning of the novel. For it is as if, in a system which rests on exploitation and injustice the virtues of courage, honesty and intelligence can be maintained only at the cost of schizophrenia.

Conrad perhaps did not see it quite in this way, and possibly the novel tells us more than he himself consciously knew. Because he could not envisage a viable third world ideology, mature realization is reserved to the Europeans whom he nevertheless perceives as "helpless" pawns in the "whole scheme of things." By reducing the natives to a chorus, and by separating the Europeans into blind activists and helpless observers, Conrad reproduced the division of labor within the metropolis and the dependency relationships underpinning the whole capitalist structure.

In *Nostromo,* the characters are, in a sense, allegorical or, at least, representative in the Lukacsian sense. In *One Hundred Years of Solitude*, on the other hand, the Buendías represent nothing but themselves; for there is no identifiable signified for which they are the signifiers. Consider, for instance, the José Arcadio who has circumnavigated the globe seven times and on his return to Macondo Indian-wrestles five men at a time in the local bar. The barkeeper, Catarino, "bet him twelve pesos stat he could not move the counter, José Arcadio pulled it out of the place, lifted it over his head and put it in the street. It took eleven men to put it back."[13] What singles out this activity is its gratuitousness, the fact that it has no other purpose than pleasure. This refusal to put their talents—whether strength, inventiveness, sexuality—to any practical end makes the Buendías quite unlike the Sampsons, Casanovas, or Napoleons they might have been. Their activities are confined, apparently by choice, to a play world which has the noninstrumentality of fiction itself. Thus, the founder, José Arcadio, who uses his scientific instruments to conceive "a notion of space that allowed him to navigate across unknown seas, to visit uninhabited territories and to establish relations with splendid beings without having to leave his study," is quite different from the Renaissance scientists whose discoveries were closely connected with maritime expansion. Moreover, José Arcadio clearly prefers his imaginary world. It is therefore fitting that the Buendía line should come to an end with the narcissistic José Arcadio, who drowns in a lily pond, and the incestuous Aureliano, who deciphers his own past.

By flouting exogamy, the founder of Macondo has, in reality, rejected the primal taboo on which society has been built; for social man communicates through exchange and differentiation, a transaction in which exogamy has an important role. Without the incest taboo, society and culture become impossible.[14] But in the realm of fiction, the utopian is still available. Hence, Macondo's economy system does not demand exploitation or master-slave relationships. There is a money economy, which includes *reales* and *pesos*; but except for vegetables and fruit, Úrsula's toffee animals, and José Arcadio's golden fish, nothing is *produced*. Instead of serv-

ing to differentiate status, the fish are used to *identify* the Colonel's follow-
ers during the civil war. Once the war is over, the Colonel can manufacture new fish only by melting down the old in a circular production system. Thus, Macondo neither recognizes the incest taboo nor engages
in the processes of exchange and capital accumulation on which the
economy of the Western world was built. Surplus production—when it
occurs—simply results in increased consumption. After the devastating
rainstorms that ruin Macondo, domestic animals are raffled according to a
system that reduces the possibility of anyone's accumulating wealth, for
the winners consume their prizes on the spot:

> At dusk food and drink stands would be set up in the courtyard and many
> of those who were favored would slaughter the animals they had won right
> there on the condition that someone else supply the liquor and music,
> so that without having wanted to, Aureliano Segundo suddenly found him-
> self playing the accordeon again and participating in modest tourneys of
> voracity.

This is the reverse of a work ethic. Indeed, apart from the banana plantation and domestic labor, which is, by definition, unproductive, work is
overshadowed in Macondo by festivity and play. The production of the toffee animals and the golden fish is a kind of game. Thus, Macondo posits in
Marcusian terms the free play of human faculties "*outside* the realm of
alienated labor" and the negation of the "performance principle."[15]
Úrsula's toffee animals, Aureliano's golden fish, Aureliano Segundo's lottery belong to the realm of freedom and fulfillment, not of work. Similarly, the invention of a boat to navigate Macondo's swiftly running river,
the discovery of a route to the sea, and knowledge that the world is round
do not have any practical application, whereas, historically, they were all
linked to the expansion of the West. And this separation of play from work
and function corresponds to the line between the real and the imaginary.

Because they have chosen this Utopia of play, the Buendías cannot,
however, aspire to the apotheosis of history. For this reason, their lives and
deaths, though pathetic, never have the exemplary force of historical
events. They frequently die obscurely, like the José Arcadio whose execution is a casual event, witnessed fortuitously by Rebeca, who "had scarcely
time to wave him goodbye." The Colonel, once supreme commander of
the revolutionary forces "with jurisdiction and command from one border
to another," dies without glory; and people soon forget the person behind
the street name that was intended to commemorate him. His feats of arms
fail to achieve the status of history, being merely unconfirmed rumors that

he had been "victorious in Villanueva, defeated in Guacamayal, eaten by
Motilone Indians, had died in one of the swamp villages and had risen
again in Urumita." To his family, he appears as a "mythic warrior" who
had "placed a distance of three meters between himself and the rest of the
world"; and this mythic space that distances the Colonel from other
human beings is, in reality, around all the Buendías.

To have history at all, we suppose a design in which events have more
than individual or family significance and hence become part of a public
and civic discourse. But in Macondo, events that should be included in
such discourse are actively forgotten, rather than commemorated, so that
the hundreds of victims of a massacre are wiped from the memory of men
even before their bodies are thrown into the sea. Gerineldo Márquez's funeral procession becomes not an apotheosis of great deeds but their negation. In pouring rain, the procession carries a coffin draped with a shame-
ful flag "that had been rejected by more honorable veterans":

> On the coffin they had also placed the saber with tassels of silver and cop-
> per, the same one that Colonel Gerineldo Márquez used to hang on the
> coat rack in order to go into Amaranta's sewing room unarmed. Behind the
> cart, some barefoot and all of them with their pants rolled up, splashing in
> the mud were the last survivors of the surrender of Neerlandia, carrying a
> drover's staff in one hand and in the other a wreath of paper flowers that
> had become discolored in the rain. They appeared like an unreal vision
> along the street, which still bore the name of Colonel Aureliano Buendía.

We are reminded of the fact that the epigraph of one of García Márquez's
earlier novels had been taken from Creon's speech in Sophocles' *Antigone* in
which he had condemned Polynices to the worst of fates—that of remaining unburied and a prey to the scavenging birds.[16] Not to honor the dead is
to condemn them to oblivion; yet, for the dead to be consecrated, there
must be society and history or, at least, a tribal memory. None of these are
possible in Macondo so that those objects which in other cultures serve as
historical and social symbols—the victor's saber, the flag, the flowers that
symbolize regeneration—here become the symbols of defeat, fragility, or
simply of private life. Thus, the Buendías are not only without a society in
a real sense but in consequence are without social symbols and myths that
serve to keep the past alive and hence to give a sense of continuity.[17]

The gulf between history and fiction is therefore complete. The
Buendías' flight from the pirates, their incest, and their defiance of physical
laws put them outside any possible social organization and even absolved
them, in some instances, from the law of gravity. Like the Spanish galleon

that José Arcadio finds in the jungle, they occupy a privileged space that should protect them from the ravages of time. But the tragedy of Macondo is precisely this: that the immortality and universality traditionally promised to those who dedicate themselves to art are denied them. The privileged space of Macondo is constantly invaded by alien forces and is susceptible to destruction by natural catastrophe. The carnival princesses are killed by real gunfire. The platitudinous declaration read by the army officers to the plantation strikers is backed up by real arms. Imagination is no match for this reality:

> The captain gave the order to fire and fourteen machine guns answered at once. But it all seemed like a farce. It was as if the machine guns had been loaded with caps because their panting rattle could be heard and their incandescent spitting could be seen, but not the slightest reaction was perceived, not a cry, not even a sigh among the compact crowd that seemed petrified by an instantaneous invulnerability.

Because it takes place in Macondo, the massacre seems like carnival or theater. What does it destroy, anyway, but figments of the imagination? Among the dead, there are even intruders from novels by Carpentier, Cortázar, and Carlos Fuentes. What is swept away is only "the whorish world where Úrsula Iguarán had sold so many little candy animals." Yet in bringing about this confrontation, García Márquez reveals the limitations of his imaginary universe.[18]

For Macondo is the space available to the liberal imagination in Latin America. By this I mean that if we take as the liberal ideal respect for individual freedom, the possibility of self-development with as little authoritarian or arbitrary interference as possible, and "civilized" discourse and relationships, then plainly these conditions can exist only in an imaginary Latin American state; any novelist who pretends to be mimetic or adopts "truth to life" as a strategy will also find it difficult to reproduce characters like those "autonomous" beings of, say, the nineteenth- and twentieth-century English novel.[19] By freeing themselves from the mimetic and by cutting the ropes that tied the "baloon of fiction" to the ground, many Latin American novelists writing in the 1960s constructed a space in which freedom and dialogue became possible. One has only to think of Lezama Lima's *Paradiso*, for example, or Cortázar's *Rayuela*, or, of course, *One Hundred Years of Solitude*. Significantly, recent novels by Roa Bastos, Alejo Carpentier, and García Márquez[20] himself have centered on the extreme power and freedom of dictators in Latin America. And, equally significant, all these novels are in the form of monologues. In contrast, *One Hundred Years of Soli-*

tude presents a set of characters who (except for the Colonel) are untainted by the original sin of power, and Macondo represents an ideal space in which to set in motion the *individual* virtues of heroism and intellectual daring. Since the "bourgeois" novel cannot provide a model, García Márquez adopts the tone of the archaic storyteller who captures his listeners' attention by promising them untold marvels.

The storyteller is, of course, not constrained by verisimilitude. For centuries, oral tradition in Latin America transmitted the tales of knightly deeds and the exploits of obscure saints; and such traditions have even represented a focus of resistance to the homogenization and submission to print culture that came with "modernization" in a dependency context. However, though García Márquez can reproduce the storyteller's enjoyment of the marvelous, he cannot reproduce the living relationship to a community that oral tradition implies, and he is doomed to the solitude of print. In order to rescue pleasure and the libido from the crushing effects of systematization and homogeneity, he constructs a Utopia whose inhabitants defy what Marcuse calls "the performance principle," which is based on the deferment of gratification.[21] Furthermore, within the text of the novel there is a distinction between the "instrumental" writing of decrees and proclamations and the "gratuitous" nature of the Buendías' activities. And this distinction, in turn, reflects a separation, common among avantgarde writers from Flaubert onward between the "instrumentality" of ordinary language and the "noninstrumentality" of poetic language.[22] In *One Hundred Years of Solitude, written* labels have to be devised to remind people of the *function* of things only when the entire populataion loses its memory during a plague of insomnia. These "instrumental" labels are rendered useless when the gypsy Melquíades restores sleep and memory with a magic potion. It is the alchemist Melquíades, however, who also introduces noninstrumental writing when he begins to encode the family history in a language that they cannot read. He does this in a room that is like the space of literature itself, for in it, privileged people feel "protected by the supernatural light . . . by the sensataion of being invisible." Yet Melquíades himself is only too mortal, having a human weight, an earthly condition that kept him involved in the small problems of daily life." The alchemy of literature thus salvages what society cannot use, but it is available only to a minority of those who, like Aureliano Babilonia, are prepared to run the risk of deciphering its meaning.

It is significant that the last of the Buendías should bear the name of a civilization (Babylon) that had a god of writing and that came to an end when writing appeared on the wall, for Aureliano devotes himself to the deciphering of Melquíades's words. Yet the limitation of this solitary voyage of discovery, which is always retrospective, never totally present, becomes clear at the end of the novel. Aureliano skips whole passages in order to "ascertain the date and circumstances of his death"; yet literature can never rejoin the reality of the present, "for it was foreseen that the city of mirrors (or mirages) would be wiped out by the wind and exiled from the memory of men at the precise moment when Aureliano Babilonia would finish deciphering the parchments, and that everything written on them was unrepeatable since time immemorial and forever more, because races condemned to one hundred years of solitude did not have a second opportunity on earth."

The storyteller is silent. Scheherezade will survive for another night but must tell a different story tomorrow. This "unrepeatability" is the very mark of the creative presence in bourgeois society, distinguishing artistic creation qualitatively from the automatized, the repetitious, and the historical. Art, it was supposed, formed a zone of unalienated work within the generally alienated labor conditions of capitalism. To salvage this unalienated space, the writer severed literature from "instrumental" language and the contamination of reality, creating "another reality" whose very positing constituted a transgression of the system. We are reminded, moreover, that this "other reality" had its brief apotheosis in 1968, only one year after the publication of *One Hundred Years of Solitude,* when Paris students proclaimed "l'imagination au pouvoir." The fact that García Márquez's novel also reveals the vulnerability of the imagination has tended to be obscured by a critical reception that reflects the system's encouragement of harmless fantasy. The condition on which imagination is allowed to survive is that it should not represent any real interference (in the communications sense) with the ideology of the technical-industrial stage of dependency and hence scramble the message of the consumer society beyond all recognition. Without diminishing the real achievement of *One Hundred Years of Solitude,* it is legitimate to question the separation of reality from imagination, of play from work, when society furthers this very division and turns imagination into a safety valve for all that is not socially useful. Conrad's verisimilitude could not prevent an ideological reading of *Nostromo* that confined Latin America to the realm of the absurd; *One Hundred Years of Solitude* defiantly accepts this, but in a manner that is too disarming. The danger is that, with the real world in the hands of the multinational corporations and the mass media, literature can safely be left to the Tolkiens and the Richard Adamses.

Notes

1. Norman Sherry (ed.), *Conrad, The Critical Heritage* (London, 1973). This unsigned review was first published on November 2, 1904.

2. Ibid., p. 159.

3. Critics have long acknowledged that Conrad drew on Edward Eastwick, *Venezuela; or, Sketches of Life in a South American Republic* (London, 1868), and G. F. Masterman, *Seven Eventful Years in Paraguay* (London, 1868). Norman Sherry, *Conrad's Western World* (Cambridge, 1971), discusses the influence of Captain Basil Hall's *Extracts from a Journey Written on the Coasts of Chile, Peru and Mexico in the Years 1820, 1821, 1822* (Edinburgh, 1824) and has noted that Conrad used Alexandre Dumas (ed.), *Garibaldi, an Autobiography,* trans. William Robson (London, 1860), for Viola. In "The Original Nostromo: Conrad's Source," R.E.S., n.s., 10, no. 37 (1959), pp. 45–52, John Halverston and Ian Watt have noted the source of the silver theft anecdote as Frederick Benton Williams, *On Many Seas: The Life and Exploits of a Yankee Sailor* (1897).

4. Francis Bond Head, *Journeys across the Pampas and among the Andes* (London, 1826), first published as *Rough Notes Taken during Some Rapid Journeys across the Pampas and among the Andes* (London, 1826).

5. W. H. Hudson, *The Purple Land* (London, 1949), p. 296. This is a reset of the second edition (London, 1904).

6. I have used the Modern Library edition of *Nostromo* (New York, 1951), with an introduction by Robert Penn Warren.

7. The words are Conrad's, *Nostromo,* p. 107. Joseph Conrad's *Letters to R. B. Cunninghame Graham* (Cambridge, 1969) shed some interesting light on their relationship, especially on Cunninghame Graham's criticism of North American capitalism and his belief that in Kipling's work "the Imperial Mission" was a euphemism for "the Stock Exchange Militant." The note on *Nostromo* in C. T. Watt's introduction to the letters, pp 37, 52, offers an interesting comment on the influence of Graham's views. Graham, who had been involved in the civil war between Blancos and Colorados in the Banda Oriental (Uruguay) was, of course, a critic whose opinion of the novel Conrad valued highly, and in his letters he shows himself sensitive to Graham's comments on certain incorrect uses of Spanish: *Letters,* pp. 157–158.

8. J. A. Hobson, *Imperialism: A Study,* 3d ed. (London, 1938), p. 9.

9. I am here using the periodization that has been elaborated by "new dependency" theorists. For a brief survey, see Ronald H. Chilcote, "A Critical Synthesis of the Dependency Literature," *Latin American Perspectives* 1 (Spring 1974).

10. There is a vast critical literature on *Nostromo* of which the most "political" interpretation to date seems to be that of Irving Howe, *Politics and the Novel* (Freeport, N.Y., 1957), pp. 100–113. See also Avron Fleishman, "Class Struggle as Tragedy," in *Conrad's Politics* (Baltimore, 1967), pp. 161–184.

11. These quotations from the *History of England* (1848–1855), by Macauley, and from *Social Statics* (1852), by Herbert Spencer, are given by E. Houghton in the chapter "Optimism," *The Victorian Frame of Mind* (New Haven, Conn.: 1957), pp. 27–53.

12. This was the opinion of the anonymous *Manchester Guardian* critic to whom I have already referred. See Sherry (ed.), *Conrad: The Critical Heritage,* p. 173. Robert Penn Warren has some discussion of the issue in his introduction to the Modern Library edition of *Nostromo,* pp. xxvi–xxviii.

13. The quotations are from Gregory Rabassa's translataion, *One Hundred Years of Solitude* (New York, 1970).

14. This is forcibly expressed by Bronislaw Malinowski, *Sex and Repression in Savage Society* (New York, 1968), p. 216.

15. Herbert Marcuse, *Eros and Civilization* (New York, 1955), especially "The Aesthetic Dimension," pp. 157–179.

16. Pedro Lastra, "La tragedia como fundamento estructural en *La hojarasca*," in Helmy F. Giacoman, *Homenaje a G. García Márquez* (New York, 1972), pp. 430–456.

17. Carlos Blanco Aguinaga, "Sobre la lluvia y la historia en las ficciones de García Márquez," in *De mitologias y novelistas* (Madrid, 1975), argues along similar lines. He shows convincingly that the novel does not belong to the circular time of myth but is "linear and chronological" and that the "circularity" and "lo fantástico" represent an evanion on the author's part. At the time of writing, the collection of essays had not been published, but the article appeared in *Narradores Hispanoamericanos de hoy* (North Carolina, 1973).

18. I have dealt with this in more detail in an article "Literary History and the Dependency Context," in the *Minnesota Review* (September 1975).

19. F. R. Leavis, *The Great Tradition* (London, 1955). This is the *locus classicus* of normative criticism. Admittedly, Leavis speaks only of English tradition, but, according to his criterion ("a vital capacity for experience, a kind of reverent openness before life, and a marked moral intensity"), even Flaubert is ruled out of the great tradition, and plainly no Latin American novelist would qualify for this particular paradise.

20. I refer to Augusto Roa Bastos, *Yo el supremo* (Mexico, 1975); Alejo Carpentier, *El recurso del metodo* (Mexico, 1974); and Gabriel García Márquez, *El otoño del patriarca* (Barcelona, 1975).

21. H. Marcuse, *Eros and Civilization,* pp. 40–41.

22. This distinction has come under attack by linguists and notably by Mary Pratt in an unpublished dissertation, "Towards a Theory of Literary Discourse" (Stanford, 1975).

One Hundred Years of Solitude
as Chronicle of the Indies

IRIS M. ZAVALA

❖ ❖ ❖

IN 1936, THE SPANISH POET Juan Ramón Jiménez noted in his preface to an anthology of Cuban verse that, in Latin America, every literary movement, especially the *modernista* schools, had failed "because here [in Hispanic America] any sort of *modernismo* was unnecessary, everything being new, given that the old was not, strictly speaking, old." Time here is asynchronic, space asymmetrical. America, Juan Ramón concludes, "has all of its time within itself." This is the vision that Gabriel García Márquez gives us of Hispanic America. He looks at it with the eyes of an early chronicler or explorer. In a sense, one could say that *One Hundred Years of Solitude*[1] is a new "chronicle of the Indies."

Like Don Quixote, who went mad from reading novels of chivalry, García Márquez shakes up American reality after having nourished himself on the poetic fancies of chroniclers and travelers. The diaries, chronicles, and reports penned by conquistadors and colonizers abound in descriptions of fabulous and imaginary peoples and places, confounding truths and lies and utilizing all the elements offered by the commonplace and the everyday, by history and geography, by literature and myth. This geographic literature was wont to describing the unreal in distant settlements, inhabited by giants, filled with outsize animals and hybrid monsters.

Description is metaphor; any item of news here—and most of all man—becomes extravagant. Chroniclers, conquistadors, and missionaries transform men into colossal monstrosities, or they grant human traits to birds and beasts. Vespucci calls the indigenous peoples "reasoning animals,"[2] while López de Gómara fattens the Spaniards who settle along the River Plate with "pig-fish and men-fish"—the latter, he says, "very like the human body in all respects."[3] Pinzón brought to Spain some extremely wild creatures from Brazil, among them "one that had the body and snout of a fox, the haunches and rear paws of a simian, and the front legs like unto those of men."[4] Man in America takes on mythic proportions; he appears always as a giant or as a being near-vegetable or near-animal that is beyond modification. The continent is a magical world from which not even the conquistador can be saved. Once having arrived there, he is a new and solitary creature, and he enters a new process of regression that leads him back, and further back, to a primordial state. Did Bishop Lué of Buenos Aires truly believe that the conquistadors and colonists had engendered rams and not men in America? In town council meetings, it was lamented that the sons of conquistadors would multiply about the field, without transforming their food into human substance.[5] Columbus tells of islands where only women live and—something still more curious—he mentions two isles, Cibán and Anán, whose inhabitants are born with the tails of animals.[6] Vespucci also expressed his bewilderment via hyperbole and fable; the island of Curaçao, he writes, is populated by Penthesileas and Antaeuses, while on another Caribbean island he describes a serpent with the size and shape of a mountain goat.[7]

Extravagance and metaphor are the sole means of describing a reality as strange as it is elusive; literature and fable find themselves in a land peopled by images where everything is lived as if it were a dream, or a book, with multiple variations. A rogue here can be called "Cervantes the madman,"[8] and an extremely slow bird can be dubbed "swift parakeet," baptized with a name that is the opposite of its essence.[9]

There is nothing surprising about García Márquez's admiration for this kind of literature. On occasion he has alluded to Pigafetta, the Italian navigator who accompanied Magellan in his journey around the world between 1519 and 1522 and who authored a treatise on navigation that starts out with the sentence from Ptolemy, "The Earth is round," to which José Arcadio would add, "like an orange." Columbus was no less ingenious; the Earth for him is round, "save where it has its nipple," a description that approximates it rather to a pear.[10] For the conquistadors, the idea of the Earth's roundness takes on concrete significance in the New World. Vespucci stayed awake many times when crossing the equinoctial line, wishing to be the "author who should designate the other polar star of the Firmament."[11] In his sleeplessness, he recalls those lines from the first canto of Dante's *Purgatory*, when the poet claims to exit the Northern Hemisphere and wants to describe the Antarctic Pole:

> To the right hand I turned, and fixed my mind
> On the other pole attentive, where I saw
> Four stars ne'er seen before save by the ken
> Of our first parents. (Henry F. Cary translation)

In his *Historia natural y moral de las Indias* (1590), José de Acosta echoes the experience and certainty of other travelers when he asserts the roundness of the Earth:

> Those of us who live in Pirú [*sic*] see it with our own eyes, more clearly manifest through experience than could ever be by any reasoning or philosophical demonstration. For, in order to know that the heavens are round and that they encircle and surround the Earth everywhere, and in order not to put it in doubt, it is enough to gaze from this hemisphere at that part and region of the heavens that goes around the Earth, which the ancients never saw. It is enough to have seen and noted both Poles, over which the heavens revolve as if on hinges.[12]

It should be no surprise, then, that the patriarch Buendía makes the same discovery with experience and observation as his sole instruments. Theory and practice were the opposing sides of navigators and mariners, who needed to repudiate the speculations of philosophers and theologians by risking themselves in their undertakings. Vespucci, ever optimistic and triumphant, writes to Lorenzo de Medici, "Practice is of more value than theory."[13] The Italian lost sleep and, as he relates, shortened his life by ten years by trying to figure out longitude, consumed as he was by the same fever for magnets and astrolabes as is old Buendía.

One Hundred Years of Solitude interweaves other histories, other conquests. It makes mention, for instance, of Sir Francis Drake, the English traveler who circumnavigated the globe in 1577. Recalling his visit to Morocco, Drake tells with surprise about the inhabitants who trade in ice, which they sell in markets for mixing with wine and other beverages.[14] Neither would Colonel Aureliano Buendía forget that afternoon in which he discovered ice. On other occasions García Márquez has expressed his knowledge of and his debt to Count Keyserling and Alexander von Humboldt. In Keyserling (or von Graff, as the novelist prefers to call him, using the man's aristocratic title so as to confuse the reader), he may have read a de-

scription of the world in evolution, a world arrested on the threshold of
the anthropological age, where plants grow and life grows the moment
they are allowed to. For the German writer, this place is Kilanea,[15] but
such a creation of the world conceived as myth could well be the great
swamp, near Macondo. And did the author happen to read in Bernal Díaz
del Castillo that description of the Gargantuan banquet given by the
Viceroy Antonio de Mendoza for the Marqués del Valle?[16] More than three
hundred gentlemen and two hundred ladies were there "from nightfall to
two hours past midnight," even as some dinner guests cried out their inability to remain seated at the tables any longer while others felt distressed
at each new dish. Their echoes come to us in the gastronomical contest
between Aureliano Segundo and Camila Sagastume—a totemic woman
nicknamed "the Elephant"—in which tournament the former nearly
loses his life.

Neither does American extravagance exclude the longevity of its indigenes, the lust of its women, or the sexual voraciousness of its men.
Vespucci notes that, in the New World, people live many years and that
there were men known for tending as many as four generations of descendants.[17] The explorer calculates that they lived for 150 years; Úrsula
reaches the age of 130. On another occasion, Vespucci finds himself per-
plexed and dazzled at certain tribes and the wicked arts of their women,
who would brutally deform the sex organs of their lovers.[18] Utterly overwhelming and extravagant will be the tattooed body of José Arcadio, the
first-born, while the thirst of lustfulness will invade Petra Cotes and Pilar
Ternera.

Fiction writing profited from these geographical legends. Novels of
chivalry show constant literary reminiscences of the discoveries.[19] Such is
the case with the *Primaleón*, which in a later edition incorporates Magellan's
journey and tells of the adventures of Palantín with the monster Patagón
(the basis for the name given to the Patagonian Indians),[20] or the *Esplandián*,
with its story of the black Amazons in the kingdom of Calafia (the origins
of the name of California). Subsequent literary works also demonstrate
their debt to the New World. Scholars have singled out the relationship between Jacques Cartier's journey and Rabelais's *Gargantua and Pantagruel*.[21] It is
also well known that one of the sources for Voltaire's *Candide* was *La Florida,*
by the Inca Garcilaso de la Vega,[22] and that Antonio de León Pinelo, the
Americanist, assisted Lope de Vega more than once with the poet-play-
wright's allusions to the Indies.[23]

The lengthy tradition of writers interested in these geographical legends, and of travelers well versed in chivalric literature, is the subject of a

magnificent study by Irving A. Leonard, who cites a text by Bernal Díaz del Castillo that describes Mexico as a place that "was like the enchanted things related in the book of *Amadís*."[24] According to the historian William H. Prescott, Cortés and the Spaniards were faced with "a scene so wonderful [that it] filled their rude hearts with amazement. It seemed like enchantment; and they could find nothing to compare it with, but the magical pictures in the *Amadís of Gaul*."[25] At another point, the conquistador asks for "good fortune in battle like that of the paladin Roldán."[26]

Seen through European eyes, America was a fantastical and marvelous place. Travelers and historians conceive of the Indies as paradise. León Pinelo firmly believes that the Garden of Eden is in southern America and that the four biblical rivers are the Plate, the Amazon, the Magdalena (in present-day Colombia), and the Orinoco.[27] The same is surmised by Vespucci, who notes "marvelous things of God and Nature."[28] Peter Martyr, the courtly chronicler, is more specific. For this learned humanist the Caribbean islands are transformed into Arcadia, and Jamaica becomes the Earthly Paradise, the clay from which God fashioned the first man.[29]

The Indian women of this Arcadia turn into utterly beautiful nymphs and dryads, "sprung from fountains that were talked about in ancient fables."[30] For Fernández de Oviedo, the New World's mountains "are more admirable and shocking than Etna or Mont-Genèvre, than Vulcan or Stromboli."[31]

An interesting deviation from this mythic standard is worth mention. Gonzalo Jiménez de Quesada, the explorer of the Magdalena and founder of Bogotá, registers a very different sort of experience. He is the first to describe for us a kind of prehistoric Macondo when, on arriving at Santa Marta in 1535, he finds four squalid houses and a miserable church.[32] Soon thereafter, as he embarks on his expedition up the Magdalena River, he describes the swamp, the floodwaters, the miasmic vapors, and the cruel and monstrous vegetation that annihilates a good number of his soldiers, a historic foreshadowing of the fantastic expedition of old man Buendía.

Of course, these marvels, filled with extraordinary adventures, also have their monsters. Oviedo contends that the feats of Greek heroes, those invented fables, are "Medean whoring and witchery."[33] His imperialist euphoria reaches unprecedented heights:

May the singers of Theseus, that labyrinth, and his minotaur turn silent, for, if Truth be told, those metaphors, when reduced to their real history, are but jokes and child's play, if they are likened and compared to what in these our Indies has been seen.[34]

Martín Fernández de Navarrete, who in the early nineteenth century gathered and published accounts of Spanish travels, complained of the poetic fantasy of the discoverers, who superimposed chivalric books onto their chronicles:

> At all times, works of inventiveness and imagination have served to elucidate the truth of History and also to corrupt the seeds good customs. Chivalry novels, absurd in their composition, unbelievable in their adventures, obscene, extravagant, and harmful in their doctrine, were works of admiration and delight for peoples who, enjoying the marvelous and extraordinary, could not accommodate themselves to the truthful accounts and the harsh incapacities of History.[35]

The reference to chivalric novels is not fortuitous. These books gave the measure for the grandeur of what was happening before their own eyes. How distressed Peter Martyr felt, he a man of such restraint, at his informants' fabulations! He, the chronicler of the Conquest from the Court, would lament the perfervid and emphatic praise of those who returned to Spain and compared "oxen with elephants, pigs with mules, but hyperbolically."[36]

As these writers did, García Márquez reveals to us the unusual aspects of the New World, along with the fantasies of chronicles and fiction. Let us remember how Melquíades discovers Macondo via the flight patterns of birds, in the same way that Columbus and other navigators let themselves be led in order to find lands unknown to them. According to some nautical historians, before the inventing and perfecting of the compass, sailors used to release birds that would lead them to land.[37]

A ship's log book, then, yet also a tale of adventure that narrates the deeds of knights errant. As in chivalric novels, the Aurelianos and José Arcadios, like the Amadíses, Esplandiáns, and Palmeríns, are members of a line of heroes in mythic realms. *One Hundred Years of Solitude*, besides being a chronicle of the Americas, is the family tree of its founders. The place name itself so indicates; judging by the definition given by Francisco J. Santamaría in his *Diccionario general de americanismos*, "macondo" is a popular form that, in Colombia, is applied to a corpulent tree of the baobab family, similar to the *ceiba*. Right next to a gigantic *ceiba* tree, outside Macondo, is where Colonel Aureliano Buendía breathes his last. The chosen people represent the birth and evolution of Latin America, as well as the genealogical stock of its conquistadors and colonizers. Úrsula and José Arcadio Buendía are the pioneer captains who arrive in order to found their family lineage in the swamp where "el mundo era tan reciente, que muchas cosas carecían de nombre" (9) [the world was so recent that many things lacked names (11)].

Another writer of Hispanic America, Ezequiel Martínez Estrada, had formerly conceived of this hemisphere as a dream, a land populated by images whose grandeur and amplitude give them an illusory impression, a magical continent where "the New World, just discovered, was not yet fixed on the planet, nor did it have any form."[38] The captains-general arrived dreaming, and those who got rid of them continued to dream, too. In these lands described by García Márquez and his Argentine fellow writer, men live in solitude, isolation, surrounded by distances, and the history of the Buendías, with its repetitions of José Arcadios and Aurelianos, Úrsulas and Amarantas, is—like the knights errant's—that of a family line condemned to solitude in a magical world.

LET US NOW CONCENTRATE on the history of Macondo, a lost city somewhere in Spanish America, and on the Buendía clan, a family haunted by the danger that some descendant could be born with the tail of a pig, as happened in remote times.[39] According to Úrsula, even he who lacks a tail—as does the Colonel—might as well have one.

Though the author gives no precise dates or facts and mixes history and geography so as to confound and prevent any identification, he does offer some signs for reconstructing the past. Judging by its geographical location, Macondo would be situated at the same point of Santa Marta, the first city founded in Nueva Granada, to whose east is Riohacha, the past, and to whose south is the swamp. Santa Marta is also the site of the death of Bolívar, represented in part by the Colonel, who shares in the goal of unifying all of the federalist forces in Central America. However, the dislocations of time make the Colonel's wars go from Independence through the end of the nineteenth century. Their struggles stand for all the disruptions and calamities that ensue before the Yankee invasion. The British pirates Drake and Raleigh are followed by the good neighbors from the North. It's important to note that the United Fruit empire was located chiefly in Santa Marta, where it controlled not only crops and workers but also railroads, ships, housing, and finance. Santa Marta had the same railroad in the country, just as the Banana Company is behind the arrival of the first train in Macondo, "the innocent yellow train" that has the town disconcerted. The Banana Company, like its model United Fruit, disrupts and destroys.

The novel escapes the tyranny of time and tends toward simultaneity, intermixing eras, characters, historical figures, and situations. It would therefore be risky to hazard any chronological guesses. According to the author, the story of Macondo ends in 1928, the year of his own birth. Simple arithmetic allows us to suppose that the solitary century of Macondo starts out in 1828. Of course, if we bear in mind that José Arcadio Buendía and Úrsula get married about three hundred years after the pirate Drake had attacked and raided Riohacha, causing consternation and stupor in Úrsula's great-grandmother (who, startled and scared, sat on a lighted stove), then we would still be living within the one hundred years of solitude even as I write, in 1971, and on through the 1990s. On the other hand, how could we fail to identify the fictive massacre of workers in Macondo with the other, all too real action that, in 1928, led to between fifteen hundred and three thousand dead and wounded among workers who had gathered in the square of a village near Santa Marta![40] Still, all these hypotheses are little more than idle speculations of a reader, for we already know that "Melquíades no había ordenado los hechos en el tiempo convencional de los hombres, sino que concentró un siglo de episodios cotidianos de modo que todo coexistiera en un instante" (350) [Melquíades had not put events in the order of man's conventional time, but had concentrated a century of daily episodes in such a way that they coexisted in an instant (382)].

The chapters do not follow a linear structure but rather present several plots that, with leaps forward and backward in time, interweave the past history of each character. The sequence is neither chronological nor logical; the reader fulfills the function of an historian, with facts and lives being set in order. The first five chapters describe the idyllic phase of Macondo, its genesis. The small settlement, "una aldea de veinte casas de barro y cañabrava construidas a la orilla de un río con aguas diáfanas" (a village of twenty adobe houses, built on the bank of a river of clear water), grows and evolves gradually before our eyes. Macondo is a center colonized by pilgrims who herald from elsewhere. Some, like José Arcadio Buendía and Úrsula, are fleeing the past; others join in for the sake of adventure and to test their luck. They will all be the future aristocracy.

Despite the settlers' isolation, the references to the world outside are fairly constant. Difficult access notwithstanding, one day Melquíades's tribe arrives at the village, led by bird calls. Melquíades dazzles José Arcadio Buendía; he speaks of Macedonia, of distant civilizations. He has died many times and, as frequently, has lived again, always being reborn and always elderly, as indicated by the name of his tribe: the Naciancenes, undoubtedly a reminiscence of St. Gregory Nazianzus,[41] often cited by the chroniclers. Melquíades signifies progress; with him there arrives word of inventions and discoveries, already old news across the swamp from Macondo, but unsuspected in the town, where everything is anachronistic and arrives ill timed. The gypsy brings the magnifying glass, the astrolabe, and alchemy.

José Arcadio Buendía is seduced by a hunger for knowledge and the fascination of science. "En el mundo están ocurriendo cosas increíbles. Ahí mismo, al otro lado del río, hay toda clase de aparatos mágicos, mientras nosotros seguimos viviendo como burros" (15) [Incredible things are happening in the world. Right there across the river there are all kinds of magical instruments while we keep on living like donkeys (17)]. José Arcadio, the patriarch, the founder, who decides and organizes and creates everything in his own image and likeness and under whose leadership the streets had been traced and the settlement transformed into a great, orderly, hard-working village, will stray ever further from his prime spirit of social initiative. Old Buendía is seized by a rage for magnets, for astronomical computations, for dreams of transmuting metals, an insatiable thirst to know all of the world's marvels. The seeker of progress cuts himself off from reality, increasingly convinced that knowledge equals superiority. He wishes to learn from Nature the way to harness it in order to gain total domination of the universe. Power and knowledge for him are synonymous; knowing equals controlling. In his hands the magnifying glass becomes a battlefield weapon, and he composes a manual that he sends to the authorities for the purposes of putting it in the hands of the military and training them in "las complicadas artes de la guerra solar" (11) [the complicated art of solar war (13)].

Melquíades—the Enlightenment, science, knowledge for knowledge's sake—attempts to dissuade him, without success. The alchemy lab becomes in José Arcadio Buendía's hands a money-minting machine; Úrsula's colonial coins have to be multiplied as many times as one can subdivide quicksilver (CAS, 14; OYS, 12).

The discovery of ice makes him think of transforming the geography and the climate—building houses made of ice, fantastical igloos in a torrid zone that would cease to be a sweltering spot and turn into a wintry city. The subject of ice is one of the central ideas in the book; in the dream of José Arcadio Buendía, Macondo is a city with frozen mirrors on its house walls. In Macondo, as in Spanish America, everything is but a reflection of the real, and its dwellers copy, seek progress elsewhere, imitate, and do not create. Everything has always been imported—first by the tribe of Melquíades, later by the Banana Company, which transforms the town and makes it "naufragar en una prosperidad de milagro" (168), or, as the English version puts it, has Macondo "swamped in a miraculous prosperity" (185).

Avid for progress and science, José Arcadio Buendía requests "el con-
curso de todos para abrir una trocha que pusiera a Macondo con los
grandes inventos" (16) [the assembled group to open a way that would put
Macondo in contact with the great inventions (19)]. Symbolically, this
would be the northward route; the East leads to the past, to the former
town of Riohacha; to the South there was the great swamp; and the North
was "la única posibilidad de contacto con la civilización" (17) [the only possibility of contact with civilization (19)]. The reckless adventure of José Arcadio Buendía will lead them to a place where "el mundo se volvió triste
para siempre" (17) [the world became eternally sad (20)]. There they find a
paradise of humidity and silence, prior to original sin, where their boots
sink and their machetes destroy bloody irises and golden salamanders.
With their lungs overwhelmed by the suffocating odor of blood and their
lives totally dependent on the compass, one morning they find a Spanish
galleon, symbol of the colony. Macondo, Spanish America, is a solitary
colony and, worst of all, is an island. José Arcadio Buendía's exclamation—
"¡Carajo! Macondo está rodeado de agua por todas partes" (18) God damn
it! Macondo is surrounded by water on all sides (21)]—takes us back to the
old Renaissance concept of island versus continent. For the first navigators,
continents were only those lands within the *orbis terrarum*—Europe and the
Mediterranean.[42] The word "continent" had at the time a denotation that
was purely cultural and historical, not geographical. The insular Macondo
hence doesn't belong to the West; it is not part of the European world but
rather is an isolated place, incapable of achieving the progress that comes
from the North, where there are tramways, postal services, and machines.
Doubtless, a pointless land that has been ill born! Since the Conquest it has
aroused only unbridled greed. How regretfully did the good Father Bartolomé las Casas exclaim that in this New World all was plagues and death:

> So much damage! So many calamities! So many kingdoms depopulated! So
> many stories of souls! . . . So many and such unforgivable sins have been
> committed! So much blindness, and such disregard of conscience![43]

It is Úrsula who will find the way to the outside world. After disappear-
ing for five months, she returns with "hombres y mujeres como ellos, de
cabellos lacios y piel parda, que hablaban su misma lengua y se lamentaban
de los mismos dolores" [men and women like them, with straight hair and
dark skin, who spoke the same langauge and complained of the same
pains]. Incredibly, "[v]enían del otro lado de la ciénaga, a sólo dos días de
viaje, donde había pueblos que recibían el correo todos los meses y
conocían todas las máquinas del bienestar" (38) [they came from the other

side of the swamp, only two days away, where there were towns that received mail every month in the year and where they were familiar with the implements of good living (43)].

On Úrsula's return the inhabitants are stricken with the insomnia plague, which produces forgetfulness and makes everyone see the dreams of others. The allegory is clear: Macondo, America, is a mirage, a dream. Everything repeats itself in a constant circle. The José Arcadios and the Aurelianos are always the same ones, united, like the twins of Arcadio and Santa Sofía de la Piedad, their identities blurred even in death. Time always spins on itself. The history of the family is a machine with unavoidable repetitions, a turning wheel whose axle gradually wears out. Úrsula reiterates it several times: "Es como si el tiempo diera vueltas en redondo y hubiéramos vuelto al principio" (169, 192, 285) [It's as if time had turned around and we were back at the beginning" (185, 209, 310)]. America is an anachronistic land, a journey inside-out of time. Once again García Márquez coincides with Martínez Estrada, who explains the discovery voyage by saying, "Each day of navigation the caravels retraced one hundred years. The voyage was made across the ages, receding from the epoch of the compass and of the printing press to that of chiseled stone."[44] The continent is an old land where nothing new takes place, and where what is reproduced are merely the personal variants of many histories now long forgotten.[45]

The repetition of names and the intense inbreeding occur because of an intense sexuality not lacking in its hints of humor. García Márquez exploits dramatic situations by always showing their ridiculous side: Úrsula's great-great-grandmother sat on a lighted stove and gives off a singed odor; Úrsula and her husband, José Arcadio, live together for a year, and she continues to be a virgin out of fear of engendering a child with the tail of a pig; José Arcadio, their first son, has a colossal sex organ. The displaced erotic impulses of this family are projected onto the world of fantasy: Rebeca eats dirt so as to suppress her sexual appetites; Amaranta knits and dreams about her nephew; Arcadio is attracted to his own mother; Remedios, the Beauty, never understands why women complicate their lives with corsets and petticoats and sews a burlap cassock, which she slips over her, always giving the impression of being naked, "que según ella entendía las cosas, era la única forma decente de estar en casa" (199) [which according to her lights was the only decent way to be when at home" (217)]. Aureliano José plunges into war in order to forget his obsession with Amaranta; there he discovers that a man had married his aunt "que además era su prima, y cuyo hijo terminó siendo abuelo de sí mismo" (who was also his own cousin, and whose son ended up being his own grandfather). Encouraged, he asks an old fighter if it's possible to marry one's aunt:

> No sólo se puede—le contestó un soldado,—sino que estamos haciendo esta guerra contra los curas para que uno se pueda casar con su propia madre. (132)

> [He not only can do that," a soldier answered him, "but we're fighting this war against the priests so a person can marry his own mother.] (145)

All these experiences and quests, however, fail to unify the family. The line consumes itself after exhausting all human possibilities. Macondo's is a world fertilized by autogenesis and destroyed by self-cannibalization.

And yet, should we wonder at this free sexuality, this cannibalism? We already know from the navigators that the American indigenes went about as naked as they had been born, and indeed shamelessly, which made a prudish, cautious Vespucci exclaim that "If all were to be related concerning the little shame they have, it would be bordering on impropriety, therefore it is better to suppress it."[46]

As the work moves along, the village changes, and its story becomes further complicated with new Buendías. Still, the fervid activity of the town, lined with acacias and almond trees, allows us to envision another, newer colony, this time a more serious one: that of U.S. imperialism represented by the Banana Company, known in real life as United Fruit. Everything is unhinged and transformed by the tumultuous and ill-timed invasion of foreigners preceded by the gringo Mr. Herbert, but

> [N]adie sabía aún qué era lo que buscaban o si en verdad no eran más que filántropos, y ya habían ocasionado un trastorno colosal, mucho más perturbador que el de los antiguos gitanos, pero menos transitorio y comprensible. (197)

> [No one yet knew what they were after or whether they were actually nothing but philanthropists, and they had already caused a colossal disturbance, much more than that of the old gypsies, but less transitory and comprehensible.] (214)

Under the sway of the Banana Compnay, Macondo will become "un campamento de casas de madera y de zinc" (40) [a field of wooden houses with zinc roofs (45)], very far from the prosperous, well-guided town founded by the first Buendía. The last Aureliano, still in his adolescence, will give us another version of the same history, whereby Macondo

lo desordenó y lo corrompió y lo exprimió la compañia bananera, cuyos in-
genieros provocaron el diluvio como pretexto para eludir compromisos con
los trabajadores. (295)

[was disordered and corrupted and suppressed by the banana company,
whose engineers brought on the deluge as a pretext to avoid promises made
to the workers.] (321)

In the end, nothing is true. No one remembers the colonel, and the Banana Company had never existed. The last survivors are cast adrift on the
ebb tide of a world now concluded, of which only nostalgia remains (CAS,
328; OYS, 358). On that immense land there arose a reality not liable to
modification, and at the end the precarious labors of man are destroyed.
Houses and family lines disappear. Things had settled in without casting
roots and never held their true place. Not even outrageous sexual appetites
help men last, for everything always ends in tragedy and terminal solitude.

Macondo is happiest when prehistoric and precolonial. Isolated both
from the East, where Europe is located, and from the boggy South of
America, and subject to the laws of progress that come from the Anglo-
Saxon North, it becomes all disrupted and turned upside down. The world
sown by the inventions of the first José Arcadio, the wars of Colonel Aureliano Buendía, the Banana Company, the massacre of workers, and the
rain that lasts almost five years all provoke its own extinction.

Little remains of the chronicle of the Buendías and Macondo. We read
the book written by Melquíades, who, as in chivalry novels, fulfills the
double function of chronicler and necromancer, and through whom we
see the descendants of the old patriarch file past.[47] The José Arcadios were
impulsive and enterprising, but they were marked with a tragic sign; the
Aurelianos were withdrawn, but with lucid minds. The former were insatiable globetrotters, the latter, artists who crafted little gold fishes in an
alchemy lab, which in their hands becomes the workshop of artificers.
That room, also housing the parchments of Melquíades, is a ramshackle,
dirty place in the eyes of the José Arcadios, a clean and well-ordered one
for the Aurelianos.

And it is from an Aureliano and an Amaranta—she an emancipated
and determined woman, raised in Europe—that there will be born the
child with the tail of a pig who will bring the line to an end. This last Aureliano, dubbed "Babilonia" by the author, will be the decipherer of the
century-old papers of a wise Melquíades, that chronicle of solitary beings,
abandoned to themselves, incapable of integrating to life. As he reads his

own story and recognizes his own family stock, Aureliano Babilonia knows he'll never arrive at the concluding line, for the epic of the Buendías

> sería arrasada por el viento y desterrada de la memoria de los hombres . . . y todo lo escrito desde siempre y para siempre, porque las estirpes condenadas a cien años de soledad no tenían una segunda oportunidad sobre la tierra. (351)

> [would be wiped out by the wind and exiled from the memory of men . . . and everything on them was unrepeatable since time immemorial and forever more, because races condemned to one hundred years of solitude did not have a second opportunity on earth.] (383)

In an interview with Miguel Fernández Braso, García Márquez explained that the best novels are those that "disturb us not only with their social and political content, but by their power to penetrate reality, and better still if they're able to turn reality upside down and show how it is on the other side."[48] His own approach, he explains, is a system for exploiting reality, yet without realist prejudices. And *One Hundred Years of Solitude*, he adds, is a work of liberation. How could it not be so? The American world is a senseless world that was ill born. Those who, like José Arcadio Buendía, seek the route of the Anglo-Saxon North for the sake of utility and progress will only lead us into the oppression of speculators and capitalists who, as in the novel *Leaf Storm,* proceed to wring us dry. Their sole legacy, if they do not bog down in a miraculous prosperity, is to be left with "los desperdicios de los desperdicios" [the dregs of the dregs].

> aldeas arruinadas, con cuatro almacenes pobres y oscuros, ocupados por gente cesante y rencorosa, a quien atormentaba el recuerdo de un país próspero y la amargura de un presente agobiado y estático.

> [a ruined village was left here, with four poor, dark stores; occupied by unemployed and angry people who were tormented by a prosperous past and the bitterness of an overwhelming and static present.][49]

Notes

This essay was translated by Gene H. Bell-Villada.

1. Juan Ramón's essay is in *La poesía cubana en 1936*, Havana, 1937, p. xvii. For *Cien años de soledad*, I cite the original edition from Editorial Sudamericana, Buenos Aires, 1967. [For English quotations, the translation cited is by Gregory Rabassa (New York: Avon, 1971).]

2. Americo Vespucci, *El nuevo mundo: Cartas relativas a sus viajes y descubrimientos.* Textos en italiano, español e inglés. Estudio preliminar de Roberto Levillier (Buenos Aires: Editorial Nova, 1951), p. 147 (Spanish), p. 290 (English). The English translation is from C. Edwards Lester, *The Life and Voyages of Americus Vespuccius* (New Haven, Conn.: H. Mansfield, 1850).

3. *Historia general de las Indias* (Barcelona: Editorial Ibevia, 1965), p. 158.

4. *Exploradores y conquistadores de Indias: Relatos geográficos* (Madrid: Instituto Escuela, 1964), p. 72.

5. Cited in Ezequiel Martínez Estrada, *Radiografía de la pampa* (Buenos Aires: Editorial Losada, 1933), p. 28.

6. Cf. Martín Fernández de Navarrete, *Colección de los viajes y descubrimientos que hicieron por mar los españoles desde el fin del siglo XV,* vol. 75 (Madrid: Biblioteca de Autores Españoles, 1953), p. 178.

7. Ibid., p. 143.

8. Bernal Díaz del Castillo, *Historia de la conquista de la Nueva España* (Mexico City: Fondo de Cultura Económica, 1966), p. 30.

9. Gonzalo Hernández de Oviedo, *Historia natural de las Indias,* in *Exploradores,* p. 85.

10. Fernández de Navarrete, *Colección,* p. 213.

11. Vespucci, *Nuevo mundo,* p. 103 (Spanish), p. 273 (English).

12. José de Acosta, *Historia natural y moral de las Indias* (Mexico City: Fondo de Cultura Económica, 1967), p. 17.

13. Vespucci, *Nuevo mundo,* p. 107 (Spanish), p. 276 (English).

14. Sir Francis Drake, *The World Encompassed* (London: Hakluyt Society, 1854), p. 14.

15. Hermann Graff von Keyserling, *The Travel Diary of a Philosopher,* trans. J. Holroyd Reece (London: Jonathan Cape 1933), pp. 577–583.

16. Díaz del Castillo, *Historia de la conquista,* pp. 506–507.

17. Vespucci, *Nuevo mundo,* p. 149 (Spanish), p. 291 (English).

18. Ibid.

19. See the excellent article by Marcel Bataillon, "Acerca de los patagones. Retractio," in *Filología* 8 (1962), 27–45.

20. See María Rosa Lida de Malkiel, "Para la toponimia argentina: Patagonia," *Hispanic Review* 20 (1952), 283–289.

21. Bataillon, "Acerca de los patagones," p. 33.

22. See the notes by Roger Petit to the Classiques Larousse edition of this work.

23. Cf. the preface by Agustín Millares Carlo to *El Epítome de Pinel* (Washington, D.C.: Panamerican Union, 1958), p. xv.

24. Irving A. Leonard, *Books of the Brave: Being an Account of Books and Men in the Spanish Conquest and Settlement of the Sixteenth-Century New World* (Cambridge, Mass.: Harvard University Press, 1949), p. 43.

25. William H. Prescott, *The Conquest of Mexico* (New York: A. L. Burt, c. 1909), p. 360.

26. Díaz del Castillo, *Historia de la conquista,* p. 110.

27. Cf. Antonio Rodríguez de León Pinelo, *El paraíso en el Nuevo Mundo: Comentario apologético, historia natural y peregrina de las Indias Occidentales* (Lima: Imprenta Torres Aguirre, 1943).

28. Vespucci, *Nuevo mundo,* p. 145 (Spanish). The English version omits this phrase.

29. Cited in Alberto Salas, *Tres cronistas de México* (Mexico City: Fondo de Cultura Económica, 1959), p. 44.

30. Ibid., p. 45.

31. Ibid., p. 86.

32. Cf. R. B. Cunninghame Graham, *The Conquest of New Granada: Being the Life of Gonzalo Jiménez de Quesada* (New York: Cooper Square, 1967), p. 9.

33. Salas, *Tres cronistas,* p. 82.

34. Ibid.

35. Fernández de Navarrete, *Colección,* p. 11.

36. Salas, *Tres cronistas,* pp. 37–38.

37. Fernández de Navarrete, *Colección,* pp. 283, 433.

38. Ezequiel Martínez Estrada, *X-Ray of the Pampa,* trans. Alain Swietlicki (Austin: University of Texas Press, 1971), p. 3.

39. Let us remember that the son of an aunt of Úrsula's, married to an uncle of José Arcadio Buendía's, had been born with the tail of a pig.

40. See the classic study by Charles David Kepner, *The Banana Empire: A Case Study of Economic Imperialism* (New York: Vanguard, 1935), pp. 328–329.

41. This saint is often cited by a number of chroniclers. Cf. *El Epítome,* and de Acosta, *La historia natural,* pp. 31 ff.

42. Cf. Wilcombe E. Washburn, "The Meaning of the 'Discovery' in the Fifteenth and Sixteenth Centuries," *American Historical Review* 68 (1962), 1–21.

43. Bartolomé Las Casas, *Historia de las Indias* (Mexico: Fondo de Cultura Económica, 1965), 2d ed., vol. 1, pp. 12–13.

44. Martínez Estrada, *X-Ray of the Pampa,* p. 84.

45. Ibid., p. 104.

46. Vespucci, *Nuevo mundo,* p. 111 (Spanish), p. 277 (English).

47. There are certain traits shared by *One Hundred Years* and chivalric novels. In the late Medieval works, the tale was often based on some ancient parchment that the author claimed to have discovered and translated, thereby giving the impression that the events were derived from an historical document. The purported manuscript tended to be written in exotic languages that were hard to decipher.

The wizards and sages who appear in the Amadís volumes have the twin characteristics of historians and sorcerers.

48. Miguel Fernández Braso, *Gabriel García Márquez: Una conversación infinita* (Madrid: Editorial Azur, 1969), p. 65.

49. Gabriel García Márquez, *La hojarasca* (Buenos Aires: Editorial Sudamericana, 1972), p. 110; *Leaf Storm and Other Stories*, trans. Gregory Rabassa (New York: Harper & Row, 1972), title piece, p. 79.

Banana Strike and Military Massacre

One Hundred Years of Solitude *and* *What Happened in 1928*

GENE H. BELL-VILLADA

◆　◆　◆

T HE EPISODE OF THE BANANA STRIKE and military repres-
sion in *One Hundred Years of Solitude* constitutes the highest point in García Márquez's extensive chronicle of Macondo. It is a vivid and dramatic
scene, packed with sociopolitical suspense, capped with sanguinary horror, and followed by uncanny official silence and a fantastical rain. Moreover, it is the last occasion in which the Macondoites and their Buendía
leaders will collectively resist the meddlings of a high-handed central government.[1] With the army occupation and repression, the townspeople will
lose once and for all the scant political autonomy still remaining them.
With the five-year cloudburst, courtesy of the Banana Company, the decline of Macondo as historical subject and vital entity will be greatly accelerated. The biblical windstorm that sweeps everything off in the concluding paragraph only completes an inexorable cycle of physical and spiritual
degradation.

In musical analysis it is often noted that the climax of a composition
tends to occur at a point approximately five-sevenths (5/7) of the work's
duration. Such happens to be the case with García Márquez's superbly
constructed, now-classic novel. In the Avon paperback edition of the book,
consisting of 372 printed pages, the strike and the massacre take place
in what are pages 270–280 of the actual text.[2] The fraction 270 over 372

can be reduced to 54 over 74—or roughly, five-sevenths. What transpires in the remaining two-sevenths is a bittersweet and melancholy dénouement, involving (among other things) the successive deaths of Úrsula, Pilar Ternera, the Segundo twins, and the last of the José Arcadios and Aurelianos.

United States imperialism, a subject by no means new to Latin American letters, has attracted a good number of ranking Hispanic authors over the last hundred years. Among Pablo Neruda's most anthologized single works is his forty-two-line attack on "La United Fruit Co.," first printed in his grand epic of the Americas, the *Canto general* (1950), where one also finds other equally impassioned protest poems about U.S. banking and mining firms and their local military puppets. In the field of narrative, an author of the genius of César Vallejo, the great Peruvian lyricist, published in 1931 his socialist-realist novel *El tungsteno* (Tungsten);[3] and Miguel Ángel Asturias, the Guatemalan who was awarded the 1967 Nobel Prize, labored throughout the 1950s on his ambitious and lengthy United Fruit trilogy, comprising the novels subsequently Englished as *Strong Wind, The Green Pope,* and *The Eyes of the Interred.*[4]

The subject matter itself proved a stumbling block to these two authors. For want of a novelistic formula suitable both to their narrative raw material and their ideological world view, the resulting novels generally fail as art—notwithstanding Vallejo's and Asturias's formidable literary gifts. It was García Márquez's fortunate lot to hit upon a narrative approach that would definitively sidestep and transcend the notorious pitfalls of anti-Yankee protest fiction. Indeed, the magic and serenity of voice of the Colombian's Banana Company sequence are at the same high level as can be found anywhere in *One Hundred Years of Solitude.* I have taught this book in American college classrooms since 1971; to date I have encountered no student complaints regarding the Banana episode, which, on the contrary, affects them profoundly. It is also worth noting that the literary critics who look with disfavor upon García Márquez's subtale of explanation, resistance, and slaughter are very much in the minority.[5]

My aim in this essay is twofold. First, I shall examine García Márquez's Banana Company episodes as formal narrative, with a view to elucidating their high artistry and possibly explaining why that section works so well. And, second, I shall be setting forth the historical facts that served García Márquez as basis for his Banana chapters. Strange as it seems, there has been minimal research done on the extent to which the great novelist built those episodes around a very real strike and repression that, in 1928, swept across the entirety of Colombia's Banana Zone, from the old Caribbean town of Santa Marta to García Márquez's inland village of Aracataca.⁶ What we see happening in the banana fields of Macondo is narrative, is novel, is fiction; but it is also basically a true story, a piece of history carefully reconstructed, and then artfully exaggerated.

What is paradoxical is that the strike and massacre, despite their centrality to *One Hundred Years of Solitude*, scarcely call attention to themselves. On the contrary, the walkout and reprisals are presented simply as one more event in the string of occurrences starting out with the exodus from Riohacha (Colombia's northeasternmost town) and terminating with the apocalypse of the wind storm in imaginary Macondo. When we think of titles such as *Tungsten* or *The Green Pope*, we know from the outset what their narratives are about and deal with. By contrast, it could never be said of *One Hundred Years of Solitude* that it is a literary polemic against Yankee imperialism, though its plot does encompass that touchiest of topics. No doubt, social struggles are extremely important, are perhaps the most important thing—but they are not the only thing. The simple wisdom of García Márquez originates in his having acknowledged for Macondo the coexistence of such realities as love and sex, of eating and merrymaking, of aging and dying and other human processes and practices, which keep taking place, if not with total independence from the Banana Company, at least with rules and dynamics of their own. (We might say that García Márquez narrates in an intuitive way what Louis Althusser explains, presents, and theorizes in a scholastic way.)

And so in those very same Banana Company chapters one also finds scenes that depict the gourmandizing and dissipation of Aureliano Segundo, the torrid romance of Meme and Mauricio, and the languid evolution and abrupt ascension of young, virginal Remedios, the Beauty. No doubt, The Struggle Goes On, as a 1970s left-wing motto would say, but, Fruit Company or no Fruit Company, life and death go on, too. Colonel Aureliano Buendía wastes away in bitter solitude and dies urinating before the chestnut tree; his sister Amaranta finishes weaving her shroud just before she perishes at nightfall; and an old nun shows up with a basket bearing the infant Aureliano, bastard son of Meme and the last character to live in the book. Hence, alongside the Banana Firm's time present there persists the elder Buendías' time past, even as there appear the seeds of time future in Aureliano Babilonia, witness-to-be of the closing moments and privileged reader of/in Melquíades's text.

Not that these developments unfold in a space wholly free and separate from Banana Company control. On the contrary, there are links that, while casual on the face of it, are actually decisive. For instance, the hapless stranger who, from ogling the femme fatale Remedios in the shower, slips and cracks his skull is one of the countless out-of-towners who have converged upon Macondo in search of Company largesse. In the same way, Meme befriends some American teenagers, and it is through Patricia Brown, daughter of the manager of the firm, that she meets her lover-to-be Mauricio, himself a mechanic's apprentice for the Company.

García Márquez's narrator doesn't insist upon those connecting links. The Fruit Company may set the stage and create conditions for such escapades, but these in turn have sufficient existence and vitality, a narrative density and textured art all their own. This differs substantially from the Austurias trilogy, where virtually everything from sex to baseball occurs in the inescapable shadow of Tropical Banana Inc., fount and origin of the thousand-page work's actions and atmosphere. It is no accident that the best scenes in Vallejo's much briefer *Tungsten* are those that have the least to do with the mining firm and deal instead with intimate power relations between the sexes.

The relative autonomy of the non-Banana scenes in the same chapters of *One Hundred Years of Solitude* becomes most manifest in their comic quality. Few would disagree that the traits and conduct of, say, Aureliano Segundo or Remedios, the Beauty, are uncommonly funny. What we have here is not anything like Shakespearian comic relief, however, but the power of levity itself, a dynamic of plebeian drollery and physical humor (of the carnivalesque, if you will) that is equal in its force and validity to the harsh matter of embattled workers and repressive troops, with its dark dynamic of horror and tragedy.

García Márquez's own Yankees are pure caricature but are drawn with such virtuoso precision and elaborate complexity that, both in aesthetic effect and in narrative significance, the portraits are fully achieved. The scene in which the Buendías guest Mr. Herbert tastes a banana, opens his toolbox, and then successively applies to the innocent fruit his optical instruments, special scapel, pharmacist's scale, gunsmith's calipers, and thermometer and photometer is a perfect satire of our notorious mercantile-technological fix, our mania for bringing to bear the latest and most sophisticated hardware onto the simplest of things (213).[7] At some point in his career, García Márquez appears to have understood that too solemn a vision of U.S. imperialism contributes nothing to the art of friction and that on the other hand there exists a rich potential in exaggerating and ridiculing those technological obsessions of ours that, even in the years since his novel was first published, have become baroque and even grotesque.

García Márquez explained to me in an interview that his Yankees are depicted as the Macondoites perceive them—a key aspect of his novel.[8] To us in our time, American global power—with its worldwide extractive and agricultural, manufacturing, marketing, financial, military, and media apparatus—is a fact we routinely take for granted as a given. For early twentieth-century Macondoites, however, the "gringos" are a novelty, and it is thus that García Márquez succeeds in defamiliarizing his Americans, "making strange" their wondrous technology and their "languid wives in muslin dresses and large veiled hats," and the almost fantastical milieu of their town across the tracks, with its "streets lined with palm trees, houses with screened windows, small white tables on the terraces, . . . and extensive blue lawns with peacocks and quails" (214).

Such a description suggests Los Angeles in the 1910s (or in the movie *El Norte*'s 1980s). In the context of a tropical and less-developed Macondo, however, the entire ensemble is intrusive, virtually something from another planet. Neither the townspeople nor we readers can hope to penetrate that colonial enclave, save for Meme's consortings with the Browns, and even then all is seen through her tender adolescent eyes. The narrator of *One Hundred Years of Solitude* is of the omniscient kind, as critics often note, but the actual bounds of such omniscience lie precisely in the electrified fence surrounding and protecting the gringos' separate reality.

By so depicting his Americans, García Márquez adhered to the first and basic rule of every good writer—namely "Write about what you know best." In contrast, a serious flaw of Asturias's banana trilogy is that the Guatemalan author made the mistake of inventing protagonists who are Yankees, even going so far as to portray them from within. The artistic result is terribly defective and false; from the outset readers are aware that Asturias lacks thorough knowledge of his materials, inasmuch as his Americans simply don't sound or feel like Americans. For example, we are informed that the Banana adventurer Lester Mead speaks English with an Oxford accent.[9] And in an episode in *Strong Wind*, the Banana Company executives take to quoting, from memory, long passages from Shakespeare's *Othello*—all this without the slightest hint of parody (no post-Modernist harbinger of Barthelme here).[10] Anyone minimally acquainted with the subculture of United States entrepreneurialism knows full well that Asturias's portraits are, to say the least, improbable. Similarly the gringos of Asturias's trilogy, as well as those of Vallejo's *Tungsten*, speak a perfect un-accented Spanish, with no syntactic or phonetic peculiarities of their own.

García Márquez did read Asturias in the 1950s and early 1960s, quite possibly in order to learn from the elder writer's mistakes. It's well worth noting that, in all the Banana Company–related episodes in *One Hundred Years of Solitude*, there is but a single occasion in which an American character is directly quoted, and that rare utterance is relayed to us secondhand, via an unreliable source. I am referring to the government's proclamation that, following assurances that the strike had been peacefully settled, cites Mr. Brown as affirming that labor negotiations will resume "When the rain stops. As long as the rain lasts we're suspending all activities" (287).[11] The truth is that the rain will fall for almost a half decade and heap ruin on Macondo.

In his numerous interviews and journalistic writings, García Márquez always demonstrates an excellent knowledge of United States history and culture. Moreover, he lived in New York in 1960 and 1961, and then, en route to Mexico, he traveled through the southern states (where, owing to Jim Crow laws, he and his family experienced some difficulty in finding hotel rooms). And yet he has never presumed to know the more intimately psychological, existential aspect of American life. Nevertheless, the Colombian novelist was to make the most out of his small-town Caribbean point of view, transforming this perspective into a narrative strength and casting the mold for the satirical vision he at last articulates toward that most classic of U.S. agribusiness firms.

The Banana episodes themselves benefit from the author's formal and narrative genius—for example, the humor in the reference to Virginia hams and in the useless copper-colored pills that the children rip off for use as bingo markers. Moreover, in contrast to Asturias's amorphous and rambling prolixity, García Márquez's myriad symmetries and repetitions keep any loose ends carefully under control. The sudden arrival of Americans in Macondo is the second such intrusion by outsiders, the first having been that of the Conservatives; in the wake of the gringos we find once again the sextet of opportunistic lawyers dressed in black; and, in the same way that José Arcadio Buendía and Colonel Aureliano Buendía had been prime leaders in the anti-Conservative resistance, José Arcadio Segundo now becomes a prominent agitator in the struggle against the Banana Company. And, finally, instead of allowing himself to be carried away by the sensationalism of the massacre, García Márquez goes well beyond it, steers our attention away from it with his wild fantasies of Orwellian oblivion and five-year rains, the work, respectively, of the Government and the Company. In all, it is a panoramic sociopolitical subplot constructed with utmost craftsmanship and imagination.

THE BANANA COMPANY CHAPTERS in García Márquez's book adhere quite closely to the actual facts of the great strike of 1928 (the year also of the novelist's birth in Aracataca).[12] The historical record of the United Fruit Company's operation in Colombia furnishes a textbook case of overseas imperialism and colonialism, a story vividly suggestive of a novel by Conrad, Foster, Graham Greene—or García Márquez. From what were comparatively modest holdings around 1900. United's dominions in the northern, coastal portions of Colombia expanded rapidly to become a state-within-a-state and the de facto power in that region. In addition to the best lands, United had its own railroads, general stores, and telegraph system; with its network of canals it monopolized irrigation; and its water practices violated Colombia's Civil Code.[13] Its labor policies left much to be desired, and already in 1918 United Fruit had responded to protests over low wages with a promise to consult with Company headquarters in Boston. The promise came to nothing.[14]

By 1925 a number of anarchist and communist labor unions were formulating strike plans and preparing organizers.[15] On 6 October 1928, the strike leadership confronted management with its list of demands. The first and most basic of these was that the Company acknowledge the fact that it had employees, inasmuch as its labor recruitment method had been one of relying solely on subcontractors who rounded up workers for United, a tactic whereby the firm had successfully evaded national laws regarding employee safety and security.[16] The strike organizers also demanded "hygienic dwelling places," "social hygiene," "a day of rest in seven," and "the establishment of hospitals in sufficient numbers."[17] Last but not least, they wanted an end to the system of paying the worker in credit slips, with which he had been obligated to purchase his provisions, at high prices, in Company comissaries. With this practice the firm had further reduced its labor costs and also steered clientele away from local merchants, who, not surprisingly, felt no love for United Fruit.[18]

Meanwhile, tensions had been mounting, and the Company manager Thomas Bradshaw feigned absence from Santa Marta. But, according to congressional testimony by the union leader Alberto Castrillón, "the simple truth is that he was merely trying to evade any negotiations whatsoever with the workers and their demands. After several days' search . . . he was casually found . . . while arranging the purchase of an automobile, and he absolutely refused to deal with the workers, and in a rather surly voice he declared them legally incompetent for negotiations of any kind, *given that the Company had no workers.*"[19]

With the talks at an impasse, the thirty-two thousand workers went out on strike on 7 October. The response of the Conservative government in distant Bogotá was a military occupation of the Banana Zone. The soldiers themselves were eventually put to work cutting and shipping banana bunches as strikebreakers. In spite of repressive laws and constant intimidation the workers stood fast, and on 5 December the government declared a state of siege.

That night a few hundred workers and their families assembled in the central plaza at Ciénaga, a town located some thirty miles north of Aracataca. At 1 A.M., General Carlos Cortés Vargas sent an army detachment to make a show of strength at the plaza. The state of siege announcement was read out loud to the strikers, and they were given five minutes to disperse. The five minutes ticked by, and they were given just one more. And finally a massive barrage of gun fire broke out.[20] The proprietor of a nearby hotel heard someone screaming "¡AY MI MADRE!" (a common Spanish exclamation, roughly equivalent to "Oh my God!").[21] Several witnesses reported having seen the bodies thrown into trucks, which then headed toward the sea. A few months later, it would be revealed that the Fruit Company had been directly paying off the military, lodging the officers in hotel rooms and sending complimentary beer, food, and cigarettes to the grunts.[22]

The massacre was followed by a reign of terror. Hundreds of labor leaders were arrested—a railroad foreman would recall having been on a fourteen-car train, filled with detained workers and headed toward Aracataca. Concerning casualties for the entire strike, General Cortés Vargas would cite a figure of forty dead and one hundred wounded, whereas Alberto Castrillón calculated four hundred dead in the plaza alone, and for the strike a total of fifteen hundred dead and three thousand wounded.[23] Shortly thereafter, a young Liberal representative named Jorge Eliécer Gaitán would promote hearings about the affair and climax his now-celebrated congressional investigation with an eloquent philippic denouncing the scale of the reprisals and also the inordinate power of United Fruit. (Gaitán was to become the most legendary politician in Colombia's entire history and would surely have attained the presidency had he not been gunned down in public by a Conservative assassin in 1948.) Among Gaitán's witnesses in the 1929 hearings was the treasurer of Aracataca, Nicolás R. Márquez, maternal grandfather of the baby boy Gabriel García Márquez.[24]

In this recounting of the events of 1928, I have largely restricted myself to the material retained and elaborated upon by García Márquez in *One Hundred Years of Solitude*. Here are a few initial examples from the labor side.

"The workers demanded that they not be obligated to cut and load bananas on Sundays" (275). They protest against "the lack of sanitary facilities
in their living quarters, the nonexistence of medical facilities," and their
"not being paid in real money but in scrip, which was good only to buy Virginia hams in the company comissaries" (278).

At first, management's tactic is—physical evasion.

> As soon as he found out about the agreement, Mr. Brown hitched his luxu-
> rious glassed-in coach to the train and disappeared from Macondo along
> with the more prominent representatives of his company. Nonetheless,
> some workers found one of them the following Saturday in a brothel and
> they made him sign a copy of the sheet with the demands while he was
> naked with the women who had helped to entrap him. The mournful
> lawyers showed in court that that man had nothing to do with the com-
> pany and in order that no one doubt their arguments they had him jailed as
> an imposter. Later on, Mr. Brown was surprised traveling incognito in a
> third-class coach and they made him sign another copy of the demands. On
> the following day he appeared before the judges with his hair dyed black
> and speaking flawless Spanish. The lawyers showed that the man was not
> Mr. Jack Brown, the superintendent of the banana company, born in
> Prattville, Alabama, but a harmless vendor of medicinal plants, born in Ma-
> condo and baptized there with the name of Dagoberto Fonseca.

What García Márquez has done here is to take the real-life manager
Thomas Bradshaw's attempted escape (as we saw reported by Alberto Castrillón) and then (1) magically elaborate the episode with the passing reference to Mr. Brown's glassed-in coach, (2) alter the capture of Thomas
Bradshaw during an automobile purchase, to the surprise entrapment of a
supposed imposter by some pro-labor prostitutes, (3) invent the incident of
Mr. Brown being nabbed in a third-class railroad car, and (4) further add
the fantastical courtroom exorcisms concerning the identity of Mr. Brown.

In higher court, García Márquez's six lawyers skillfully argue that the
workers' demand "lacked all validity for the simple reason that the company did not have, never had had, and never would have any workers in its
service because they were all hired on a temporary and occasional basis"
(280). Agreeing with this position, the court solemnly decrees that "the
workers did not exist."

In the wake of the martial law declaration, there arrive three army
regiments to cut and ship the bananas and thereby break the strike, and
the union leader José Arcadio Segundo is thrown in jail. The massacre
order is signed by General Carlos Cortés Vargas (García Márquez thus re-

tains the full name), and the protesters are given five minutes to disperse. At the outset of the slaughter, someone cries out, "Aaaay, mi madre!" (rendered as "Aaaaagh, Mother" in Rabassa's translation). García Márquez replaces the multiple trucks sighted by witnesses with his mysterious two-hundred-car train seen only by José Arcadio Segundo. Of the figures being debated with regard to casualties, the novelist seems simply to have chosen the highest of them all, the three thousand wounded cited by the strike organizer Alberto Castrillón.

To this combined historical-fictional account I wish to add an experience of my own. In August 1982 I visited García Márquez's original hometown of Aracataca. During my few hours' stay, I saw certain basic realities from up close, for example the two-block trek leading from the local church to the town cemetery, strikingly similar to the street to be walked by the stout-hearted woman at the end of García Márquez's powerful short story "Tuesday Siesta." It was a sultry, noisy lunch hour when I strolled down that road, and as I entered the cemetery the first gravestones I noticed were for Mercedes and Ester Ternera, the family name of Pilar Ternera, the erotic and freewheeling madam in *One Hundred Years of Solitude*.[25]

But my "Macondian" experience would reach a kind of climax when the youthful General Secretary of the town introduced me to an elderly retiree, who for years had worked as a timekeeper (he used the English word) for United Fruit. His brothers had also been Company employees, and he remembered with great wistfulness the glory days of Banana prosperity, when there was lots of money to spare and folks would dance the native *cumbia* with peso bills burning away in their upheld hands.

I asked him what he thought about the strikers. This is what he answered. "Look, those people only caused problems and ruined everything. And let me tell you, all that stuff about massacres or whatever, its all just a story. Lies. It never happened. The most *I* heard of was two guys shot. Look, if there really were all those dead, then you tell me, where'd they dump the corpses?" Thus spoke the senior citizen, in those words more or less, and at that point I became especially aware of the extent to which García Márquez works from reality. Finally, as a capstone to these symbioses between history and fiction, I must make an observation regarding García Márquez's prophetic strain. In 1972, Senator Claiborne Pell (D-R.I.) revealed that, for twenty-five years, the Department of Defense had been pursuing weather modification research and moreover, that, since 1967, in order "to reduce trafficability along infiltration routes," the U.S. Armed Forces had been seeding clouds to cause rains along the so-called Ho Chi Minh trail in Laos.[26]

To a certain degree, the Banana strike and military repression are to the history and literature of Colombia what the Napoleonic invasion and retreat were to the history and literature of Russia. In both cases, one is faced with great events that bring to mind noble abstractions such as national sovereignty but that also have to do with matters so basic as the lives, sufferings, and survival of entire peoples. In the aftermath of these events there arise new, liberalizing elements within each society (Decembrists in Russia, Gaitán in Colombia), its consensus shaken by the harsh deeds of a more developed, more prosperous foreign invader. And, what for us matters most, those historic events play a key role in two panoramic novels, one by Tolstoy and another by García Márquez.

There is today in Ciénaga's central plaza an impressive memorial to the victims of the United Fruit massacre, a monumental fifty-foot statue of an Afro-Colombian field worker, machete in hand. For simple reasons of accessibility, few non-Colombians will ever set eyes on that commemorative sculpture. But millions worldwide have read and will read the chapter depicting the strike and repression in *One Hundred Years of Solitude*. Most readers of classic novels know that Napoleon Bonaparte invaded Russia. Perhaps some day they will also know that an American agribusiness firm invaded Colombia and that the massacre in Macondo isn't "all just a story."

Notes

1. In Colombia, the Conservatives have traditionally been a centralizing force, whereas the Liberals have consistently struggled for regional autonomy. In practice, however, the differences between them sometimes tend to get blurred.

2. Gabriel García Márquez, *One Hundred Years of Solitude*, trans. Gregory Rabassa (New York: Avon Books, 1971). Though in this edition the novel ends on a page numbered 383, the actual text of the book does not begin until p. 11.

3. César Vallejo, *El tungsteno* (Madrid: Editorial Cenit, 1931).

4. All three trans. Gregory Rabassa (New York: Seymour Lawrence/Delacorte, respectively, 1968, 1971, and 1973).

5. One such rare dissenting opinion is that of Alexander Coleman, "Beyond *One Hundred Years of Solitude*," *New Boston Review*, January 1977, p. 22. Coleman believes the Banana Company portions to be aesthetically inferior, on the grounds that the workers' strike and military massacre present "a catastrophic conflict in tone" with the rest of the book. "It is as if a chapter from *The Grapes of Wrath* were intercalated into the *Amadis of Gaul*."

6. Among the few works that examine the Banana strike, one can cite the

following: Zavala (in this volume), Mena (1972), and Janes (1984). (See Selected Bibliography, at the end of this volume.)

7. All page references will be provided within the body of the text.

8. As García Márquez observed to me, "The Yankees are depicted the way the local people saw them. . . ." See the interview in this volume.

9. "He spoke Oxford English." Miguel Angel Asturias, *Strong Wind*, p. 31.

10. Ibid., p. 92.

11. In the original, Mr. Brown's alleged comment is in standard, correct Spanish: "Será cuando escampe. Mientras dure la lluvia, suspendemos toda clase de actividades." Gabriel García Márquez, *Cien años de soledad* (Buenos Aires: Editorial Sudamericana, 1969), p. 262.

12. In García Márquez's own words to me, "That sequence sticks closely to the facts of the United Fruit strike of 1928. . . . The only exaggeration is in the number of dead, though it does fit the proportions of the novel. So instead of hundreds dead, I upped it to thousands." See the interview in this volume.

13. Miguel Urrutia, *The Development of the Colombian Labor Movement* (New Haven: Yale University Press, 1969), p. 99. Charles David Kepner, Jr., and Jay Henry Soothill, *The Banana Empire: A Case Study of Economic Imperialism* (New York: Vanguard, 1935), p. 290.

14. Urrutia, p. 22.

15. Ibid.

16. Ibid., p. 102.

17. Kepner and Soothill, p. 329.

18. Ibid., p. 319; Urrutia, p. 99.

19. Alberto Castrillón, *120 días bajo el terror militar* (Bogotá: Editorial Tupac Amaru, 1974), p. 33. Translation mine. Emphasis in the original.

20. Urrutia, p. 105.

21. Anon., *1928: La masacre en las bananeras* (Bogotá: Ediciones Libres, 1972), p. 120. This pamphlet is a transcript of Jorge Eliécer Gaitán's 1929 hearings before the Colombian congress.

22. Kepner and Soothill, p. 327.

23. Ibid., p. 329.

24. *1928: La masacre*, pp. 47–48.

25. For an account of that visit, see Bell-Villada, "Journey to Macondo . . . " in Selected Bibliography.

26. Joseph Hanlon, "Military Rainmaking," *The Phoenix* (Boston), June 7, 1972, p. 20.

The Dark Side of Magical Realism

Science, Oppression, and Apocalypse in One Hundred Years of Solitude

BRIAN CONNIFF

◆　　◆　　◆

IN CRITICISM OF THE LATIN AMERICAN NOVEL, "magical realism" has typically been described as an impulse to create a fictive world that can somehow compete with the "insatiable fount of creation" that is Latin America's actual history.[1] This concept of magical realism received perhaps its most influential endorsement in the Nobel Prize acceptance speech of Gabriel García Márquez. The famous Colombian novelist began this speech, suggestively enough, with an account of the "meticulous log" kept by Magellan's navigator, Antonia Pigafetta. In the course of this fateful exploration of the "Southern American continent," the imaginative Florentine recorded such oddities as "a monstrosity of an animal with the head and ears of a mule, the body of a camel, the hooves of a deer, and the neigh of a horse" (207). In the course of his Nobel speech, García Márquez recorded many less imaginative but equally improbable facts—"in the past eleven years twenty million Latin American children have died before their second birthday. Nearly one hundred and twenty thousand have disappeared as a consequence of repression. . . . A country created from all these Latin Americans in exile or enforced emigration would have a larger population than Norway" ("Solitude of Latin America" 208, 209)—on and on, as if he were trying to combat a plague of amnesia.

In such a "disorderly reality," García Márquez explained, the "poets and beggars, musicians and prophets, soldiers and scoundrels" of Colombia had been forced to respond to one of the saddest and most productive challenges in modern literature: "the want of conventional resources to make our life credible" (208–209). Fortunately, conventional resources were not everything. So, according to conventional wisdom, "magical realism" was born, offering the type of hope that García Márquez tried to provide, in that famous speech, when he said that the writer can somehow "bring light to this very chamber with his words" (208). Perhaps magical realism might allow the writer to create in his work a "minor utopia," like the one inhabited by Amaranta Úrsula and the next to last Aureliano at the end of *One Hundred Years of Solitude,* a fictive order that might somehow, like the birth of a child, affirm life in the face of the most brutal oppression. It was a novelistic act analogous to pulling a rabbit, or a child with a tail of a pig, out of a hat. It was magic.

Needless to say, critics have been quick to make use of such a powerful precept. "Magical realism" has typically been seen as the redemption of fiction in the face of a reality that is still becoming progressively more disorderly. But some critics have noted that the term, as it has most often been used, has always lent itself to certain simplifications. Most important, it has sometimes served as "an ideological stratagem to collapse many different kinds of writing, and many different political perspectives, into one single, usually escapist, concept" (Martin 102). Still, the overall optimism needs further qualification. In fact, there is another side of "magical realism," just as there is another side of magic. Not only can the conjuror make rabbits and flowers and crazed revolutionaries appear instantly, but he can also make them disappear, just as instantly. Although critics have not been quick to notice, García Márquez also sensed this darker side of magical realism. Unlike his "master" "William Faulkner thirty-two years before, he could not "refuse to admit the end of mankind." Apocalypse, he was forced to admit, had become "for the first time in the history of humanity . . . simply a scientific possibility" ("Solitude of Latin America" 211). By the end of *One Hundred Years of Solitude,* apocalypse had become, perhaps for the first time in the history of the novel, just one more calamity on "this planet of misfortune" (211). When apocalypse does occur, García Márquez suggested, it will be pervaded, like so many events toward the end of *One Hundred Years of Solitude,* by a strange air of eternal repetition. It will be only the logical conclusion of the progress already brought by "advanced" ideas. In the disorderly modern world, magical realism is not merely an expression of hope; it is also a "resource" that can depict such a "scientific possibility." That is, it can depict events strange enough, and oppressive enough, to make apocalypse appear not only credible but inevitable.

On the first page of *One Hundred Years of Solitude,* such a strange event occurs, an event that will recur, over and over, like the ceaseless repetition—of names and incest, solitude and nostalgia, madness and failed revolutions—that haunts the house of Buendía: the gypsies come to Macondo. For a long time, they will come every year, always "with an uproar of pipes and kettledrums," and always with new inventions, until the wars make such trips too dangerous, and the natives become too indifferent; but their first appearance is the most impressive, and the most ominous. They first appear in a distant past, "when the world was so recent that many things lacked names, and in order to indicate them it was necessary to point" (11). Into this "primitive world" the gypsies bring an omen of the future, an invention of great wonder and potential: the magnet.

Melquíades, the "heavy gypsy with the untamed beard," calls this invention "the eighth wonder of the learned alchemists of Macedonia" (11). He drags it around, from house to house so that everyone can see pots and pans fly through the air, nails and screws pull out of the woodwork, long-lost objects reappear. Like any great missionary of progress, Melquíades is concerned with enlightening the natives, so he also provides an explanation: "Things have a life of their own. . . . It's simply a matter of waking up their souls" (11).

But José Arcadio Buendía, the first citizen of Macondo, has an idea of his own. Prophet, patriarch, inventor, and murderer—José Arcadio is not a man to forsake progress. He is, in fact, "the most enterprising man ever to be seen in the village" (18). His "unbridled imagination" often takes him, along with anyone he can convince to follow, "beyond the genius of nature, and even beyond miracles and magic," just as he once led a handful of men and women on an "absurd journey" in search of the sea, the journey that resulted in the founding of their inland village (31–32). Confronted with the marvelous magnet, José Arcadio feels that it is necessary to discover a useful application. Whereas Melquíades is content to mystify the natives, José Arcadio must look, with a wonder of his own, toward the future. He comes up with an idea that is portentious, just as his technological imagination will be fatal. Through a process no one else seems to understand, he calculates that it must be possible to use this marvelous invention "to extract gold from the bowels of the earth" (12). A "brilliant idea," to a man like José Arcadio, should translate into a well-deserved profit.[2] Even though Melquíades is honest and tells him that this idea will not work, José Arcadio begins to search for "gold enough and more to pave the floors of the house." He trades in "his mule and a pair of goats for the two magnetized ingots" and explores "every inch of the region"; but he fails to find anything he considers valuable. All he finds is "a suit of fifteenth-century armor that had all of its pieces soldered together with rust and inside of which there was the hollow resonance of an enormous stone-filled gourd" (12). Searching for gold, José Arcadio finds the remains of Spanish imperialism.

The following March, when the gypsies next appear in Macondo, they bring a telescope and a magnifying glass, "the latest discovery of the Jews of Amsterdam." Once again, Melquíades provides an explanation—"Science has eliminated distance"—and, not surprisingly, he once again mystifies the natives (12). His theory of the elimination of distance, like his theory of magnetic souls, is a fusion of chicanery and "advanced" science—and it is just as prophetic as José Arcadio's accidental discovery of the suit of armor. Even though the natives, José Arcadio in particular, are unable to understand the principles of Melquíades' discoveries, they are all too willing to assume that it is because they are not "wordly" or "advanced" enough. Melquíades's perspective, unlike theirs, is "global"; he has circled the world many times; he seems to know "what there was on the other side of things" (15). Perhaps he even believes he is being honest when he tries to comfort them by promising that such a perspective will soon be available to everyone, through the wonders of science, with no disruption of domestic tranquility, without the inconvenience of travel: "In a short time, man will be able to see what is happening in any place of the world without leaving his own house" (12).

But Melquíades's "theoretical" approach to science, just like José Arcadio's "practical" approach, suffers from a fatal blindness. Both of them are willing to assume that science is essentially democratizing. They do not understand that José Arcadio's misdirected discovery of the rusted armor, and its "calcified skeleton," has already brought to Macondo a vision of "progress" that is both mystifying and applied—but not democratizing. Years later, after the prolonged senility and death of José Arcadio, after the innumerable deaths of Melquíades, Macondo will eventually see the outside world—which José Arcadio tried so hard to discover, which Melquíades leads them to believe he knows completely—and science will be responsible. But, by then, the chicanery of the gypsies will only be displaced by more sophisticated and more determined exploitation.

For the moment, however, José Arcadio is simply inspired by the magnifying glass, so he allows his fantasies to transport him, once again, closer to an "outside" reality that he badly misunderstands. After watching another of the gypsies' demonstrations, in which the magnifying glass is used to set a pile of hay on fire, he immediately decides that this invention has even greater potential than the magnet because it can prove useful as an "instrument of war." Ignoring the protests of Melquíades, and ignoring the legitimate fears of his wife, José Arcadio is compelled, once again, to invest in an invention. This time, he uses a more progressive currency, the two magnetized ingots and three "colonial coins." His enthusiasm prevents him from noticing that his currency is being debased. Many years later, gold, and even colonial coins, will be superseded by the banana company's scrip, whish is "good only to buy Virginia ham in the company commissaries" (278); but José Arcadio will never be able to understand how the debasement of the currency helps support the domination of his people.[3] He is happy to dream of progress, to experiment, to burn himself, to almost set the house on fire, and to finally complete "a manual of startling instructional clarity and an irresistible power of conviction" (13)—thus linking, for the first time in the history of Macondo, and without noticing, scientific discovery and political rhetoric.

Then, in his zeal to improve his village, José Arcadio makes the greatest of his many misjudgments: he sends his manual to "the military authorities" (13). With it, he sends all the scientific evidence he considers appropriate, "numerous descriptions of his experiments and several pages of explanatory sketches" (13). He is determined to leave no doubt that he is ready to do his part for the perfection of military technology: if called upon, he will even "train them himself in the complicated art of solar war" (13). Nothing happens. At least, nothing happens in Macondo. But it is clearly not José Arcadio's fault that the government fails to respond. He has even anticipated Star Wars.

José Arcadio never quite recovers from his disappointment at having been denied the excitement of futuristic wars. Melquíades tries to console him with more "new" discoveries: an astrolabe, a compass, a sextant, and the alchemical equipment that Colonel Aureliano Buendía will later use to make the little gold fishes that will ultimately, and ironically, become the symbol of failed subversion.[4] José Arcadio does revive his spirits just long enough to prove that "The earth is round line an orange" (14). By this time, however, his dedication to science only convinces Úrsula, and most everyone else, that he has lost what little was left of his mind. Later, when confronted with the marvel of ice, he will imagine an entire city constructed entirely of the fantastic substance; he will create a memory machine in an attempt to combat Macondo's plague of somnambulistic insomnia; he will spend sleepless nights trying to apply the principle of the pendulum to oxcarts, to harrows, "to everything that was useful when put into motion"; he will even try to execute a daguerreotype of God—but he will continue to lose faith in the reality of his fantasies. So his family must fight a losing battle, struggling to keep him from "being dragged by his imagination into a delirium from which he would not recover" (80). Finally, they all have to be content with his strange senility, interrupted only by prophecies in Latin.

The tragedy of José Arcadio Buendía is that his infatuation with science allows the government to exploit a passion that was, initially, a "spirit of social initiative." His first creations were the traps and cages he used to fill all the houses in the village with birds. He made sure that the houses were placed "in such a way that from all of them one could reach the river and draw water with the same effort" (18); he saw that no house received more sun than another. He was, from the start, a type of "model citizen," useful to his people. It is the appearance of "advanced" science in Macondo that makes him, virtually overnight, useful to authority: "That spirit of social initiative disappeared in a short time, pulled away by the fever of magnets, the astronomical calculations, the dreams of transmutation, and the urge to discover the wonders of the world" (18). That is how his faith in progress, and the faith of his people, is betrayed.

But more important than José Arcadio's tragic disappointment, more important than his invested dubloons—which Melquíades returns in any case—even more important than his final senility, is the fact that he resolves his debate with the gypsy. Throughout the rest of the novel, scientific discoveries will continue to serve two purposes: science will mystify the citizens of Macondo and will lead to their exploitation. The novel's arresting first sentence suggests that these two purposes have always been inseparable: "Many years later, as he faced the firing squad, Colonel Aureliano Buendia was to remember that distant afternoon when his father took him to discover ice" (11). But, perhaps, if his father had avoided such discoveries, Aureliano Buendía might never have wound up before a firing squad of his own government.

The equally arresting ending of the novel is a full-scale denial of José Arcadio's ill-begotten dream. The novel's "apocalyptic closure" is a denial of progress, as conceived by either the scientist or the politician, and a momentary glimpse of the world that might have been, if the great patriarch had not been so carried away with his idea of the future—if he had tried, instead, to understand history. Only Amaranta Úrsula and Aureliano, the last adults in the line of the Buendías, see "the uncertainty of the future" with enough demystified clarity to forsake progress,"to turn their hearts toward the past"; only they are not exploited (375). Their child, Aureliano, is "the only one in a century who had been engendered with love"—but by then it is too late (378). They cannot enjoy their primal, "dominant obsessions" for long; they cannot remain "floating in an empty universe where the only everyday and eternal reality was love" (374).[5] They are confronted, instead, with an end that is as ridiculous as their family's beginning: "The first of the line is tied to a tree and the last is being eaten by the ants" (381). The world has not progressed one bit. In fact, the key to understanding the present, and all of history, is not in the science so valued by José Arcadio but in Melquíades's ancient manuscripts, written in Sanskrit. Macondo is finally devoured by the "prehistoric hunger" of the ants, then obliterated by "the wrath of the biblical hurricane" (383).

Because he is the man of technology, the man of science-as-progress, who brings together, more than anyone else, mystification and exploitation, José Arcadio is never able to foresee this end, just as he is never able to turn his obsessive nature toward love, just as he is never able to admit the kind of association that occurs to Colonel Aureliano Buendía when he faces the firing squad. He never understands, as Úrsula does, that time is circular. He never really pays any attention to the suit of armor from the past, so he never learns that the rusted coat of armor anticipates the soldiers and machine guns that will support the banana company, that the imperialism of the past prefigures the imperialism of the future. In this sense, Úrsula is capable of learning; José Arcadio is not. Úrsula learns, at least, that her schemes for prosperity have set her up to be betrayed. Ultimately, José Arcadio cannot understand any of these things because his view of the world shares too much with the oppressors who will take over his village in the delirium of banana fever; in other words, whether he realizes it or not, his horizon is determined by the interests he serves. As John Incledon has written, José Arcadio's fascination with scientific inventions—as sources of wealth, power, control—"reveals a frantic desire to grasp and manage his world" (53).

The difference between José Arcadio and the other residents of Macondo—who think he is crazy, when they are not following him—is merely that he is a useful citizen of the active type, whereas they are useful citizens of the passive type. The only exceptions are Colonel Aureliano Buendía and his men, but their revolutions always take place outside of Macondo. José Arcadio is doomed because he has convinced himself that "Right across the river there are all kinds of magical instruments while we keep on living like donkeys" (17). His greatest fear is that he might die "without receiving the benefits of science" (21). The village is doomed by the same belief that magic—in particular, advanced technology—is valuable in itself, uplifting, and the privileged possession of the outside world. Once the people believe that science, like all uplifting things, must come from elsewhere, that the outside world is better because it is more "advanced," then imperialism becomes much easier to justify. The gypsies' "discoveries" are always excessively foreign. Later, the residents of Macondo easily convince themselves of the innate superiority of Italian music and French sexual techniques. The Crespi brothers' business in mechanical toys, aided by their foreign looks and foreign manners, develops into a "hothouse of fantasy" (108).

If the government had only understood this inclination when they received José Arcadio's manual on solar war, it could have saved itself a lot of time. But José Arcadio's plans did not convince it that Macondo was a regular hothouse of applied fantasy; in this sense, it did not fully appreciate its "natural resources" until it learned from Mr. Brown and the Banana Company.

For their part, the villagers never understand what all these foreign wonders do to them. Like José Arcadio when he bumps into the suit of armor, they let their infatuation with the promises of the future render them incapable of uncovering their past: "Dazzled by so many and such marvelous inventions, the people of Macondo did not know where their amazement began" (211). They merely enjoy, with more moderation than José Arcadio, the excitement of closing the "technical gap" that has separated them from the "outside world."6 The bearers of science are always exoticized. At the same time, the villagers' "primitive" past is rendered so insignificant that it is not worth remembering. To them, the important things have always happened somewhere else—and their future will be determined by somebody else.

Many years later, when the government massacres thousands of civilians in order to crush a union strike, no one except José Arcadio Segundo, great-grandson of the first José Arcadio, will even be capable of remembering "the insatiable and methodical shears of the machine guns" (284). As for the rest, they will remember only what they have been taught to remember by the technocrats and by the government that supports them: "Nothing has happened in Macondo, nothing has ever happened, and nothing ever will happen. This is a happy town" (287). In this "modern" world, things always happen somewhere else. The Banana Company, with the help of the government, is raising the village's standard of living, so it must be benevolent. It cannot be responsible for a massacre. The irony that José Arcadio Segundo has the name of his great-grandfather is just one of the novel's, and history's countless circles, one more indication that, despite their "progress"—or, in fact, because of their "progress"—the oppressed have been unable to learn what is really important.

The first José Arcadio has a quality of many characters in García Márquez' fiction: he is so strange, so absurd, that it seems he must be real. José Arcadio Segundo is, in this sense, his precise opposite. He sees the events of the government massacre with a clarity that suggests he is unreal. So when government troops enter the room where he has given up hiding, they cannot see him, even though they are looking right at the place where he believes he is sitting. Opposition, to such a government, must be invisible. It makes no difference that they did not actually kill him, that he jumped off the train on which the corpses had been "piled up in the same way in which they transported bunches of bananas" (284). He is merely left alone, once again, to decipher Melquíades's ancient manuscripts.

In the end, however, José Arcadio Segundo shares something important with the first José Arcadio. "The events that would deal Macondo its fatal blow"—the strike, the public unrest, the massacre, and its aftermath—take shape at the precise moment that the train begins to control the events of the novel (272). Transportation, in Colombia, has inescapable links to the desire for "progress." Auerliano Triste's initial sketch of Macondo's railroad "was a direct descendent of the plans with which José Arcadio Buendia had illustrated his project for solar warfare." Aureliano Triste believed that the railroad was necessary "not only for the modernization of his business but to link the town with the rest of the world" (209). Only Úrsula, who had seen so much of the suffering that results from such schemes, understood that "time was going in a circle"; only she knew enough to fear modernization that came from "the rest of the world" (209).

The train also allows Fernanda to travel back to the dismal, distant city of her birth. She has never stopped thinking of the villagers of Macondo as barbarians; and she is so intent on her desire to sequester her daughter in a convent, away from the "savagery" of the Caribbean zone, that she does not even see "the shady, endless banana groves on both sides of the tracks," or "the oxcarts on the dusty roads loaded down with bunches of bananas," or "the skeleton of the Spanish galleon" (273). At this point it is clear that she has failed in her attempt to colonize Macondo with the manners and rituals of the inland cities; but her "internal colonialism" has been superseded, without her noticing it, by the brutal imperialism of the Banana Company. When Fernanda returns to Macondo, the train is protected by policemen with guns. Macondo's "fatal blow" is under way. José Arcadio

Segundo has already organized the workers in a strike against the Banana Company, and he has already been "pointed out as the agent of an international conspiracy against public order" (276). Fernanda's two rides on the train are opposite in direction, but tell of a single effect: "civilization," modernization, and progress are finally assured, even in Macondo—if not with "proper" manners and gold chamberpots, then with guns.

The train is, if anything, even more symbolic of this "progress" in Colombia than it is in Macondo. Under the dictatorship of General Rafael Reyes (1904–1909), "British capital was, for the first time, invested in Colombian railways in substantial amounts" (Safford 232). Not surprisingly, this period saw the completion of the railway between Bogota and the Magdalena River; "Macondo" was irreversibly linked to the "outside world." But, of course, that was only the start: "As the transportation improvements of 1904 to 1940 began to knit together a national market, significant innovations occurred in other economic sectors," and it was the nationalization of Colombia's railways that made many such "innovations" possible (Safford 232–234). In the period of the strikes against the United Fruit Company, in particular, reorganization of the railroads was a central issue of American diplomacy in Colombia. The National City Bank and the First National Bank of Boston refused to extend short-term credits until a railroad bill was passed. By 1931, they demanded, in their negotiations with the Colombian government, an even greater control: "that the railroad system be taken out of the hands of the government and placed under the direction of professional management" (Randall 64). In his description of the banana strike, García Márquez makes the implications obvious: the same trains that send bananas and profits to the north transport the murdered bodies to the sea. There—both the government and the "professional management" hope—they will disappear, even from history.

The repeated follies of José Arcadio—like the name and hereditary stubbornness of his great-grandson, like Úrsula's pronouncements, like the end of the novel—are attempts on the part of García Márquez to assert that history is, in some sense, circular. The "primitive" past of Latin America, like that of Macondo, might have provided countless omens of Colombia's future, if anyone had paid attention—that is, if anyone had avoided the delirium of progress. From the first half of the nineteenth century, the combination of foreigners and trains was devastating, in Argentina, in Chile, in Guatemala, in Mexico, and in Uruguay. With their public services, especially the railroads, controlled by foreigners, or by governments serving foreigners—first from Paraguay, then principally from Britain, then principally from the United States—these countries faced extraordinary military expenditures, "a frenzied increase in imports," and growing debts, subject to inflationary manipulation. In Galeano's words, they mortgaged their futures in advance, moving away from economic freedom and political sovereignty" (216–219). Later, in Colombia, the tendency to see railroads as "forerunners of progress" would be just one more failure to remember. For García Márquez, such an assertion of history's circularity is not merely a matter of philosophical speculation; it is a calculated attempt to make the outrages of oppression, ancient and recent, visible again; it is an attempt to make Colombian history credible.

After the massacre, when the train from which he has escaped slips off into the night, "with its nocturnal and stealthy velocity," on its way to dump more than three thousand murdered bodies into the ocean, José Arcadio Segundo cannot see it in the darkness; the last things he sees are "the dark shapes of the soldiers with their emplaced machine guns" (285).[7] Perhaps José Arcadio Segundo came to understand such progress as his great-grandfather could not, and perhaps that is why the government's search squad could not see *him*. For men indoctrinated by such a government, opposition must not exist.

For such men, the past must disappear. That is why they seem so improbable, and so real. That is why a "resource" like "magical realism" is needed to depict them. And that is why the novel's famous "apocalyptic closure" is not only credible but also anticlimactic. Apocalypse is merely the darkest side of "magical realism," in which the "magic" and the "realism" are most completely fused, in which the most unimaginable event is the most inevitable. The "biblical hurricane" that "exiles" Macondo "from the memory of men" is "full of voices from the past, the murmurs of ancient geraniums, sighs of disenchantment that preceded the most tenacious nostalgia" (383). The ceaseless repetitions of the novel lead to this final conviction that apocalypse is only one more "scientific possibility," which the "primitive world" understands only after it is too late. Apocalypse is only the logical consequence of imperialist oppression, supported by science. The "events" that bring about the end of Macondo were actually determined much earlier, even before the trains came. The end began the first time the gypsies appeared with their foreign discoveries.

Notes

1. Gabriel García Márquez, in "The Solitude of Latin America: Nobel Address, 1982," describes Latin American history as such a fount (208). Gerald Martin provides a detailed and critical summary of this criticism in his essay.

2. I have borrowed this idea from Ariel Dorfman's *The Empire's Old Clothes*: "having a 'brilliant idea' is not only what allows a contestant to win in the game of life. It is also a sign that such a victory is well deserved" (35). In the United States, the belief in such radical insight is one component of our mystification of ideas, in particular our mystification of science. We want to believe that certain people have privileged access to the truth and that they have, therefore, a "natural" authority over those people who lack such insight. Dorfman explains how the government of the United States has tried to cultivate this ideology in Latin America—even through such apparently innocuous vehicles as Donald Duck, the Lone Ranger, and Babar the Elephant—as part of our effort at domination. In *How to Read Donald Duck,* referring to the United States's assistance in the overthrow of the Allende government, Dorfman and Armand Mattelart write: "There were, however, two items which were not blocked: planes, tanks, ships, and technical assistance for the Chilean armed forces; and magazines, TV serials, advertising, and public opinion polls for the Chilean mass media" (9).

3. In his study of nineteenth-century European colonialism, Ralph Schnerb writes of Latin America: "These republics' histories may be said to be that of the economic obligations they incur to the all-absorbing world of European finance," obligations that were quickly exacerbated by "inflation, which produces depreciation of the currency," Eduardo Galeano adds, "The use of debt as an instrument of blackmail is not, as we can see, a recent American invention" (217–218).

4. Perhaps it is no coincidence that Colonel Aureliano Buendía is both the revolutionary and the alchemist—that he is, like José Arcadio Segundo, the heir of both Úrsula's indominability and Melquíades's manuscripts. For the Latin American who would resist domination, a knowledge of transformation, even alchemy, might be much more practical than it would at first appear. Galeano suggests such a connection, at least metaphorically, in his *Open Veins of Latin America,* a book that would be immensely popular in Colombia a few years after its initial publication in 1971: "Our defeat was always implicit in the victory of others; our wealth has always generated our poverty by nourishing the prosperity of others—the empires and their native overseers. In the colonial and neocolonial alchemy, gold changes into scrap metal and food into poison" (12).

5. The final situation of Amaranta Úrsula and Aureliano will become increasingly important as criticism begins to address García Márquez's recent novel, *Love in the Time of Cholera.* As Thomas Pynchon suggests, with some trepidation, in his review of that novel, critics will inevitably ask "how far" that novel, so dominated by love, has departed from the more "political" concerns of *One Hundred Years of Solitude* and *The Autumn of the Patriarch:* "we have come a meaningful distance from Macondo, the magical village in *One Hundred Years of Solitude.* . . . It would be presumptuous to speak of moving 'beyond' *One Hundred Years of Solitude,* but clearly García Márquez

has moved somewhere else, not least into deeper awareness of the ways in which, as Florentino comes to learn, "nobody teaches life anything" (49).

6. I have borrowed the phrase "technical gap," as well as the basic idea of this passage, from Dorfman's reading of Babar the Elephant in *The Empire's Old Clothes*. Of course, there are systems—of ownership, of trade, of education—that keep the gap from actually closing, despite the useful illusion of progress. In this regard see Galeano, especially the section appropriately entitled "The Goddess Technology Doesn't Speak Spanish" (265–268). Dorfman's explanation of the capitalist's equation of childhood and underdevelopment is also worth noting, especially in reference to José Arcadio's later senility. Once he abandons his hope of reaching the "outside world's" level of civilization, José Arcadio destroys his scientific equipment and allows himself to lapse into his "second childhood," to be spoonfed by Úrsula.

7. Later, José Arcadio Segundo would tell little Aureliano his "personal interpretation of what the banana company had meant to Macondo" (322). But no one would want to believe Aureliano, either; "one would have thought that he was telling a hallucinated version, because it was radically opposed to the false one that historians had created and consecrated in the schoolbooks" (322). In *Gabriel García Márquez: Writer of Colombia*, Stephen Minta provides a brief, useful summary of the surviving accounts of the 1928 strike against the United Fruit Company in Cienaga. Accounts differ, of course, in their estimates of the number murdered. Cortes Vargas, who signed the decree that "declared the strikers to be a bunch of hoodlums" and "authorized the army to shoot to kill," and whose name appears unchanged in *One Hundred Years of Solitude,* wrote his own account, in which he claims that only nine were killed. Officially sanctioned accounts typically mention "the menace of Bolshevism." But perhaps the most telling document is a telegram from the Head of the U.S. Legation in Colombia to the U.S. Secretary of State: "I have the honor to report that the Bogota representative of the United Fruit Company told me yesterday that the total number of strikers killed by the Colombian military exceed one thousand" (171).

Works Cited

Dorfman, Ariel. *The Empire's Old Clothes*. Trans. Clark Hansen. New York: Pantheon, 1983.

Dorfman, Ariel, and Armand Mattelart. *How to Read Donald Duck*. Trans. David Kunzle. New York: International General, 1975.

Galeano, Eduardo. *Open Veins of Latin America*. Trans. Cedric Belfrage. New York: Monthly Review, 1973.

García Márquez, Gabriel. *Autumn of the Patriarch*. Trans. Grefory Rabassa. New York: Harper, 1976.

————. *Love in the Time of Cholera*. Trans. Edith Grossman. New York: Knopf, 1988.

————. *One Hundred Years of Solitude*. Trans. Gregory Rabassa. New York: Avon, 1970.

————. "The Solitude of Latin America: Nobel Address 1982." McGuirk and Cardwell. 207–211.

Incledon, John. "Writing and Incest in *One Hundred Years of Solitude*." *Critical Perspectives on Gabriel García Márquez*. Ed. Bradley A. Shaw and Nora Vera-Godwin. Lincoln: Society of Spanish and Spanish-American Studies, 1986. 51–64.

Martin, Gerald. "On 'Magical' and Social Realism in García Márquez." McGuirk and Cardwell. 95–116.

McGuirk, Bernard, and Richard Cardwell, eds. *Gabriel García Márquez: New Readings*. Cambridge: Cambridge University Press, 1987.

Minta, Stephen. *Gabriel García Márquez: Writer of Colombia*. London: Cape, 1987.

Pynchon, Thomas. "The Heart's Eternal Vow." Review of *Love in the Time of Cholera*, by Gabriel García Márquez. *New York Times Book Review*. 10 April 1988: 1, 47–49.

Randall, Stephen J. *The Diplomacy of Modernization: Colombian-American Relations, 1920–1940*. Toronto: University of Toronto Press, 1976.

Safford, Frank. *The Ideal of the Practical: Colombia's Struggle to Form a Technical Elite*. Austin: University of Texas Press, 1976.

Schnerb, Robert. *Le XIXe siècle: l'apogée de l'expansion européenne, 1815–1914*. Paris: Gallimard, 1968.

Streams Out of Control

The Latin American Plot

CARLOS RINCÓN

◆　◆　◆

> Now more than ever, and in the future more than
> now, everybody's personal identity, and every col-
> lective hope, depend on complex mediation be-
> tween the local and the global.
>
> —Marshall Berman

Booksellers in front of the University of Teheran hawk
their wares heaped on tables in a bazaar-like atmosphere: *"One Hundred
Years of Solitude /* one hundred pages for one hundred *tuman."* In the vast
spaces of what used to be the Soviet Union, in Samarkanda and in Yerivan,
in Tiblisi and in Alma Ata, Gabriel García Márquez's novel circulated in
magnitisdat, clandestine recorded cassettes that were the oral version of the
written *samisdat,* unofficial, counterofficial. This occurred at a time when
scarcely anyone was noticing that the Soviet Union, with its noncapitalist
version of modernity, was a multiple and extremely varied conglomerate
of different peoples, ethnic groups, and civilizations in the Euro-Asiatic
space. Before *perestroika* came on the scene, when the incompatibility between political "opening" and a one-party system, between the modernizing process of economic reform and the structures of real socialism, became somewhat apparent, the texts of García Márquez had a special
destiny in Moscow itself. Transformed by the *magnitisdat* into a multiplicity
of voices, they occupied their own space for half a decade, outside the opposition between hagiography and demonology, shielded from the tumultuous process of decanonization and the end of personality cults. In spite
of millions of official editions, the *magnitisdat* copies commanded the same
hefty price as the cassettes of the legendary poet-singer Vladimir Vysorsky.

Under the predominance of the Russian tongue, what symbolic demands and necessities could lead to the intercultural transfer of such a
highly specialized written product to its oral restoration to a community
(read out loud or recited from memory), thanks to chromium dioxide
tape and electronic acoustic reproduction? And, after the Iranian Revolution and its overwhelming consequences, would it be legitimate to enter
into this calculation economic resources, techniques of printing, the logic
of a book's internal organization (title, number of pages, chapter divisions)
as part of a will to dialogue, a recognition of the non-Islamic (i.e., something distinct from the inability for self-representation, self-understand-
ing, and self-awareness that is the key theme of Orientalist discourse?)[1] The
possibilities of appropriating these texts according to the specific codes of
perception and deciphering of the postcolonial Muslim world and those
of a multiethnic and multinational state whose collapse no one foresaw
present a decisive fact. These dissimilar recipients possessed cultural and
symbolic resources that would be revalued and activated, thanks to a
great transfer of South-South cultural capital. Questions of working-in-
representation come into play in this transference, in postcolonial images
and languages, as Gayatri Chakravorty Spivak formulates in her question"
"Can the Subaltern Speak?" Because of this relationship, local cultures
that depend on the historical condition of place and find themselves included in and marked by the process of cultural globalization have their
own authority over that very process.

The presence of Jorge de Burgos in the epistemological-detective novel
The Name of the Rose, and just a few years later as a blind man named
"Borges" in the postcolonial fiction of the Magrheb author Tahar ben
Jalloun, evinces a double process: the delegitimazation of the master-code
parallel to the proliferation of *petite histoire* that accompanies the crisis of
metanarratives and the role of Latin American fiction in articulating these
phenomena in the context of the literature of the 1980s. The reception of
the texts of García Márquez in the United States is a crucial index to the
fragmentation, dissociation, dislocation, and cultural decentralization that
crystallize in this reception and that are detectable in books ranging from
Williams Kennedy's *Ironweed,* Alice Walker's *The Color Purple,* Toni Morrison's
Song of Solomon, to John Nichol's *The Milagro Beanfield War* and the visible bor-
rowings from the Colombian novelist in Anne Tyler's *Dinner at the Homesick
Restaurant,* to Paul Theroux's *The Mosquito Coast,* or even John Updike's *The
Coup.* America's supreme metafictionists Robert Coover, John Barth, and,
most especially, Thomas Pynchon (*Vineland*) have notably appropriated
García Márquez's texts. With this appropriation, the metaphorical-

topological images of the position of marginality obtain their own dynamic, which appears as an imaginative strategy demonstrating what the universal system represses—a strategy for putting the margins into the center. The principles of renarrativizing texts to construct new tales and rewriting known and highly codified genres form an element of the streams of cultural capital that also have been direct, in spite of a secular relationship of inequality, toward a South-North flow.

Recent Latin American narrative has become an integral part of the permanent stock and prospective programming of the main European and U.S. publishing houses. Something similar occurs with the more specific product of Latin American television, the *telenovela,* the spread of which in Western Europe coincides with the deregulation of television channels. The Brazilian productions have also obtained popularity in Asia and in Africa south of the Sahara. In 1985, Polish television viewers considered *A escrava Isaura* the best television program of the last decade; in Beijing, during the period when Deng Xiaoping tried "opening up" the country to the outside world, television owners rented out seats in their houses to those wanting to watch *The Tale of the White Slave.*

In the past twenty years, emigration from the countryside to the cities has been much more accelerated in Latin America than in other continents. Seventy percent of Latin America's population now live in cities, and capital cities house between a third and a quarter of the population of their country. Under these conditions, in Latin America the phenomenon of greatest cultural relevance in the 1980s was the change in social life that came with the introduction of new electronic technologies in mass media as part of the general cultural consequences of the technical transformation of social communication. At the same time, Latin American societies also were gradually perceived as part of a cultural market in the process of industrialization and globalization. One of the basic characteristics of this process was the rise of urban cultures without territorial memory, now directly linked to the audiovisual media. This lack of a point of territorial reference is a phenomenon generated in the criss-crossing of action of new technologies and their products, a phenomenon of their influence even when not in use.[2]

The accelerated and amplified expansion of the cities; the drastic change in urban political culture visible at the end of the populist movements; the appearance of television presidents; the transformation of communication and the social imaginary under the action of the media; the ungovernable scenes of catastrophe (ecological disasters, rampant insecurity, epidemics, and the breakdown of public services, etc.); the changes in the use of urban space are among the many items on the agenda of the recent urban process on the subcontinent. Here I am particularly interested in the cultural sphere in the complex, flexible strategies that were negotiated in this decade-long process: the incorporation of large social groups, whose basic cultural capital is so-called *cultura popular*,[3] into the structures of urban life with its implicit access to forms of internationalized consumption. Such strategies and models can basically be characterized as inconsistent with the hierarchical binarism of center versus margin characteristic of the ideological universe of the 1970s, that of Manichean absolute opposites.

Certainly, recent tactics for the selection, adaptation, and refunctionalization of certain products and practices in the international globalization culture provide a substratum of cultural memory. This substratum consists of secular and discontinuous cultural codes characteristic of a heterogeneous cultural tradition of the subcontinent's colonial and national societies. But in the midst of eclectic transactional strategies and mechanisms that incorporate, tame, and adapt heterogeneous fragments of the dominant global cultural regime to the new urban culture of the actual Latin American societies, a specifically contemporaneous mutation can be substantiated. This mutation is related to an aesthetic of excess, discontinuity, and bricolage that manages a mass culture with its ideology of consumption and planned obsolescence.

There are certain ironic and parodic traits of a recycling nature with this new urban culture—multiple manifestations of the politics of diversity in its style of appropriation (decoded and recorded) and in the operations of resemantization that are carried out within this context. This leads to carnavalesque combinations, to some degree democratized in overstimulating pastiches of elements, icons, and even complete sectors of the mass media industry, and more generally to the contemporary capitalist culture with its profit structure. This playful characteristic, with which supposedly fossilized single-cultural identities become unfrozen, expresses the simultaneous heterogeneous Latin American cultural experience of premodern under development of modernity and the reality of postmodernism as a social, political, and cultural configuration.

It is worth emphasizing that this definitory element of jocular disruptive cultural practice, appropriate to today's Latin American urban centers, is also found in the new mixed cultures that have risen from the immigration of "Latinos" to the United States. It is well known that this massive emigration, which has resulted in the Latinamericanization of the United States, particular in the regions of California, Texas, and New York, has led to the creation of the Chicano and Nuyorican cultures. Referring to this type of phenomena, Tzvetan Todorov notes that "the constant interaction of the cultures [leads to] the formation of hybrid cultures."[4] In addition to this formation of mixed cultures, there are extremely varied forms of cultural practices by emigrants for whom neither the ghetto nor the melting pot provides a cultural solution. For them the answer is not legitimization by inclusion or identification with dominant cultural norms, nor a recalcitrant cultural resistance through complicity counter-identification. Instead, a spectrum of responses to the power of institutions and discourses is invoked that constitutes an ambivalently positioned "Latin" subject. This spectrum puts the romance of the Latin-marginal parodically on the scene.

The memories of Esperanza's childhood in the fiction of Sandra Cisneros is an illustration of this key element, also characteristic of a specific cultural form like the Chicano version of rock in its stylistic multiplicity. In rock music, the aesthetic of the cover version has been considered as a democratic principle of intertextuality. In this way it expresses not a "single cultural identity," but rather the "negotiation of mixed or transitional cultural identities."[5] In order to constitute provisional interrelational identities, Chicano rock and roll music (with its mixture of rhythms and Latin American instruments, Mexican songs with blues melody) treats ethnicity "as plastic and openended. For [Chicano rock musicians], ethnicity is as much a dynamic construct as an inherited fact, as much a strategic response to the present as an immutable series of practices and beliefs derived from the past."[6] This form of ethnic minority culture formation plays a crucial role in developing a photo from the unprinted negative of the technoculture, because inclusion of Chicano musicians from the technoculture leads them "to cultivate a sophisticated capacity for ambiguity, Juxtaposition and irony."[7]

Because the question of streams of cultural capital in Latin American societies includes such diverse processes as the South-South transference of symbolic products, and the massive and permanent presence of the media in daily Latin American life (with its imagistic construction of the real, its forms of perception, speech patterns, categories of thought coined by the vast proliferation of images and the transformation of social communication), and because the consideration of these streams demands at least two perspectives (to understand the character of the direction in which it moves and the exchange and negotiations between cultures that it creates), I am going to attempt to map out the situation. One must take into account the demand to escape the subordination of one language, cultural experience, and identity to another.[8] In sections two and three, I will concern myself with the transference and reception of literature in the South and in the North; Latin American *telenovelas* are the subject of the fourth section. In section five, I will reconstruct some of the principal strands of the Latin American urban culture of the 1980s.

In discussing these currents of cultural capital, one must understand that this process has taken place in the course of ten "lost" years characterized by processes of democratization at a time when all existing models of economic development were bankrupt; the exaggerated growth of the informal economy sector; the propagation of neoliberal corrective measures, and attempts to join the world market and embrace its new forms of capital accumulation.

THERE ARE TWO WRITERS whose texts determined, and continue to determine, the image of Latin American fiction projected beyond all geographical, political, and intellectual frontiers: Gabriel García Márquez and Jorge Luis Borges. Having to condense a bit, and considering the enormous amount of cultural resources that have led to a reevaluation of his work, I will limit my comments to García Márquez, whose *One Hundred Years of Solitude*,[9] like the other pivotal works of recent international literature, such as Thomas Pynchon's *V*[10] or Italo Calvino's *If on a Winter's Night a Traveler*,[11] pays tribute to the Lord of the Labyrinth.

Pierre Bourdieu has stressed that a "work" of art exists as a symbolic object given value only if it is received by spectators "capable of recognizing and knowing it as such."[12] At the same time, he distances himself from those who use the notion of literary "institution" to do away with one of the most significant characteristics of the functioning of the literary field: its very low level of institutionality. As shown by the reception of *One Hundred Years of Solitude* in such far-flung and diverse corners of the world ad the People's Republic of China or the Arab-Muslim world, the first thing that must be captured in this reception, at the level of the experience of reading, is an operation of direct or oblique self-recognition by readers. In this manner, after the appearance of the Lebanese translation from the French of *One Hundred Years of Solitude,* in 1981, Abdelkader Rabia wrote:

> To open the pages of the novel in the Arab language is to discover a captivating world, and for the Arab reader, an easy rediscover of the atmosphere of *A Thousand and One Nights,* an admitted source of inspiration for García Márquez, is today, in this second half of the twentieth century, one of the giants of world literature.[13]

The role of the texts of García Márquez in Deng Xiaopings's China in the period of "opening up," as well as their welcome reception in the peripheral Soviet republics and in Japan, show that this effect of emotive and situational self-recognition is repeated in the most unexpected latitudes, constantly adjusting itself to extremely varied conceptions of ego, beliefs, morality, and reality. The program initiated by Deng in 1978 had as its point of departure a tacit verification of the economic disaster and the failure of the social transformation attempted by a Stalinist-line party that understood itself as "the only organization capable of centralizing the leadership of the struggle of the proletariat" and that, according to Lui Shaogi, described its character as determined by "our party's political struggle and political life, its ideological education and political leadership."[14]   Deng's reform, with its emphasis on economic efficiency and managerial competence, marked the beginning of the end of the Marxism-Leninism-Mao Zedong Party as the only instrument capable of channeling the great torrent of the Chinese people. In this context, after the devastation of Mao's Cultural Revolution, since the beginning of the 1980s until the events at Tiananmen Square in which the army upheld the power of the Party, the cultural movement *Xungen Wenxue* (scar literature) proposed as its goal a type of present-day archeology: the establishment of a plurality of identities corresponding to the heterogeneity of the times and spaces of the diverse ethnic groups, peoples, and cultures of that immense country. The intellectuals of *Xungen Wenxue,* and especially its writers such as Mo Yan and Liu Zhenyun, with their hallucinatory and frequently eroticized fiction and chronicles, had as their model the text of García Márquez.

As far as readers and writers in Japan, a country where a culture of traditional behavior is coupled with a postmodern concept of reality, the reception of Garcías Márquez's functions as the reflection of their own abundant narrative resources. This presupposes a challenge that leads the West to both a self-conscious declaration of its rationality in the garb of modernity and its dependence on the forms of the Other to mark its own boundaries of rationality. Thus, Macondo is in Kikirikij, the village that proclaims its independence from the Empire of the Rising Sun in the celebrated satirical-marvelous utopian book of the same name by Inoue Hisashi. Moreover, the two elements of Japanese cultural and literary tradition, ignored by the West, facilitated Japanese readers' reception of García Márquez. Buddhism includes the concept of *mujo,* which can be roughly paraphrased as uncertainty, immanence of change, mutability of forms within the human condition. Second, the combination of the marvelous with the everyday, the display of encyclopedic knowledge about the life of ghosts, of the uninterrupted chaos of civil wars, characterizes the great parodic, episodic, and self-referential fiction of *Gesaku* prose. *Gesaku,* unlike the other great cultural form of the Edo period, *Kabuki* drama, could never be correlated with the narrow modern European concept of *Weltliteratur.* In contrast, Japanese readers could easily see García Márquez as the most prestigious of narrators in the *Gesaku* tradition, as a Japanese narrator *avant la lettre.*

The figure of a triangle helps one to understand the activation of both repressed narrative sources and resources in the peripheral regions of the Soviet Union that accompanied the appropriation of the texts of García Márquez. One side of this figure is constituted by the liberation of a new epic attitude capable both of including myth and of mythologizing, as demonstrated in the work of masters such as Fazil Iskander, Yuri Rytieu, Yuvan Shestalov, and Bulat Okudshava, who read *One Hundred Years of Solitude* as a synthesis of the novel and epos under the sign of myth. The second side of the triangle is made up of texts written on the periphery of the former Soviet Union, such as the novels of the Siberian Valentín Rasputin, Armenians such as Shabua Amiredzhibi and Grant Matevosian, or Baltic narrators such as Youzas Bultushis, which neither opposed nor supported the Russian hegemony. Their attitude is one of nonidentification. This second side plays with the demands for verisimilitude and the borders of official censorship and self-censorship. The two sides of this triangle rest on a common base that is made up of the great discovery by Tschingis Aitmatov and Vazil Zemliak: the signification of Macondo as a compressed space and an organizing point of the world, a topological entity foreign to the West, that is, *omphalos,* center of the universe.

The search with the aid of fiction for identities of class, ethnicity, gender, religion, and culture in the midst of processes of modernization is a visible characteristic of the reception of García Márquez in the peripheral regions of the former Soviet Union.[15] This can be seen in films such as Nikita Michalkov's *Urga* (1990), a fairy tale about the friendship between a Mongol shepherd and a Russian truckdriver, which combines Gengis Khan, plastic, fifty different types of green, and the deafening sounds of discotheques. Michalkov playfully winks at the spectator with his recognizable allusion to the fictions of García Márquez, in the same manner that Polanski, in his nostalgic film *Chinatown* (1973), names the hotel "Macondo" and thereby gives a clue to his reading of the modernization of Los Angeles.

These texts and films, as well as the films of magic realism such as *Urga* or the realistic magic in the prose of Hisashi (which laughingly questions

Japanese modernity), Mo Yan's or Zulfikar Ghose's, are evidence that, since the beginning of the 1980s the handling of magic realism had ceased to be the privilege of Latin Americans. Devices of narrative theme and organization (such as the multiplication of hyperbolic action, character, and the marvelously narrated world, of the writing process and the splitting of the narrative subject into divers instances) that appear as characteristic of recent Latin American narrative are no longer exclusive to their fiction. At the beginning of the decade, we find three novels that allow us to measure the enrichment brought by the currents of Latin American cultural capital. Two of these novels are by well-known authors of that period, Günther Grass and Aitmatov, while the other is by a writer unknown at that time—Salman Rushdie.

In the introduction to his 1980 novel *I kolsche weka dlitsja den,* Aitmatov, whose ethnic group Kirghis still maintains some nomadic characteristics, invokes *expresis verbis* form García Márquez and emulates as well Gogol and Bulgakov (who until then did not form part of the "[multi]national heritage" of the Soviet Union), as cultivators of "fantastic realism." Into this retrospective fiction of memory about the landscape of the Kazakhstan steppes, a science fiction tale is interjected. This subgenre, which crystallized as a complement to the modern, and which in postmodern literature had a role similar to that of the detective story in modern literature, is united with a Central Asian legend about a man who is turned into a slave because he lost the memory of his culture. In novels like this, using living oral culture as a resource, the articulation of ethnic and cultural identities gives rise to an ethical reflection on the history of the century.

Besides the dramatic events in Yugoslavia and the former Soviet Union, the evolution on the 1980s of postcolonial India reconfirms the growing impression that the nation, sustained by the idea of unity, is a social model that simply does not fit at the dawn of the twenty-first century. Accounts of the military assault on the Golden Temple in Amritsar, the riots in Ayodhya, the assassinations of Indira and Rajiv Gandhi, and the bellicose declarations of the high castes of Hindus in the face of the short-lived intentions of Prime Minister Singh to take into account the demands for separate lands by Muslims in Kashmir, Sikhs in Punjab, and the United Liberation Front of Assam showed how illusory the desires of the British imperialists were to "unify India," and the fantasy of the "Raj."

At the beginning of the 1980s, Salman Rushdie, storyteller of Bombay and Cambridge, narrated the history of the 1001 children born during the night of August 15, 1947, by the same forceps as the modern state of India. *Midnight's Children* recounts the impossible world of the 581 who survived, even though some possessed the gift of infallible memory, the clairvoyance and telepathic vision to handle the midnight conference that was supposed to bring them together. They divide into groups according to their ethnic, religious, linguistic, social, and ideological interests, and Indira Gandhi takes up the task of undermining the entire conference. In this network of fiction and familiar history, Macondo shines through in the hyperreal image of Calcutta, and García Márquez's patriarch is reincarnated in the form of the terrible widow with hair parted in the middle. But it is in the power of the self-representational fable and the treatment of the question of nation that one can best measure the extent of the postcolonial reception of García Márquez's texts. The distance between Salman Rushdie's first novel, *Grimis* (1975), and *Midnight's Children* (1981) shows that, with the transference of cultural capital South-South, the question of self-representation of cultural difference comes into play in a specific way. Its very heterogeneous collection of fractured local solutions is integrated into globalizing structures that are engendering new forms of social life, economic orders, and communities of readership. From these aspects, *The Autumn of the Patriarch* appears as the text that contributes decisively to the revalorization by narrators in what was then known as the third world of their own cultural resources in order to confront postcolonial challenges. This revalorization is confirmed in the fiction about demented patriarchal dictators constructed by the Congolese novelist Soni Labou Tansi or the fiction of the Benghali writer Amitav Ghosh.

IN A SITUATION ONE SUPPOSES was understandable in metaphorical-topological terms of space and territory, in the imagery of metropol and periphery, center and margin, position and boundary, inside and outside, the reception of the text of García Márquez contributed decisively to the deconstruction of the very structures of the antique-seeming map of the world of political and cultural relations evoked by this system of metaphors. The great carnavalesque fictions of García Márquez affected the hierarchies prevalent in the processes of writing as symbolic-cultural remodelings. In the South-South transfer, they not only helped put into question the usurpation of signifying and representing functions but also, by activating uncultivated self-representational resources, stimulated the production of texts, which, by adopting a marginal place for themselves, brought the margins into the center by applying a deconstructive critique to the dominant self-historism of the West. In the South-North transfer, the results are parallel, as demonstrated by the reception of García Márquez in the Islamic-Arabic and the Northern countries.

Said has pointed out that the Orient has been not an interlocutor for Europe but its silent Other. Since the Enlightenment, "Oriental" history was considered a stage that should be left behind in the dialects of spirit, the emancipation of the rational subject, the hermeneutic of meaning. Historians of literature even resorted to Keats or Hölderlin to put forward the thesis that the Orient surrendered its historical relevance.[16] In order to put into perspective the present situation of Arab narrators, with their changes in literary paradigms and the disappearance of the aura of modern metropolitan classics, Jamel Eddine Bencheik notes: "Latin American literature—and, above all, that of García Márquez—has transformed the 'new novel,' or, perhaps better said, the contemporary novel. García Márquez is a kind of guide in the new quest for fiction."[17] It is within this proliferating network of the margins that Farazdak, Omar Ibn Ali Rubia, Abu Navas, Ibn Haldunly, and another dozen classics of the pre-Islamic era and of the Abadidas become tied to García Márquez with the use of intertextual strategies in *Les 1001 années de la Nostalgie* by Rachid Bodjedra.

With regard to the reception of García Márquez in the North, the change of orientations brought about by this reception encouraged writers to find their own particular voice and actually to begin writing. This phenomenon occurred across America and Europe, from Jayne Anne Philipps and Angela Carter to Patrik Süskind. The curious and significant self-designation involved in the new versions of the "history of the world," which Günter Grass, Burnes, or T. Coraghessan Boyle put forth in a carnavalesque form, reveals a change. If the modernist aesthetic project in a sense constituted a critique of modernity and a refusal to endorse its celebratory grand narratives, contemporary fiction assumes and practices an incredulity with regard to metanarratives, those universal guiding mythologies and principles, accepting instead the inevitability of a plurality of perspectives and the dissolution of various older aesthetic and ideological polarities and boundaries. The attentive and reflective readings of García Márquez's fiction stabilized a set of key aesthetic strategies. Combined, these textual objects and practices can be seen as definitory in contemporary fiction. Barth designated it as "postmodernist fiction" in his second manifesto. Larry McCaffery observes:

> If a single work may be said to have provided a model for the direction of postmodern fiction of the 1970s and 1980s, it is probably García Márquez's *One Hundred Years of Solitude,* a work that admirably and brilliantly combines experimental impulses with a powerful sense of political and social reality.

Indeed, García Márquez's masterpiece perfectly embodies a tendency found in much of the best recent fiction—that is, it uses experimental strategies to discover new methods of reconnecting with the world outside the page, outside of language.[18]

With this common denominator, one can legitimately correlate Barth's *Letters*, William Gaddis's *JR*, William Kennedy's *Ironweed*, and Rushdie's *Midnight's Children*; similarly, with the Macondo of García Márquez, a new topography takes shape, mapped out in works such as Pynchon's *Vineland*, or Aitmatov's *Buranny*, Rachid Boudjedra's *Manama*, Beat Starchy's *Innerwald*, and the Japanese master Hisashi's *Kikirikij*, articulating the contemporary polarity between globality and local cultures.

IN THE 1980S, through their mass media, Brazil and Mexico began to have a voice in the bustling hubbub of the world information order previously dominated by the North. Brazilian entrepreneurs expanded toward Europe and entered the world audiovisual market with a product without which it would be difficult to imagine the world today: the *telenovelas*. In Mexican media, the same epochal turning point had taken place, and President Carlos Salinas de Gortari sought to include Mexico in the trade agreement that had just been negotiated between the United States and Canada. *Rede Globo,* the fourth largest network in the world, obtained control of the Italian affiliate of the French company *Telemontecarlo. Televisa* of Mexico, the second largest Latin American media consortium, fomented the establishment of radio and television stations in the United States, a lucrative and promising future market that the Monterrey Group today controls as a monopoly.

The Latin Americans have been very successful in marketing their own distinct production of *telenovelas.* Both *Rede Globo* of Brazil and *Televisa* of Mexico have found that the *telenovelas* are one of the most profitable components of their exportable products. With the need for television companies to guarantee revenue for several years at the lowest cost possible within the framework of deregularization, the know-how of the program production industry in Mexico and Brazil, as well as the *telenovelas,* had its impact on the industrial rhythms of production and the structure of programming. The production cost of a *telenovela* is less than thirty thousand dollars an hour, less than half the production cost of a single soap opera in the United States. "It is an essentially Latin American genre, because it characterized us, it identifies us," as the *telenovela* author Ignacio Cabrujas has declared.[19] Furthermore, the genre has developed significant variants resulting from an encounter between form and memory, between the lift of the countries and their cultural heterogeneity.

Several theorists see television as constituting the postmodern psychocultural condition—a world of simulations detached from any reference to the "real," circulating and performing exchanges in centerless flows. Ann Kaplan uses rock video clips and Lawrence Grossber's *Miami Vice* as examples of this phenomenon. Grossberg described the series in this fashion:

> *Miami Vice* is . . . all on the surface. And the surface is nothing but a collection of quotations from our own collective historical debris, a mobile game of Trivia. . . . The narrative is less important than the images. . . . Narrative closure becomes a mere convenience of the medium. And the spectator as subject all but disappears in the rapid editing and rather uncomfortable camera angles.[20]

Kaplan distinguished five types of video clips, couching her argument in negative terms:

> What characterized the postmodernist video is its refusal to take a clear position vis-à-vis its images, its habit of hedging along the line of not communicating a clear signified. In postmodernist videos, as not in the other specific types, each element of a text is undercut by others: narrative in undercut by pastiche, signifying is undercut by images that do not line up in a coherent chain, the text is flattened out creating a two-dimensional effect and the refusal of a clear position of the spectator within the filmic world.[21]

These unstable determinations in a negative light almost always represent a constant. For example, in his analysis of the cult video "Road to Nowhere," Dick Hebdige stresses that the video creates "a space of subliminal narrative *suggestions* which is neither 'realist' nor 'modernist' . . . encouraging neither identification nor critical reflection."[22]

There cannot be a sharper contrast within the actual development of cultural production, marketing, and consumption on a global scale than that between the characteristic aesthetics of these cultural artifacts and the symbolic order of the *telenovelas*. The revealing paradox of change in contemporary culture, as a passage from modernity to postmodernity, resides here in the international success of the *telenovels,* wherein signs are the *function* of a reference to the world, which can be explained only as a result of a product emerging from this terrain of transformation. Because of this, the *telenovela* is defined by the cultural matrices that function within it, rather than by its codes or content. More than the texts themselves or the daily rites of reception, attention is focused on two other factors: one is the social actors who intervene in the circulation of the *telenovela,* possessing abilities and knowledge that, constituted in memory, become a prism for the reading that different social groups, sexes, or ethnic, regional, or national groups carry out. The second factor is the existence of a collective imaginary from which these groups project their identity.[23] As the media theoretician Jesús Martín Barbero has shown, social demand and cultural dynamics are tangled up in the logic of the market, giving rise to re-elaborations and recuperation of *Ungleichzetigkeiten* within a discourse that combines the new audiovisual technologies with a slide show of narration and archaic recognition.[24]

The newspaper serial as a narrative genre that corresponds to deep layers of a collective imaginary, only through which it obtains entry into the historical memory of the Latin American societies, has its present-day version in the *telenovela.* In the genre of newspaper serials, conflict, dramaturgy, action, and narrative language are interwoven, and "the dramatic effects" result in the "expression of a moral exigency."[25] The mixture of temporalities and of extremely varied discourses in the *telenovelas* assumes the technoperceptive transformation of the new urban masses carried along by the electronic audiovisual media. But, at the same time, mechanisms of recognition, untied with a symbolic weave of interpellation and the sensation of feeling oneself interpellated (and, because of this, related in a specific way to the constitution of subjectivity) supposes another class of realities. To recognize oneself in the newspaper serial or *telenovela* presupposes a psychosocial substratum: to participate in a primordial sociability in which the determinate factor is kinship, the neighborhood, the place of origin and friendships, with all their fidelities.

Within specific explorations of the discrepancies of temporality, power, and development between the anthropologist and his constructed object, Johannes Fabian hypothesizes a concept of culture that is primarily a conglomerate of matrices and practices of knowledge and behavior.[26] Jean Franco has similarly given new dimensions to the category of the *popular,* understanding it as a specification of a particular *cultura popular* on the basis of the existence and handling of cultural competencies different from those of the hegemonic.[27] High culture and popular culture, as well as industrial culture and forms of mass communication, appear today as parts of a structuring and destructuring matrix eminently appropriate to the time-space-money experience of urban life in contemporary societies of Latin America. It is worth repeating that today the traditional and the modern are not found in opposition to each other and that the division among high culture, *cultura popular,* and the industrial culture (as exclusive and closed categories) is meaningless. Therefore, forms of mass communication have resulted in new processes for the production and distribution of culture, a result that cannot be accounted for by simpleminded technological determinism, the mobilization of desire and fantasy in the context of a politics of distraction, or the promotion of a culture of consumerism. The *telenovela,* upon activating these matrixes of *cultura popular,* with its archaic narrative typical of newspaper serials and the visual tale of publicity as discourse, manages to interpellate millions of people on every continent who are now included in processes of such an accelerated modernization that it has reached the status of a historical transition. The *telenovela* has thus become an interstitial receptacle for strategies of transforming negotiations around socially constituted subjectivities.

IN THE LAST DECADE, Medellín became the world capital of illegal narcotraffic. Among the multiple strategies employed by cocaine businessmen was that of violence as a device of defense and pressure. Within this context, new forms of rendering services came into existence, including those of young *sicarios,* "hired assassins."[28] From the point of view of the multitemporal heterogeneity that characterizes the cultural modernity of Latin American societies, Medellín and its *sicarios* had almost an emblematic significance. In this case, the processes of economic and symbolic reconversion, which peasants were undergoing in their adaptation to urban life, were the objects of an intense compression of time. New cultural forms and products of modernization could not substitute for what *sicarios* considered traditional or for what they took to be their own identity. Rather, there was a knitting together of distinct modalities of symbolic development. It involved not a superimposition but rather a fluid elaboration of definitions of identity and culture. An investigation of participatory sociology among the *sicarios* is the multitemporal heterogeneity characteristic of the cultures they make up and that gives its own particular stamp to modernity within its limits in Latin America.

Alonso Salazar's study distinguishes the first layer, that of traditional culture oriented by the mythology of the not-so-distant mining and agricultural colonialization of the region. The Catholic popular religiosity and a strong sense of profit and retaliation are derived from that experience. The second layer he distinguishes has to do with the processes of urbanization in the first part of the century and, at the same time, with more recent forms of population scattering: the *malevo* culture and the salsa, that is, the world of the tango and the barrio, together with the cult of the Argentine singer Carlos Gardel, killed in an airplane accident in Medellín. To this *machista* and aescetic culture is joined a culture of the body and an enjoyment of libidinal discharge arriving from the Caribbean, with its salsa music. Finally, and as revealed in the discourse of the *sicarios,* there is a uniquely modern culture. This is defined by the values of consumption as a source of enjoyment of creature comforts and prestige, a sense of the ephemeral, and a language corresponding to the norms of the audiovisual dominated by discontinuous images.[29] With the redefinition thus accomplished within a modernizing perspective, the (traditional) cult and the (traditionally) popular (with its authentication and ritualization of identity) and the culture of the mass media (with its industrialization of cultural production), a new crossbreeding or syncretic synthesis does not arise. Rather, a simultaneous mixture and a cultural hodgepodge are the determinant results. With these new mixed cultures and their transitional cultural identities, the mass media become the access channel to modernity.

Another of the strong currents that give tension to the new urban cultures is deterritorialization, which spawns new cultural forms, above all among youth. A key sector of the unbalanced national demographic pyramids has as its experience an audiovisual culture (television, music, video clips, game machines), not tied to any territory, with the use made of the culture being its decisive element. In a broad sense, one could even talk about strategies of reterritorialization, of forms of recycling, recuperation, and resignification, and of an attempt to come to grips with the elements, components, and icons of global culture offered by the media. Here, as in the case of rock music and audiotechnology, the relationship between two or more codes is carried out with the help of modes of connotation that give them added meaning. The social recourse to multiple codes, the ironic play of the signs with televised spectacularity is, to mention as example, the regulating strategy of the emergence of the figure of *Superbarrio* after the 1985 earthquake in Mexico City. The Mexican-masked icon comes from a world that makes spectacles of the good and evil of wrestling, and, to the degree that the encoding and decoding of the world exists in a parodic fashion through its Superheroes (Superman, Batman), it adopts a double-voiced or culturally hybrid form permitting it, in the everyday reality of the megapolis, to put itself at the service of the needy.

This process of hybridization not only escapes the scheme of an intercultural mixing of heterogeneous elements into a synthesis of theories of *mestizaje;* it also puts into question the cultural politics giving hegemonic groups or their elites a modern character and reduces the traditional to the popular sectors, at the same time putting forth the massification of the consumption of cultural goods as a step toward cultural development. The modernization of the sector would be in this form a task of private capital, while the State has to concentrate on conservation of patrimony. Néstor García Canclini makes this clear in his study on forms, in which borders between the *popular,* the high culture, and the mass media have been moved with the obsolescence of the old repertories, encyclopedias, and mental cultural maps. The empirical analysis of these processes, especially in the borders themselves, as in the case of Tijuana, in which there has resulted a space of exchange, fusion, and transformation of cultural identities that are always related, demonstrates the character of the far-reaching process from the point of view of the flows of cultural capital it accomplishes.[30] Under conditions of uneven and combined development, as different as the historical-cultural processes are in the various Latin American countries and regions, these cultures are today the rule, rather than the exception.

Notes

1. Edward Said, *Orientalism* (London: Routledge & Kegan Paul, 1978).

2. Jesús Martín Barbero, *De los medios a las mediaciones* (México: Gustavo Gili, 1987).

3. Jean Franco, "What's in a Name? Popular Culture Theories and Their Limitations," *Studies in Latin American Popular Culture* 1.1 (1982) 5–14; William Rowe and Vivian Schelling, *Memory and Modernity: Popular Culture in Latin America* (London and New York: Verso, 1991) 49–150.

4. Tzvetan Todorov, "Le croisement des cultures," *Communications* 43 (1986) 22.

5. Angela MacRobbie, "Postmodernism and Popular Culture," *Postmodernism: ICA Documents,* ed. Lisa Appagnanesi (London: ICA, 1986) 5:57.

6. Georg Lipsitz, "Cruising around the Historical Bloc: Postmodernism and Popular Music in East Los Angeles," *Cultural Critique* 5 (1986–1987) 169–170.

7. Ibid., 159.

8. Jean-François Lyotard, *Le postmodernisme expliqué aux enfants* (Paris: Galilée, 1986) 43–64.

9. García Márquez, *Cien años de soledad* (Buenos Aires: Editorial Sudamericana, 1969); English translation: *One Hundred Years of Solitude,* 1st ed. (New York: Harper & Row, 1970).

10. Thomas Pynchon, *V,* 1st Perennial Fiction Library (New York: Harper & Row, 1986, c1963).

11. Italo Calvino, *Se una notte d'inverno un viaggiatore* (Turin: Einaudi, 1979); English translation: *If on a Winter's Night a Traveler* (New York: Harcourt Brace Jovanovich, 1981).

12. Pierre Bourdieus, "Le champ littéraire: préables critiques et principes de méthode," *Lendemains* 10.36 (1985) 7.

13. Abdelkader Rabia, "Gabriel García Márquez et sa fortune dans les pays arabes," *Recherches et Etudes Comparatistes Ibero-Françaises de la Sorbonne* 3 (1981) 96.

14. Stalin, *Leninism* (Moscow: International Publishers, 1933) 78; Lui Shaoqui, *Three Essays on Party-Building* (Beijing: Foreign Languages Press, 1980) 181.

15. This is also true of the Chinese reception of García Márquez (Jiang Yuanlun, "Chutu. Dangai xiaoushuo zhong de yizhong wenhua xianxiang." *Dushu* 10 [1986] 85).

16. Edward Said, "Orientalism Reconsidered," *Literature, Politics and Theory: Papers from the Essex Conference 1976–1984,* ed. Francis Baker, Peter Hulme, Margaret Iversen, and Diana Lonley (London and New York: Methuen, 1986) 215–218,

17. Rabia, "Marquez et sa fortune" 96.

18. Larry McCaffery, *Postmodern Fiction: A Bio-Bibliographical Guide* (New York, Westport, London: Greenwood, 1985) xxv–xxvi.

19. José Ignacio Cabrujas, "Telenovela nuestra de cada día," *Comunicación* 47 (1984) 11.

20. Lawrence Grossberg, "The In-Difference of Television," *Screen* 28.2 (1987).

21. Ann Kaplan, *Rocking around the Clock, Music, Television: Postmodernism and Popular Culture* (London and New York: Methuen, 1987) 6.

22. Dick Hebdige, *Hiding in the Light: On Images and Things* (London: Comedia, 1988) 237.

23. See Gladys Daza Hernández, *TV Cultura: los jóvenes en el proceso de enculturación* (Bogotá: Nueva América, 1989); Renato Ortiz et al., *Telenovela: história e produção* (Petropolis: Vozes, 1989); José Marquez de Melo, *Produção e exportação de ficâo televisual brasileira* (Sâo Paulo: UNESCO, 1987); M. Wilton de Sousa, *A rosa púrpura de cada día: trajetoria de vida e cotidiano de receptors de telenovela* (Sâo Paulo: USP, 1986).

24. See Jesús Martín Barbero, *De los medios a las mediaciones* (México: Gustavo Gili, 1987); "Televisión, melodrama y vida cotidiana," *Diálogos de la comunicación* 17 (1987); "Matrices culturales de las telenovelas," *Estudios sobre culturals contemporáneas* 4–5 (1988). Michael Dobbs of the *Washington Post* indicates that the airing of Mexican *telenovelas* has been the salvation of former Soviet state television and comments: "When *The Rich Also Weep* is aired on Ostanki Television, dubbed in Russian, life in the former Soviet Union slows to a standstill. Wars are suspended as soap-obsessed fighters flop down in front of TV sets. The water pressure goes up. The number of burglaries goes down. Fields are abandoned" ("Age of TV Dawns in Russia; Fans Swoon over Mexican Soap Opera," *International Herald Tribune,* Paris, September 9, 1992).

25. Peter Brooks, "Une esthétique de l'étonnement: le mélodrame," *Poétique* 19 (1974) 356. See Marlyse Meyer, *De Folhetins* (Rio de Janeiro: Centro Interdisciplinar de

Estudos Contemporâneos, 1990); Silvia Oroz, *O Cinema de lágrimas da América Latina* (Rio de Janeiro: Rio Fundo Editorial, 1992).

26. Johannes Fabian, *Time and the Other: How Anthropology Makes Its Object* (New York: Columbia University Press, 1983).

27. Franco, "What's in a Name?"

28. Ciro Krauthausen and Luis Fernando Sarmiento, *Cocaina & Co* (Bogotá: Tercer Mundo, 1991) 85–90.

29. Alonso Salazar, *No nacimos pa' semilla* (Bogotá: CINEP, 1990) 183–212.

30. Néstor García Canclini, *Culturas híbridas. Estrategias para entrar y salir de la modernidad* (México: Grijalbo, 1989) 263–328.

Selected Bibliography

Arenas, Reinaldo. "En la ciudad de los espejismos." *Casa de las Américas* (Havana) 7, no. 48 (May–June 1968): 134–138. Reprinted in *Sobre García Márquez*, edited by Pedro Simón Martínez (q.v.), pp. 139–146.

Arnau, Carmen. *El mundo mítico de Gabriel García Márquez*. Barcelona: Ediciones Península, 1971.

Bell-Villada, Gene H. *García Márquez: The Man and His Work*. Chapel Hill: University of North Carolina Press, 1990.

———. "Journey to Macondo in Search of García Márquez." *Boston Review* 8, no. 2 (March–April 1983): 25–27.

———. "Names and Narrative Pattern in *One Hundred Years of Solitude*." *Latin American Literary Review* 9, no. 18 (1981): 37–46.

Beltrán Almería, Luis. "La revuelta del futuro: Mito e historia en *Cien años de soledad*." *Cuadernos Hispanoamericanos* 535 (January 1995): 23–38.

Benedetti, Mario. "García Márquez o la vigilia dentro del sueño." In *Letras del continente mestizo*, pp. 180–189. Montevideo: Arca, 1967.

Brotherston, Gordon. "An End to Secular Solitude: Gabriel García Márquez." In *The Emergence of the Latin American Novel*, pp. 122–135. New York: Cambridge University Press, 1977.

Carrillo, Germán Darío. *La narrativa de Gabriel García Márquez*. Madrid: Ediciones de Arte y Bibliofilia, 1975.

Castro, Juan Antonio. "*Cien años de soledad* o la crisis de la utopía." In *Homenaje a Gabriel García Márquez: Variaciones interpretativas en torno a su obra*, edited by Helmy F. Giacoman (q.v.), pp. 267–277.

Dorfman, Ariel. "La muerte como acto imaginativo en *Cien años de soledad*." In *Homenaje a Gabriel García Márquez: Variaciones interpretativas en torno a su obra*, edited by Helmy F. Giacoman (q.v.), pp. 107–138.

Earle, Peter, ed. *García Márquez: El escritor y la crítica*. Madrid: Taurus, 1981.

Fau, Margarita Eustella. *Gabriel García Márquez: An Annotated Bibliography, 1947–1979*. Westport, Conn.: Greenwood Press, 1980.

Fau, Margarita Eustella, and Nelly S. de González. *Bibliographic Guide to Gabriel García Márquez, 1979–1985*. Westport, Conn.: Greenwood Press, 1986.

Gallagher, D. P. "Gabriel García Márquez." In *Modern Latin American Literature*, pp. 144–163. New York: Oxford University Press, 1973.

García Márquez, Gabriel. *The Fragrance of Guava: Plinio Apuleio Mendoza in Conversation with Gabriel García Márquez*. Translated by Ann Wright. London: Verso, 1983.

Giacoman, Helmy F., ed. *Homenaje a Gabriel García Márquez: Variaciones interpretativas en torno a su obra*. Long Island City, N.Y.: Las Américas, 1972.

Gutiérrez Mouat, Ricardo. "*Cien años de soledad* y el mito farmacopéyico del realismo mágico." *Revista de Estudios Hispánicos* 17–18 (1990–1991): 267–279.

Harss, Luis. "Gabriel García Márquez o la cuerda floja." In *Los nuestros*, pp. 381–419. Buenos Aires: Editorial Sudamericana, 1966.

Harss, Luis, and Barbara Dohmann. "Gabriel García Márquez, or the Lost Chord." In *Into the Mainstream: Conversations with Latin American Writers*, pp. 310–341. New York: Harper and Row, 1967.

Irvine, Dean J. "Fables of the Years: Postcolonialism, Postmodernism, and Magic Realism in *Cien años de soledad* [One Hundred Years of Solitude]." *Ariel: A Review of International English Literature* 29, no. 4 (October 1998): 53–80.

Janes, Regina. *Gabriel García Márquez: Revolutions in Wonderland*. Columbia: University of Missouri Press, 1981.

———. "Liberals, Conservatives, and Bananas: Colombian Politics in the Fiction of Gabriel García Márquez." *Hispanófila*, no. 82 (September 1984): 79–102.

Lerner, Isaías. "A propósito de *Cien años de soledad*." *Cuadernos Americanos*, año 28, vol. 162, no. 1 (January–February 1969): 186–200. Reprinted in *Homenaje a Gabriel García Márquez: Variaciones interpretativas en torno a su obra*, edited by Helmy F. Giacoman (q.v.), pp. 251–265.

Levine, Suzanne Jill. *El espejo hablado: Un estudio de "Cien años de soledad."* Caracas: Monte Avila, 1975.

López Mejía, Adelaida. "Debt, Delirium, and Cultural Exchange in *Cien años de soledad*." *Revista de Estudios Hispánicos* 29 (1995): 1–25.

López Mejía, Adelaida. "Women Who Bleed to Death: Gabriel García Márquez's 'Sense of an Ending.'" *Revista Hispánica Moderna* 52, no. 1 (1999): 135–150.

Ludmer, Josefina. *"Cien años de soledad": Una interpretación.* Buenos Aires: Editorial Tiempo Contemporáneo, 1972.

Martínez, Pedro Simón, ed. *Sobre García Márquez.* Montevideo: Biblioteca de Marcha, 1971.

McGuirk, Bernard, and Richard Cardwell, eds. *Gabriel García Márquez: New Readings.* New York: Cambridge University Press, 1987.

McMurray, George R. *Gabriel García Márquez.* New York: Frederick Ungar, 1977.

Mena, Lucila Inés. "La huelga de la compañía bananera como expresión de lo 'real maravilloso' americano en *Cien años de soledad.*" *Bulletin Hispanique* 74 (1972): 379–405.

Minta, Stephen. *Gabriel García Márquez: Writer of Colombia.* London: Jonathan Cape, 1987.

Oberhelman, Harley D. *The Presence of Faulkner in the Writings of Gabriel García Márquez.* Lubbock: Texas Tech Press, 1980.

Ortega, Julio, ed., with the assistance of Claudia Elliott. *Gabriel García Márquez and the Powers of Fiction.* Austin: University of Texas Press, 1988.

Palencia-Roth, Michael. *Gabriel García Márquez: La línea, el círculo y la metamorfosis del mito.* Madrid: Gredos, 1983.

Parra, Mauricio. "La crítica de la razón instrumental en *Cien años de soledad* o la posibilidad de la excentricidad." *La Torre: Revista de la Universidad de Puerto Rico* 2, no. 3 (January–March 1997): 73–85.

Rama, Ángel. "Un novelista de la violencia americana." In *Homenaje a Gabriel García Márquez: Variaciones interpretativas en torno a su obra,* edited by Helmy F. Giacoman (q.v.), pp. 57–72.

Rodríguez Monegal, Emir. "Novedad y anacronismo de *Cien años de soledad.*" In *Homenaje a Gabriel García Márquez: Variaciones interpretativas en torno a su obra,* edited by Helmy F. Giacoman (q.v.), pp. 15–42.

Roses, Lorraine. "A Code of Many Colors: Biblical Intertextuality in *One Hundred Years of Solitude.*" In *Justina: Homenaje a Justina Ruiz de Conde en su Ochenta Cumpleaños,* ed. Elena Gascón-Vera and Joy Renjilian-Burgy, pp. 171–178. Erie, Pa.: ALDEEU, 1992.

Saldívar, Dasso. *García Márquez: El viaje a la semilla: La biografía.* Madrid: Alfaguara, 1997.

Shaw, Bradley A., and Nora Vera-Goodwin, eds. *Critical Perspectives on Gabriel García Márquez.* Lincoln, Neb.: Society of Spanish and Spanish-American Studies, 1986.

Vargas Llosa, Mario. *García Márquez: Historia de un deicidio.* Barcelona: Barral, 1971.

Volkening, Ernesto. "Anotado al margen de *Cien años de soledad.*" In *Sobre García*

Márquez, edited by Pedro Simón Martínez (q.v.), pp. 178–206.

Wilkie, James W., Edna Monzón de Wilkie, and María Herrera-Sobek. "Elitelore and Folklore: Theory and a Test Case in *One Hundred Years of Solitude*." *Journal of Latin American Lore* 4 (1978): 183–223.

Williams, Raymond L. *Gabriel García Márquez*. Boston: Twayne, 1984.

Zamora, Lois Parkinson, and Wendy Faris, eds. *Magical Realism: Theory, History, Community*. Durham, N.C.: Duke University Press, 1995.